UNBEATABLE

TOM OSBORNE AND THE
GREATEST ERA OF NEBRASKA FOOTBALL

HENRY J. CORDES OF THE Omaha World-Herald

UNBEATABLE

TOM OSBORNE AND THE
GREATEST ERA OF NEBRASKA FOOTBALL

BY HENRY J. CORDES

Omaha World-Herald

EDITOR
Dan Sullivan

DESIGNER
Christine Zueck-Watkins

PHOTO EDITOR
Jolene McHugh

CONTRIBUTING EDITORS
Duane Retzlaff, Bob Glissmann, Jim Anderson

PHOTOGRAPHERS
Bill Batson, Jeff Beiermann, Jeff Bundy, James R. Burnett,
Jeffrey Z. Carney, Kiley Cruse, James Denney, Rebecca S. Gratz,
Rich Janda, Phil Johnson, Rudy Smith

EXECUTIVE EDITOR
Mike Reilly

PRESIDENT AND PUBLISHER
Terry Kroeger

Omaha World-Herald Co.
1314 Douglas St. Omaha, NE 68102-1811
First Edition
ISBN: 978-0-615-71539-1
Printed by Walsworth Publishing Co. Marceline, MO

Table of Contents

AS SOON AS THE KICK LEFT BYRON BENNETT'S UNSTEADY RIGHT FOOT, it was clear it had no chance, fluttering off into the warm Miami night. Tom Osborne, who had been intently gnawing his gum and watching from the sidelines, wordlessly pursed his lips and looked away.

Once again, his Nebraska Cornhuskers had fallen excruciatingly short in the quest for a national championship. For a state and legion of fans who over two decades had longed for a title more than just about anything in life,

it was another sign that their much-admired coach couldn't win the big one.

But as Osborne sat down in a lawn chair beneath a palm tree early the next morning to tape his weekly TV show, the coach's face radiated with satisfaction. He had the appearance of a man who knew a secret, and looking back, he did.

Nebraska was back. Osborne knew the Huskers now had the talent and the team to play with anyone, anywhere. At that moment, though, even Osborne could not have dreamed of the history-making success that lay just ahead for his team.

Three national championships over the next four years, a feat achieved just once before in big-time college football. Back-to-back titles in 1994 and 1995, the first consensus bookend titles in nearly four decades. A five-year record of 60-3, the best career-finishing run in history.

These were nearly unbeatable teams, and for Nebraska's ardent fans, unbeatable times.

But beyond names, games, scores and statistics, the story of those Husker teams is a human one, played out in the real world by genuine, flawed and exceptional people.

Along the way, there would be enough drama to fill a lifetime: a star player's life-threatening health condition, underdog heroes, valiant comebacks, indomitable spirit, crimes and punishments, controversy and condemnation, triumph and glory, gut-crushing defeat, a lucky break, a wayward native son's redemption, and a painful, tragic death.

And it all ended in 1997 with the architect of it all secretly planning his own exit from the field — reluctantly keeping an old promise.

While most credit for that phenomenal success has rightfully fallen to Osborne, the legendary coach would be the first to say the primary players in this narrative were the young men who wore the helmets emblazoned with those iconic red N's.

These teams were made up of a diverse and quirky mix of hardworking farm kids and slick city kids, black and white, no-name walk-ons and supposed five-star recruits, coming from every corner of the state and every region of the country.

What bound them together was a devotion to each other forged in the crucible of gridiron battles and an undying love for their coach, a man they literally shed blood for.

This is the story of the greatest era of Nebraska football.

Revisiting the Past

Tom Osborne walked into the stark visiting room in the California state correctional facility near San Diego and sat down in front of a thick pane of security glass. Soon a metal door clanked open on the other side. An imposing man walked in. Lawrence Phillips immediately recognized this visitor from his past, and a big smile lit his face. Osborne broke into his trademark little stone-faced grin.

At the time of this meeting, the day after Christmas 2009, the iconic former coach and the star running back-turned-pariah hadn't seen each other for the better part of a decade. But as they spoke, Osborne was pleasantly surprised to see how good Phillips looked. Four years inside the cold, impersonal walls of prison — with some three decades to go — had not broken Phillips. There was a glint in his eye, and he seemed happy, at peace.

Osborne told almost no one of his plans to visit his former player while the Nebraska Cornhuskers were in San Diego to play in the Holiday Bowl. And the fact he was there at all would probably have come as a shock to many. Why would Osborne show any concern for a man who had nearly destroyed his career? The man who had almost single-handedly tarnished one of the greatest coaching legacies in the history of college football?

But Osborne had always maintained that the reason he allowed Phillips to return to the field in 1995 after he violently assaulted a former girlfriend was not to win another national championship, but to help him.

> "I guess in some ways when someone's out of line, I feel a little like I would if it were one of my own children. I just can't walk away from whatever they do, good or bad."
>
> — TOM OSBORNE

Now, 14 years later, Osborne was still trying to help him. In fact, it would surprise no one who ever played for Osborne that the coach eventually turned the conversation to education.

Lawrence, Osborne told him, you ought to look into finishing that degree. Let's see if we can find a way to do that while you're here.

No, Osborne never did give up on his players. In his mind, no one was completely beyond saving. And there would always be a place in Osborne's heart for Phillips, whom Osborne had plucked as a high schooler out of a Los Angeles-area group home where he lived after being abandoned at age 12. Osborne was about as close to a father as Phillips ever had. Before Phillips threw away a chance at a Heisman Trophy and became the poster boy for much of what was wrong with big-time college football, he'd been known to nearly everyone around the Husker program as an extremely hard worker who always put the team above himself. Sitting there that day, Osborne still saw the same things in Phillips he'd seen when he first met him in 1993: a young man who was strong and incredibly tough, but also vulnerable and deeply scarred at a young age.

"I guess my feeling is that if you get to know people who do things that aren't right, there's usually some good in them," Osborne would say in a 2012 interview, sounding no different from how he did back in 1995. "It's a part of the human condition that some people end up in prison while some end up as the president of General Motors. And sometimes, the line between the two isn't as great as we think."

Maybe he was right, Osborne said, maybe he was wrong. But that's what he believed. It would seem to say something about the coach's original intentions with Phillips that all these years later, when there were no football games or championships to be won, Osborne still wanted to help him.

An awful lot had happened since Osborne and Phillips were last publicly linked, that unbelievable night in the Arizona desert when Nebraska swamped Florida's Gators to claim its second consecutive national title. Phillips had run wild on that big stage — not that a dominant Husker team had ultimately needed him to win.

With Osborne's blessing and encouragement, the two had then parted ways. Phillips left school a year early to enter the NFL draft. Osborne said he told Phillips, his agents and his handlers that the running back needed to have a support system around him. He needed to continue the counseling he'd been receiving for the anger and feelings of mistrust that seethed deep inside him.

"We're depending on him to make
good decisions. I think Lawrence will make
decisions in the best interest of the team
and the university."

— ASSISTANT COACH FRANK SOLICH ON LAWRENCE PHILLIPS,
BEFORE THE '95 SEASON

It didn't happen. Within 10 years, the player — who old teammates still swear had the talent to be one of the greatest in NFL history — had blown numerous chances to make it in the pros. He'd lost his millions, hocking at least one of his Husker championship rings in Las Vegas for $20. And most troubling, on at least five occasions, he had again lashed out violently against women.

The final straw came in 2005 when Phillips had gotten into a pickup football game with some teenagers back home near the Los Angeles Coliseum. A 30-year-old man playing with kids as young as half his age, getting back to the game he loved. But afterward, he accused the teens of stealing money and other valuables he'd set on the sidelines. They probably did. As one of the boys later told the Los Angeles Times: "He was cool until that happened. My friends are kind of crafty, and they can get in your pocket without you knowing it." Of course, that didn't excuse Phillips' reaction, which was to climb into his car and race right at the boys, striking three of them.

Once again, Phillips' rage had come back to haunt him. But this time, California authorities threw the book at him. He was convicted of the assault on those youths and of other felonies related to an earlier assault on another girlfriend. His sentence: 38 years and four months, in a state that doesn't give inmates much credit for good behavior when locked up for violent crimes. State of California Inmate G31982 isn't scheduled to be released on parole until 2032 — quite likely not during his former coach's lifetime. Phillips himself will be 57 years old by then.

In all the intervening years, the world had changed dramatically for Osborne, too. He'd retired in 1997 after winning his third national championship in four years, missed the game horribly, found a new diversion in politics, served three terms in Congress and lost a race for governor. And then he returned to the University of Nebraska as savior, stepping in as athletic director when it became clear in 2007 that the football machine he'd so painstakingly built over 25 years had completely broken down. He was the only person who could have immediately reunited the team's downtrodden and divided fan base. Now Osborne was working hard to restore Nebraska to football greatness.

And here he was sitting eye-to-eye with Phillips. As he talked to him by phone with a pane of ¾-inch glass between them, Osborne couldn't help thinking about all that Phillips had lost. "It's kind of sad to think about where he was and what could have happened," he said later.

Of course, the former coach and player also talked some football that day. Osborne told Phillips about another Californian, an up-and-coming freshman quarterback named Taylor Martinez, who was tearing things up on the scout team for Coach Bo Pelini's Huskers. He could be a pretty good one, Osborne said.

During their 45-minute visit, Osborne and Phillips didn't spend much time reminiscing about their own football days together. But it would have probably pleased them both if they could have somehow rolled back the years and returned to simpler times in Lincoln, Nebraska. Back when there was nothing in front of Osborne, Phillips and the entire Cornhusker team but hope, possibility and dreams of glory.

Unfinished Business

"It will take a total effort —
not just from the starters, but everybody.
If we do, we can go 12-0."

— TOMMIE FRAZIER BEFORE THE 1994 SEASON

The Coach

Dressed for Nebraska's searing August heat in shorts and a golf shirt, a cap shading his squinted eyes, Tom Osborne walked among his team as it collectively stretched on the faux grass surface of Memorial Stadium. Preseason practice was on for the 1994 version of the University of Nebraska's vaunted Cornhuskers. And in moments like these, Osborne, a complex yet simple man, was in his element.

He'd dryly needle a player about the girl he saw him with the other day, wondering aloud what she could see in him. He'd ask another player how his family was doing, still remembering the names of his parents, brothers and sisters from having met them years earlier on the recruiting trail. Always, there would be questions about how school was going. And it didn't matter if the player was a first-team All-American or a scout team walk-on who never saw the field on Saturday. Osborne knew and cared about them all.

For the players, especially the home-grown Nebraska kids who were raised on Big Red football, there was an aura surrounding Osborne, and their feelings for him bordered on reverence. His personality certainly wasn't going to overwhelm anyone. But there was a genuineness and integrity that shined through. With Osborne's gentle but firm way, his players didn't fear him. They feared disappointing him. "You knew he genuinely cared about you more as a person than as a football player," recalled Grant Wistrom, just a promising freshman from Missouri on the practice field that day. "Which is why guys were willing to sell out for him every day."

Osborne had won a lot of games during his 21 years as head coach at Nebraska, enough to make him a treasure in his football-crazed, native state. Everyone always said he could have been elected governor — a theory that wouldn't actually be put

"Last year we expected to be good. We were good. Same way this year."

— TOM OSBORNE, 1994 PHOTO DAY, BEFORE THE FIRST HUSKER PRACTICE to the test for another decade. But for the 57-year-old Osborne, football had never been about the games, or the wins, or the trophies, but the process. Building anew each year. Achieving perfection through practiced repetition. Scheming for the Saturday chess matches. Maximizing each team's potential.

And at the center of the process were what he would always simply and warmly refer to as "the players." Osborne above all saw himself as a teacher — educating his players not just on X's and O's, but on life. The cheers will die off. The trophies and rings will land in the closet. It all goes very quickly. But character, he'd tell them, is the thing that will carry you through life. Football was but a vehicle, a metaphor for how he wanted them to approach each day. Give great effort. Do things the right way. Be disciplined. Play for the guy next to you. Persevere in the face of adversity. Stay humble. And through it all, keep your eye on higher purposes. It's what made football most meaningful for Osborne: the process of transforming boys into men.

It was through practices like this one that Osborne's work ethic and values were ingrained in his players. The messages the players heard each day were consistent, from the methodical head coach down through every coach, trainer and staffer on the field. Kevin Steele, working with the Husker linebackers on the field that day, would later coach at other elite football schools like Alabama and Florida State. But he said there was no place quite like Nebraska. "At most other places, you went to practice to try to become a starter and to win the game," he said. "At Nebraska, it was conveyed verbally by Coach, but also by the way the process worked, that you went to practice to become the best you could be and to make the team the best it could be. Which was a completely different mind-set."

That approach would become part of the players' very DNA, and before long they'd be passing on the same messages to the younger guys. The culture under Osborne was not to shun the underclassman trying to take your job, but to take him under your wing. "If I play like I'm supposed to play, you're not going to take my job anyway," senior defensive back Barron Miles would tell the younger guys. "If I can make you better, that's gonna make our team better." When he expressed the same attitude years later while playing professionally in Canada, some guys looked at him like he was crazy. But that was Nebraska football under Tom Osborne.

A whistle sounded. Time to break up by position for group work. And before long, the sharp pop of pads was echoing off the balconies of the hallowed old stadium. It was mostly fundamental stuff — staying low, fighting off blocks, wrapping up on tackles, running through contact. There was almost always a lot of contact at an

Osborne practice, more than was typical for most college teams. Despite his professorial way and well-earned reputation as a master strategist, Osborne demanded a very, very physical style of play. This was not a dichotomy. He understood that football, at its core, is a brutally simple game: the most physically punishing team usually prevails.

Osborne turned physical football into a science. The way he had it figured, the secret to winning a game was to, on average, knock down 1½ opposing defensive players per play. If the offense took 80 snaps, he wanted to see 120 of the other guys on their backsides. It was something he had his staff closely track and chart week to week. Now, he didn't want anything dirty or unsportsmanlike. In fact, help the other guy up after you knock him down, he'd tell his players. But then knock him down again … and again … and again. By the fourth or fifth time you do it, most guys will just lose their will, give up. Those 2-yard runs will suddenly turn into 6-, 7- and 8-yard runs. That's how games are won in the fourth quarter.

Osborne thought that physical style well-suited the personality and people of the blue-collar farm state. This wasn't San Diego or South Beach. This was the cold, unforgiving Plains. And Osborne's players came to embrace and take pride in that style, willingly paying the price every day. If this practice was like a typical one, there would be six to eight players seeking medical attention — usually not the kind of thing that would lay them up for too long, but not just bruises and scrapes, either. It went with the territory. At Nebraska, the ability to both take and deliver a vicious hit was considered a badge of honor. Quarterbacks would get a tongue-lashing if they ran out of bounds. Even kickers were expected to be tough. The Huskers learned to play through the hard knocks, which only served to make them that much tougher come game day. "There is a difference between pain and injury," senior right tackle Zach Wiegert said after a particularly bruising game later that fall. "Our guys know the difference."

Wiegert, a baby-faced Fremont, Nebraska, native, was now knocking heads with his line mates just off the field in "the Pit" — a dank, hot-as-hell, below-grade practice area inside the historic Schulte Field House. At a school famous for producing top-notch offensive linemen, this was one of the most talented collections of lumber-ing bulk that line coaches Milt Tenopir and Dan Young had ever worked with. No one knew it at the time, but on the field that day were players who would become winners of the school's seventh and eighth Outland trophies, along with two other first-team All-Americans and another pair of guys who'd enjoy long NFL careers. This would also be the group to inspire "The Pipeline" nickname, becoming the

trademark for all Husker lines to come.

In fact, at every position station on the field at that moment, Osborne could see young men of exceptional size, speed, strength and agility. Just about every year, the word out of the Huskers' palatial, iron strength complex in West Stadium was that this year's team was bigger, faster and stronger than ever before. But this team really met the eyeball test.

Turner Gill, the former Husker star now serving as quarterbacks coach, checked out the footwork of the player who would ultimately supplant him as the greatest quarterback in Husker history. Tommie Frazier was only a junior, but the fierce competitor was now in his third year leading the Huskers' option attack.

At the running backs station, the well-cut Lawrence Phillips quietly flashed the power, speed and elusiveness that gave him the potential to become the school's best I-back ever. The modest sophomore from West Covina, California, had been so good as a true freshman the previous year that Osborne just had to play him. Once on the field, he ran with such toughness that it was almost impossible to get him off it. He'd play hurt.

On the next whistle, the offensive skill players gathered to run "skeleton" — a seven-on-seven passing drill. Then in a subsequent drill, the top two units ran each of Nebraska's 12 different option plays — Osborne's bread and butter. He usually spent more than 90 percent of his time around these offensive stations. The Husker offense was his baby, and come game day, he called the plays. Osborne would sooner retire than hand the duty off to an offensive coordinator, which was the practice at most big-time schools.

The perfectionist coach was also hands-on in such drills, calling out directions and encouragement in his familiar, calm monotone. The man with a doctorate in educational psychology — Dr. Tom, he was often called — believed in positive

"I-backs get a lot of the glory, but I get mine by knowing I'm throwing good blocks."

— FULLBACK JEFF MAKOVICKA, WHO WEIGHED
170 POUNDS WHEN HE WALKED ON AND PLAYED AT 215 AS A SENIOR

reinforcement. He'd rather catch a player doing something right than making a mistake. And he wouldn't usually rant when they did mess up. "We can be better here," he'd say. "We can be better." In the Vince Lombardi school of coaching, fear was the great motivator. In the Tom Osborne school, the greatest motivator was love. Osborne did at times get mad, especially if he felt the intensity or effort wasn't there. Coaches and players came to recognize that when those veins in his neck popped and his ruddy face turned a shade redder that they were in for one of their coach's rare eruptions. "Dadgummit!" Osborne would shout, using his swear word of choice. "Now run it again." It always got their attention.

You hear about teams running plays half-speed or three-quarter speed. At an Osborne practice, there were really only two speeds: all out, and go get a drink of water. "I don't even like to use the word practice," receivers coach Ron Brown recalled. "We were playing." Osborne figured the one thing in football you could always control was your effort. Play as hard as you can, and the score will take care of itself, he'd tell the players. If you do play hard and get beaten by a better team, there's no shame. And the expectation of effort was the same every week, regardless of whether the next opponent was Florida State or Central Florida.

Teammates expected effort, too. Fullback Cory Schlesinger recalled one intense practice that fall where two linemen got into a scuffle. The reason: One didn't think the other was practicing hard enough.

While Osborne was focused on the offense, his eyes were all over the field. Players and coaches would often marvel at how he never seemed to miss a thing — asking after practice why a play wasn't being defended the way coaches discussed in the morning meetings, or offering a linebacker a tip on dropping into pass coverage. "Eddie, you've got to get a little wider on that drop there," he'd say. And All-American linebacker Ed Stewart would think, "How the heck did he even see that?"

Across the field, the defense was working now under Charlie McBride, the longtime defensive coordinator who in the eyes of Husker fans was not yet the genius they would come to remember him to be. The colorful McBride was wired quite a bit differently than Osborne. Hard-nosed and fiery, he'd get in players' faces, swearing, the spittle flying, questioning whether their hearts were pumping blood or Kool-Aid. "I was scared to death of Charlie," recalled middle linebacker Phil Ellis. "He intimidated the hell out of me, from day one." It was how McBride motivated players. His philosophy: Be patient, but don't let them know you're being patient. But McBride was also fair. He yelled at everybody. Veteran players came to actually enjoy seeing wide-eyed freshmen get their introduction to McBride's ways. But the real key to McBride was that deep down, beneath that gruff exterior, he loved his players, and they knew it. As much as he rode them when they made mistakes, he'd be just as quick to give 'em a wink, a pat or a hug when they made a great play. The Blackshirts came to take great pride in playing for the man.

Besides the talent, a visitor to practice that day would also have been struck by the sheer number of players on the field — more than 160, about 40 to 50 more than was typical at other schools. Of course, every Nebraskan knew that was made possible by the Huskers' renowned walk-on program. For nearly every scholarship player like Frazier, Phillips or Wiegert on the field that day, there was another kid, usually a pretty good football player from a Nebraska farm town like Cozad, Holdrege, Albion or Battle Creek, who was paying his own way to school to be part of the Big Red.

Osborne cared deeply about the walk-ons, recruiting many of them himself. He felt the walk-on program helped unite every corner of the state behind Nebraska football. And he always said the work ethic and unselfishness in his program were products of the passion the walk-on kids brought to practice every day. Scholarship players who came to Nebraska with dreams of playing in the NFL on Sundays would later tell Osborne how profoundly the walk-ons had impacted them. After going up every day in practice against these kids who would give up a limb for the team, they couldn't help seeing there was more to this game than personal glory.

Every year, it seemed, four or five of these walk-ons would develop into major contributors through inspired work in the weight room and at practice. Osborne promised when he recruited walk-ons that if they ever cracked the top two spots on the depth chart, he would do everything possible to award them a scholarship. Such walk-on success stories were celebrated across the state. Matt Shaw, a walk-on who had risen to become the starter at tight end on this 1994 team, would later recall his opportunity to walk on at Nebraska as a great gift. "It allowed people with ordinary talents," he said, "to sometimes do extraordinary things."

But in reality, the life of most walk-ons was to largely serve as practice fodder — a role they fully understood and accepted. They'd run the opposing team's plays on scout team units, bringing the effort — and taking a beating — every day. Then perhaps by the time they were seniors, they'd get the chance to run down on kick-offs or get in for a handful of plays at the end of a blowout. It might not sound like much. But for kids whose sandlot dreams had revolved around autumn Saturdays

in Memorial Stadium, it meant the world. Now for the rest of their lives, they could say, "I played for Coach Osborne." The inability to bottle such fervor is the reason that while many schools tried to emulate the Nebraska walk-on program, none could duplicate it. "To be out there and go through some very physical practices without much intrinsic reward like having your name in the paper or getting in the game, it took a lot," Osborne later recalled of his walk-ons. "But they were so important to us. If we didn't have them, we couldn't practice like we did."

Indeed, all those bodies came in handy after the next tweet of the whistle, when the Huskers broke into what Osborne called "team work." That's when the offensive and defensive units would separately run their plays 11-on-11 against the lower-unit scouts. At most schools, team work would be run in two stations, one for the offense, one for the defense. It usually meant a lot of guys standing around not doing much while the first-stringers took most of the repetitions. But Osborne always ran four stations, two each for offense and defense.

To start team work, Frazier and the first-team offense ran through the Huskers' pass plays in the south end zone under the direction of Brown and Young. At the same time, backup quarterback Brook Berringer and the rest of the second team drilled on running plays on the west sideline under Tenopir and running backs coach Frank Solich. Osborne and Gill moved between both stations, particularly keeping an eye on the reads the quarterbacks were making.

After 18 minutes in which the two top units each had taken about 30 snaps at their stations, they switched and went at it for another 18 minutes. The work was brisk, too, with everyone expected to run up to the ball after breaking the huddle, just as in a game. At Nebraska, being the best-conditioned team on the field wasn't a goal. It was the expectation. Similarly, McBride and the other defensive coaches had the

"I don't know what heaven is like. But this must be close. It's not like some places I've been where you work on a game plan, and the head coach comes in on Thursday and changes half of it."

— DEFENSIVE COORDINATOR CHARLIE MCBRIDE

top two defensive units working simultaneously, switching off between a passing station in the north end zone and a run station on the east sideline. When the first-unit guys in their signature black practice jerseys were at work at the run station, it was usually a good idea to keep a trainer with some ice packs handy. The Blackshirts didn't like surrendering even one yard on the ground to the scout team.

Osborne's four-station system helped the two top units get in an amazing number of reps in a practice — 90 to 100 snaps each. At most schools, the top units would split a total of 90 snaps, with the vast majority going to the starters. In effect, Nebraska's top two units as a whole were getting at least double the practice time seen elsewhere. The option was a high-risk offense, with the potential for bad pitches and ball-handling errors, so such repetition was critical to instilling discipline and cutting down on drive-killing mistakes. With the number of looks both units were getting from the scout team, the players also went into games feeling they were ready for anything. Plus, with the top two units getting equal snaps, a starter couldn't get complacent. He always knew there was a guy pushing behind him who was getting a good look from the coaches. And if a starter did go down with a serious injury, there would always be a second-teamer ready who knew the plays and schemes.

Once you grasped all the intricacies of Osborne's system, it was clear Nebraska was indeed a football factory — though not in the negative sense that phrase usually connotes. Year after year, the school churned out guys who could flat-out play. "No program developed football players better than Nebraska," defensive backs coach George Darlington said. "I'm not saying that because I was part of it. I say it because it was absolutely the truth."

With the arrival of a new fall in Nebraska, some of the names on the backs of the scarlet jerseys would change. But Osborne's systems and culture remained, becoming a self-perpetuating code that came to be known as "the Nebraska Way." Any player who had played for Osborne in the previous 20 years would have been able to show up at practice on this day and fit right in, knowing the schedule, the drills and the expectations. In fact, if anyone was looking for a single reason why an Osborne team in all those years never failed to win at least nine games — or even more remarkably, how only one Osborne team in all his years ever lost to a team that finished with a losing record — that was it.

But despite that notable, machine-like consistency, Osborne and his ways seemed to fall short in the eyes of many because of his failure to bring home a national title.

That was the standard that had been set by Bob Devaney, the godfather of Nebraska football. Devaney won back-to-back titles in 1970 and 1971, helping make football in Nebraska akin to a state religion. For a flyover state of some 1.5 million people not known for much beyond agricultural commodities and Mutual of Omaha's "Wild Kingdom" on TV, football became a tremendous source of pride. Even people who didn't know football knew that Nebraska was a football school.

When Devaney hand-picked Osborne to succeed him after the 1972 season, it was expected that the gangly redhead who directed the offense of those title teams would keep the hardware coming. Osborne did succeed in bringing home 10 Big Eight crowns over the next 21 seasons, and his winning percentage was unmatched by any other active long-tenured coach. But when it came to the big prize, it seemed Osborne was jinxed, his teams so often falling just short.

One heartbreaker in particular came to define Osborne. His 1983 team had rolled undefeated into the Orange Bowl in Miami with an offense led by Gill that could have scored on NFL teams. Sports Illustrated had already dubbed it the greatest college team ever. But on a steamy night in Miami, the Huskers ended up in a classic shootout against the hometown Miami Hurricanes. When the Huskers scored a touchdown in the final minute to pull within one, Osborne was an extra-point kick away from a tie that surely would have delivered his Huskers the title.

But a steely Osborne didn't hesitate. He called for a two-point conversion attempt, going for the outright win. The image still painfully played in the heads of Husker fans: Gill rolling out and firing a pass. The ball barely tipped by Miami safety Ken Calhoun, hitting I-back Jeff Smith high on the shoulder pads and bounding to the turf, the championship hopes lying down there with it.

Just a year earlier, on that same cursed Orange Bowl field, the 1993 Huskers had suffered another gut-wrencher, falling 18-16 to Florida State. Unlike a decade earlier, Nebraska had been the big underdog this time. Osborne's Huskers had lost six straight bowl games going in, and the pundits said Nebraska didn't deserve to be on the same field as the speedy Florida teams that had come to dominate college football. The general tone of reporters' questions before the game was, "Why are you guys even here?"

But what most didn't know going into that season was that it was a different kind of Nebraska team, one that not only had players who could run with the Sunshine State speedsters, but also the heart of a champion. Great field leaders like

"Every time we touched him,
we got screamed at (by the officials).
I don't know what the deal is,
whether they're saving him for basketball."

— OUTSIDE LINEBACKER TREV ALBERTS ON QUARTERBACK CHARLIE WARD

Trev Alberts and Kevin Ramaekers had grown tired of the bowl losses and the critics and adopted a motto: Refuse to Lose. It seemed to take on a life of its own, as the Huskers week after week gutted out victories that were not always pretty.

Then back in the Orange Bowl, Alberts and Co. sacked Heisman Trophy winner Charlie Ward five times. If instant replay had been around in those days, the lone Seminole touchdown very likely would have been waved off. The running back clearly fumbled after taking a jarring blow while diving for the goal line. Despite that call and a phantom clipping penalty that wiped out a Husker punt return for a touchdown, the brilliant Frazier put Nebraska in position to win. Byron Bennett made the field goal that should have caused his name to go down in Husker glory, putting the Cinderella Huskers up 16-15 with just 1:16 left on the clock.

But then three Nebraska penalties — one when Bennett shanked the ensuing kick-off out of bounds — helped Florida State get in position for a chip-shot field goal. That put the Seminoles back up with just seconds left. Frazier still wasn't done. He found Trumane Bell running open down the middle of the field, setting up Nebraska deep in Seminole territory with just a second left. Bennett rushed back out. But from the moment he struck the ball, it was clear he had pulled the 45-yard kick far, far to the left. Once again, Osborne and the Huskers had fallen one play short.

Afterward, Florida State Coach Bobby Bowden told the press — and Husker coaches in personal letters he later wrote to them — that Nebraska had beaten his team everywhere but on the scoreboard. The Huskers had deserved to win. That Nebraska team would always go down as one of Osborne's favorites. He told his players as much in the locker room afterward. You played as well as you could have played. You did everything you could within your control to win the game. To him, that made them champions. But to the players, such sentiments were hollow. They couldn't help feeling they had let their dream slip through their fingers.

Now most of the players from that team were back out here on this practice field, including 13 starters. And the fire inside them burned as strongly as before. "Refuse to Lose" had given way to a new credo: "Unfinished Business." Even before the season opener, much had already been said and written about how the players had spent the offseason working out in Memorial Stadium with the scoreboard clocks set to 1:16, the time left in the Orange Bowl before they coughed up that final lead. It was a symbol of their resolve that this year would be different. Sometimes at the end of a grueling drill, the players would put another 1:16 on the clock and gut it out for another 76 seconds, pushing themselves harder than they thought they could. "Our goal is to be a good enough team so if we play that game again, no matter what happens or what kind of calls we get, we'll still win," Wiegert had told the Big Eight's Skywriters, an annual bus tour of conference sportswriters.

It was in the heat of those informal summer drills where games are often won or lost come fall. Now to a man, the players believed they were on the verge of something special. And when it had come time to set the team's goals for the season, they made it clear that there was only one logical goal — a national championship. They got some pushback from their coach on that. If you set such a high goal and fall short, he told them, it suggests your season has been a failure. But in the team meeting, the players were adamant. We've won a conference championship. We've had an undefeated regular season. We've done all of that. There's only one thing left to accomplish. "We all put our name and stamp on it," Aaron Graham recalled. "That was our goal: to win the national championship."

The goal was now clearly displayed on the wall in the team's South Stadium meeting room. And as the preseason was winding down toward the opener against West Virginia, Osborne liked what he'd seen of his players' attitude. But as Osborne began his 22nd year as head coach and 33rd at the university, this group still needed to prove itself to him.

Part of the beauty and mystery of this game is that every team has its own unique chemistry and personality. It remained to be seen whether this group would have the winning alchemy of talent, toughness and leadership that goes into a championship team. Osborne had learned long ago that seasons are long, and lots of things can happen, many of which you can't control. When adversity comes, as it always does, who was going to step up in this group?

Practice ended with the much-despised "gassers," a pair of 220-yard wind sprints. If a player didn't make the time required of his position, he ran another one. Then in the fading light of early evening, the players headed for the showers. Osborne walked over to a small gathering of local reporters for his regular post-practice press conference. He gave them the latest on injuries, movement on the depth chart and whatever else they wanted to know about. "Well, is that about it?" he'd ask as the questions wound down. Then Osborne started off on his regular post-practice jog, a solitary three miles around and around the empty floor of Memorial Stadium. Heart trouble a decade earlier kept Osborne diligent about this ritual, which also gave him a little time to think to himself.

In private moments like these, the coach who was now in the twilight of his career did at times contemplate what it would mean to finally win the big one. Tenopir would later recall that in his 20 years with Osborne he had never once heard his boss talk about a personal need or desire to win a national championship. And Osborne's frequent comments to the press that he was more interested in getting the most out of his team than winning trophies or rings did nothing to make fans believe the national title was a huge priority to him.

Osborne kept a sense of humor about the state's endless infatuation with winning it all. During one practice around that time, a tight end ran down the field wide open but never got the ball. As he jogged back to the huddle, he called over to Osborne, "Coach, if you'd throw to the tight end more you'd get that national championship."

"OK, that's what we'll do then," Osborne deadpanned in reply.

But if nothing else, Osborne knew that if Nebraska did win a national title, he would no longer have to answer all the questions about it. One of these years, he figured, his team was going to get over that hump. He knew well that this could be the year.

Touchdown Tommie

After taking the snap, Tommie Frazier in a wink pirouetted 270 degrees and started running down the line of scrimmage, a Husker I-back trailing behind him. Seeing the defense was flowing hard toward the sideline, Frazier suddenly cut so hard to the inside that the angle of his body appeared to defy gravity. He bulled through the arm tackle of a big West Virginia linebacker, brushing him off like a bug. Now he was running straight up the field, looking more like a running back than a quarterback. He juked to avoid a hard-charging safety, who whiffed completely. He then cut around teammate Reggie Baul, whose block cut down the last defender with any prayer to make a play. Frazier coasted to a stop after his 27-yard TD jaunt. That sent up a roar from the 12,000 Husker fans who had journeyed to New York City to witness the start of a season of high expectations.

When run to perfection, any Husker fan would tell you, option football is a beautiful thing to behold. And no one in 1994 ran the option like the sensational Tommie Frazier. Darting and dodging through the West Virginia defense, the 6-foot-2, 205-pound quarterback scored three touchdowns as the Huskers thumped West Virginia's Mountaineers 31-0 in the Kickoff Classic in New Jersey's Meadowlands.

The Huskers had put their national championship dreams at risk in agreeing to fly to the Big Apple for the special bowl-like game that annually marked the start of the college football season. They were taking on a West Virginia team that had gone through the regular season undefeated the previous year. But the players had eagerly voted to accept the invitation, even though it pushed the start of preseason

> "I wasn't even thinking about the Heisman Trophy. But every time I turned around, somebody was asking me about it."
>
> — TOMMIE FRAZIER TO REPORTERS
> AFTER BEATING WEST VIRGINIA

camp into the most blazing days of Nebraska's summer. It revealed the uncommon commitment and hunger of players who felt they had some things to prove. Indeed, while the Huskers had earned more first-place votes than any other team in the Associated Press' preseason poll, the team was ranked only fourth overall. That meant a lot of writers still believed the school that had now lost seven straight bowls was but a paper tiger.

But on a blistering Sunday afternoon in late August when the on-field temperature hit 105 degrees, the Huskers created some believers. The Nebraska defense — with three local New Jersey natives as starters — was relentless. West Virginia, which would finish the season unranked at 7-6, was held to 89 total yards, with just 8 yards rushing, its quarterback sacked eight times. Sophomore I-back Lawrence Phillips, in his first career start, ran for 126 yards on a wide variety of sweeps, counters, options, draws and dives. And Frazier was dangerously efficient at the throttle of the Huskers' option attack, running for 130 yards on just 12 carries and throwing for another 100 yards, having a hand in all four Husker TDs.

Frazier that day looked like he'd been running this offense his whole life, which wasn't quite true. He first quarterbacked the option at age 7. Now the magician was showing all his tricks. He'd patiently hold the ball and force a defender to commit to him before flipping a split-second pitch to the I-back. He'd fake the pitch and keep, turning it inside. He'd sell the run and then quickly drop back to zip a pass downfield. The Nebraska option game was so devastating against the Mountaineers that a couple of times Frazier practically walked into the end zone. And beyond his decision-making, ball-handling and running, Frazier's poise, confidence and fire showed through. With 50 national writers on hand, the buzz in the press box was that Frazier was now one of the favorites to come back to New York in December to pick up the Heisman Trophy.

That the Husker offense would be receiving rave reviews was a little ironic. For years, the writers had been saying the college game had passed Tom Osborne and his archaic, ground-pounding offense by. As the bowl losses piled up, one Washington Post writer labeled Osborne's schemes "prehistoric." While Nebraska annually ranked among the nation's leaders in rushing, even many fans had restlessly groused in the early 1990s that if Osborne didn't start throwing the ball around the field like the other top college teams, the Huskers would never again be among the nation's elite.

"Tom, you are a good head coach, and I'm proud of our clean, strong program,'' one man wrote to the Omaha World-Herald in 1991. "However, we will never know how good our athletes can play as long as our current ultraconservative offense continues."

But Osborne stubbornly clung to the option, still believing it was well-suited for Nebraska. The offense fit with the state's hard-nosed mentality. And it could sometimes get a little ridiculous trying to throw the ball in wind tunnels like Ames, Iowa, and Manhattan, Kansas. Plus, while you didn't pass much in the option, when you did, the results could often be devastating. The option game spread defenses out so much sideline to sideline that teams had little choice but to commit a safety to covering the pitch man. If a quarterback running the option suddenly dropped back to throw, a receiver would only have to beat one guy to be running alone down the field.

And contrary to the belief of some, the Nebraska running game was not simple. There were 27 different running plays in the Osborne playbook, each blocked five or six different ways and able to be run out of 12 to 15 different formations. Add in the fact that many defenses saw the option only once or twice a year, and Osborne's option attack produced as many headaches for defensive coordinators as it did bruises for their players. Tom Osborne didn't invent option football. But his coaching peers said no one ran it more creatively or effectively.

So while Osborne made lots of major changes in his program around that time, he never chucked his offense. The biggest problem, Osborne and his coaches knew, was that for years they'd had quarterbacks who were just pretty good players. What they needed was a real playmaker.

That's why the day after the Husker attack was completely throttled by Miami 22-0 in the 1992 Orange Bowl — the first time Nebraska had been shut out in 18 years — Osborne and assistant coach Kevin Steele traveled north up Florida's Gulf Coast. They were headed to Palmetto for a recruiting visit to the home of Tommie and Priscilla Frazier. Years later, Steele liked to joke that he won Tommie Jr. in a game of Spades, having spent hours playing the card game with Frazier's family. The sequence of events that would ultimately bring Tommie to Lincoln was a little more complicated than that — but no less a good story.

Steele, a linebackers coach, recruited the entire southeast United States for the Huskers, a natural role for the University of Tennessee grad who spoke with a bit of a Southern twang. Steele actually left a coaching job at his alma mater in 1990

"The only time I hear anything negative about us is when I'm in Nebraska. The people in the South are in awe of this program."

— ASSISTANT COACH KEVIN STEELE (ON RIGHT, WITH TURNER GILL)

for the chance to join Osborne's staff. After growing up the son of a high school coach and watching classic Nebraska-Oklahoma games on TV, it had been a life goal for Steele to coach with Osborne. As enamored as he was with Osborne as a coach, he'd found he was even more taken by the way Osborne carried himself as a person. Osborne was about the only man he'd met in his life who made him feel uplifted in his presence.

As part of his recruiting duties, Steele was checking out a receiver at a high school in Orlando during spring ball in 1990. "If you want to win a national championship at Nebraska," the coach there told him, "you need to go to Manatee High School and get that 10th-grade quarterback they've got there." Steele had no idea who the coach was talking about. But he well knew Manatee, a powerhouse program in Bradenton that produced four or five big-time recruits a year. And Manatee's coach, Joe Kinnan, actually studied and ran the Nebraska option offense. It sounded promising.

On a sultry afternoon the very next day, clutching a towel to wipe the sweat from his brow, Steele got his first look at Tommie Frazier. The kid was a force of nature. Tall and well-built, the junior-to-be was taking charge, pointing here, pointing there, telling everyone what to do. He had a cannon for an arm and a quick release on the ball. He had huge hands, making him an excellent ball-handler. And no one could tackle him. This guy is unbelievable, Steele thought to himself. If we can somehow get this guy to Lincoln, we'll win a whole bunch of ballgames.

By Frazier's senior year, after he'd led his high school to a two-year record of 21-3, he was a hot property. Some recruiting analysts rated him the nation's best option quarterback. Nebraska was lucky that the big schools in Frazier's home state favored drop-back throwers and weren't much interested in him as a quarterback. But Colorado, Notre Dame and Clemson — all three of which had won national championships in recent years — joined Nebraska as top suitors.

Frazier at one point was ready to commit that fall to the Buffaloes after a visit to Boulder. But Colorado fell out of the running after it signed Koy Detmer and told Frazier he was now only wanted as a defensive back. It was a decision coaches there would surely later regret: Less than a year later, freshman quarterbacks Detmer and Frazier would duel head to head in Lincoln, a game the Huskers won 52-7. While at Nebraska, Frazier never would lose to the rival Buffs. Any time he played Colorado, he acknowledged years later, it was personal.

The critical recruiting period for the Huskers came in January 1992, starting when Osborne made his official visit to the Frazier home after that huge bowl loss. A recruiting call coming right after such a humiliating setback was always tough duty. Steele recalled a similar visit a year earlier when the recruit's mom offered the beaten-down Osborne a drink. After he informed her he didn't drink, she responded, "From the way you look, you might oughta start."

Osborne seemed pretty run-down this day, too. But Frazier's father broke the ice on the poor bowl performance, telling Osborne, "Coach, you sure look better tonight than you did last night." Osborne chuckled. And Osborne in general was pretty effective in these home meetings. Parents unsure about sending their kid off to the middle of nowhere U.S.A. pretty quickly got the impression this was a guy who would take care of their son. The Fraziers were impressed by Osborne's emphasis on education. "You're going to play good football," he said, "but if you do everything you're supposed to do, you'll leave with your degree." Osborne's relaxed persona also seemed to mesh well with that of the quiet quarterback. Osborne wasn't one of those fast talkers who made recruits a bunch of promises, and he was never one to promise playing time. But if Frazier came to Lincoln, the coach said, he'd get the chance to compete for the starting job right away. Osborne made it clear that from what he could see on film, Frazier could be a difference-maker for Nebraska. The visit put Nebraska in the mix.

In the final weeks, Steele was spending so much time at Frazier's school he could have been on staff. For his NCAA-allowed one contact a week, he'd go to Manatee early in the morning and watch Frazier lift weights. He'd walk Frazier to class and then hang out with his coaches. He'd sit with him at lunch and then watch him practice basketball in the afternoon. After that, he'd spend the evening with the Fraziers at the family's tidy home in Palmetto.

Bradenton and Palmetto are part of the Sarasota metro area, and Frazier's neighborhood was not immune to the pitfalls and dangers of urban inner-city life. Just a few blocks from his home was "the corner," the place where gang members hung out and drug dealers plied their trade. Tommie's dad worked for a fruit and vegetable packing firm, his mom in a grade school cafeteria, and they strived to keep their six children active in sports and at the local youth center up the street. Tommie stayed out of trouble and was lauded at school for his work ethic. But an older brother, also a very good athlete, was in prison on a cocaine-trafficking conviction, serving as an example to Tommie of the path he needed to avoid.

Steele got to know all the Fraziers well and enjoyed his time with the close-knit family, often joining them in a game of cards. They'd been playing for three hours one evening when Tommie's mother told Steele he needed to leave — Notre Dame Coach Lou Holtz was making his official home visit. But as Priscilla walked Steele to the door, she told him, "Now, we haven't finished this Spades game. When they get through, you need to come back." Steele sat outside in his rental car for two hours until Holtz left, and then proceeded to play two more hours of cards with the Fraziers. Steele could tell Priscilla liked him and liked Nebraska. It was a good sign.

But then things got kind of dicey. Frazier was scheduled to make his official recruiting visit to Nebraska the final weekend before signing day, the last of his five official school visits. But the Tuesday before Frazier was to come to Lincoln, his sister told Steele things weren't looking good. Frazier had gotten back from his recruiting visit to South Bend, and there was now a Notre Dame magnet on the refrigerator. Even worse, he was telling his family he wanted to cancel his Nebraska trip. He was tired of the recruiting process. Priscilla urged him to make the visit, saying he had made a promise to Nebraska that he'd come. But he wasn't budging. Without a visit, Steele knew there was no way Frazier would sign. It was hard to convince city kids there was more to Nebraska than cornfields and cows if they didn't get to campus. Steele asked Priscilla to hand the phone to Tommie.

"Tommie, I understand this, but you've been given an opportunity to make five 48-hour visits so you can make the decision that's best for you," Steele told him. "In the course of a lifetime, five 48-hour visits is not a lot of time. If you cancel one of those, it would be a shame if those 48 hours could have changed the rest of your life."

Tommie still didn't commit to coming, but that didn't stop Steele from flying to Bradenton for his regular weekly visit. The coaches at Manatee offered Steele condolences. They thought it was over. But Steele didn't give up, continually prodding Frazier, and his mother didn't let up on him, either. He finally relented. "You can thank Priscilla Frazier for that," Frazier recalled years later. "She was right. I needed to be a man of my word."

So on Friday after school, Frazier and Steele boarded a privately owned Learjet — perfectly legal transportation under NCAA rules at the time — and flew to Lincoln. The visit went very well. Frazier liked the coaches and the facilities and was having a good time. But the unsung hero of Frazier's visit was Mike Grant — the heir apparent, senior-to-be quarterback who Frazier would ultimately beat out. In a perfect

"It's just my first career start at Nebraska.
There are going to be many more like this."

— TOMMIE FRAZIER, AFTER BEATING MISSOURI 34-24 IN 1992

reflection of the team-first culture Osborne had instilled in his program, Grant served as Frazier's player-host, and the two Florida natives really hit it off. Frazier liked the unity and togetherness of the team. And he felt wanted and welcomed. "It was Nebraska football at its finest," Steele recalled of Grant's performance that weekend. Twenty years later, Frazier and Grant remained good friends.

A story in the Omaha World-Herald on the Saturday of Frazier's visit caused some heartburn around the Husker football offices. It noted Frazier was in Lincoln over the weekend but quoted a recruiting analyst saying, "If Tommie should say no to Clemson and Notre Dame, it would be the biggest surprise in the United States." The coaches decided they should show it to Frazier rather than have him come upon it himself. Frazier laughed it off. That guy isn't making the decision, he said. I am.

Steele had a good feeling when he and Osborne flew home with Frazier, but the quarterback still had not made a commitment. On Monday, Steele faxed hand-written letters to Frazier's school every two hours. Then on Wednesday, signing day, Steele's big, clunky Motorola cellphone rang. It was Frazier's high school coach. Someone wants to talk to you, he said. Frazier got on the line. "Nebraska is the place I want to be."

Frazier could hear the whoops on the other end of the line, and there were a lot of high-fives and exaltations as word got around the South Stadium football offices. Stories would later circulate that Osborne actually got a little misty-eyed on hearing the word. But Steele, who witnessed the stoic coach's immediate reaction, said it was no different than if the Huskers had scored a big touchdown. "Every Husker fan in the world knows Tom's reaction," he said later. "A little smile says it all."

No Nebraska recruit since Turner Gill arrived to more fanfare than Frazier in the fall of 1992. The 18-year-old took notes in meetings and picked things up quickly. It was clear he'd been studying the offense. And with Frazier, you only had to tell him something once. He got it. There was still much to learn. Besides mastering the NU playbook, his physical tools were raw. His footwork needed attention, and he tended to fire every pass like a bazooka shot. He needed to develop more touch. But he was confident to an extreme. One of the first times the freshman sat down in the training room to have his ankles taped for practice, the subject of a national championship came up. "That's what I came here for," he said matter-of-factly.

His teammates quickly learned the freshman had kind of a split personality. Off the field, Frazier was distant and quiet, a loner. On the field, he was a brash, take-charge leader. It became legend within the program that fall how once during practice the freshman came into the huddle to find two upperclass linemen talking. Frazier grabbed one of the players by the face mask, pulled it forward and barked, "Listen up!"

The brashness and abrasiveness irritated some teammates, who saw it as a sign of arrogance. Steele and others who knew him best dispute that, saying arrogance was never part of Frazier's makeup. He was just a supremely confident guy who wanted badly to win. Regardless, teammates also quickly recognized he was a special talent — perhaps the critical piece they had been missing.

Frazier quickly rose to third on the depth chart and played a little in the first two games, scoring his first career touchdown against Middle Tennessee State. But he was also impatient. That created a minor crisis after he didn't play in the Huskers' fourth game, a blowout victory over Arizona State. Frazier showed up Monday morning in Steele's office, his jaw firmly set. "I'm going to go home and do something else," he said. It led to a serious meeting in Osborne's office with Gill, Steele, Frazier and Jack Stark, the team's psychologist.

Frazier asserted himself, saying he felt he should be starting already. Osborne told the restless freshman he wasn't ready yet, that he needed to learn the system better and work on his audibles and checks. The meeting did much to comfort Frazier and clear the air. Frazier was glad to hear where he stood and learn the things coaches felt he needed to work on. In the end, Osborne urged his young quarterback to be patient. His time would come.

His time came more quickly than any of them thought. Going into the Huskers' sixth game against Missouri, Grant was having some trouble with his back, and Osborne handed Frazier the keys to the family car. He became the first true freshman quarterback to start at Nebraska since World War II.

From there, the job was his. Frazier led the Huskers to some big victories that first year, including the Colorado blowout, and took the Huskers to a Big Eight title. But he was also at the controls during one of the Huskers' greatest upset losses of all time, a 19-10 embarrassment in Ames to an Iowa State team that won just two other games all year. He'd finish the year 5-2 as a starter, the other setback being yet another Orange Bowl loss. The young quarterback turned the ball over twice in the Huskers' 27-14 loss to Florida State, though Nebraska's performance overall was much better than in any recent bowls.

As a sophomore in 1993, Frazier blossomed, helping the Huskers reel off 11 straight victories en route to an Orange Bowl rematch with the Seminoles. In that 18-16 loss, the gritty Frazier for the first time proved to all of college football that he was a big-game quarterback. The stage and stakes didn't faze him at all, as he outplayed the Heisman Trophy-winning Ward. It was Frazier, in a losing cause, who was named the game's MVP. Frazier made big play after big play, right up until that last-second pass to Bell to set up the failed field-goal try. Against the Seminoles that night, the only thing to finally stop Frazier was the clock.

The loss left Frazier feeling he and the Huskers had blown a great opportunity. Unlike some of his teammates, he didn't feel they had been robbed by the refs. "When all was said and done," he said, "we took the lead and didn't do our jobs. We lacked a killer instinct."

Frazier's statistics were never mind-blowing, but he was a gamer. When you needed a first down, he had a knack for getting it — using his keen field vision, athleticism and sheer will to get the nose of the ball past the chain. He'd aggressively take the ball down the line on the option, and whether he kept it or pitched it, there was no hesitation, no doubt. He also developed a thorough knowledge of Osborne's system. The quarterbacks always had the freedom to switch the direction of the play or to audible into another call altogether, depending on how the defense was lining up. If a play were run into certain defensive formations, it could be dead before it even started. Osborne counted on his quarterbacks to think the same way he did and to get the Huskers out of those plays. Over time, Frazier became Osborne in pads. "They had to know it cold," Osborne recalled. "You knew when Tommie was out there, things were going to be done right."

Above all, Frazier had a competitive fire that could not be suppressed. Teammates said he could get them rolling just by looking them in the eye. He was college football's version of Michael Jordan, making all the other players around him better. Like Jordan, Frazier also expected a lot from those around him — nothing short of perfection. And if they didn't meet his standard, he wasn't shy about letting them know. Sometimes Husker coaches would have to talk to Frazier and get him to ease up on his teammates. Reserve offensive lineman Matt Hoskinson would never forget the day in practice when he made a half-hearted effort to block a defensive end on an option play. When he got back to the huddle, Frazier ruthlessly lit into him and wouldn't stop. Hoskinson was originally shocked and upset by the prickly quarterback's reaction. But over time, he also came to understand and respect it. "He was a tough and vocal leader, and he expected everyone to do (things) perfectly,"

"We, at times, didn't play all that well.
But we think we have a good team."

— TOM OSBORNE AFTER BEATING WEST VIRGINIA

Hoskinson said. "There was some resentment because of that. But at the end of the day, he made us a better football team."

Frazier never would be elected captain at Nebraska, likely because of such blowups and the fact that he wasn't the most fun guy to be around. He had few close friends on the team and tended to keep teammates, fans and everyone else at arm's length. "Tommie was kind of an acquired taste," one teammate later put it. But there also wasn't a person in the program who didn't recognize that Frazier was a leader. "He may not have been the guy you wanted to go to a movie or a party with," Ron Brown recalled. "But I know one thing: When Tommie Frazier showed up in the huddle, everyone was ready to follow him."

And now the Huskers and their fans were ready to follow him all the way back to Miami. After Frazier's first touchdown that day against the Mountaineers, the P.A. announcer at first indicated there were flags on the field. Then he corrected himself. "Excuse me, those are oranges." Husker fans' ritual toss of citrus fruit was usually reserved for late November against Oklahoma, the game that typically decided the Big Eight champion and Orange Bowl berth. But for this Nebraska team, even here in late August 1994, any other January destination would be a major disappointment.

With the convincing win, the Huskers planted a stake in the ground for the rest of college football to see. Indeed, it would boost Nebraska to the top of the polls. Not that Osborne was getting excited about such things. "If you're optimistic about Nebraska, fine," Osborne told reporters. "We'll go along with that."

The coach still saw plenty of things to work on, including cleaning up the five turnovers his team committed that day. But to paraphrase the Sinatra song, if Frazier and the Huskers could make it here in New York, they could make it anywhere. As the plane carrying Osborne, Frazier and the rest of the Huskers that evening put the majestic Manhattan skyline on the horizon, there appeared to be no limit to what they could accomplish.

A Need for Speed

A s soon as the Blackshirts recognized the play as an option right, they turned on the jets. Defensive tackle Terry Connealy, a senior from Hyannis, Nebraska, darted inside and forced the Texas Tech quarterback into an early pitch. That allowed the Husker pursuit to put a giant bull's eye on the pitch man. Backup safety Tony Veland, one of the team's hardest hitters, flew into the picture, slipped a block and popped the ball carrier low. And Grant Wistrom, seeing early-season action in his true freshman season, shed his blocker and cleaned it all up along the sideline. Only a generous spot allowed the runner to even get back to the original line of scrimmage.

"You try to run outside on Nebraska, and you take your life in your own hands," play-by-play man Brad Nessler said during the Thursday night ESPN telecast. "They run too well."

Indeed, Nebraska flashed speed all over the field on defense during its 42-16 shellacking of the Red Raiders in Lubbock. Interior linemen with the quickness to shrug off blocks and be disruptive inside. Linebackers who could run stride for stride with a wide receiver or come hard on the blitz. Cornerbacks comfortable with life on an island, able to cover the speediest wide receivers one-on-one. On this balmy Thursday night in west Texas, the Blackshirts turned out the lights on the Red Raiders, whose most effective offensive play tended to be quarterback Zebbie Lethridge scrambling for his life. "Speed, speed, speed on this football team," ESPN color analyst Gary Danielson agreed.

Those words were probably quite a revelation to many viewers given the perception that Nebraska teams were big, corn-fed and plodding. During the string of bowl losses, Husker players recalled taunts like, "Country boys, go home. You're too slow." The turnabout did not come by accident. Tom Osborne and his coaches had

"It just so happens that blocking kicks is my specialty."

— BARRON MILES AFTER HIS FOURTH BLOCKED KICK OF THE SEASON

made a concerted effort in recent years to get more speed on the field, especially on defense. In the early 1990s, Husker coaches began putting a premium on speed in recruiting. And then in the 1993 season, Osborne and veteran defensive coordinator Charlie McBride altered Nebraska's decades-old defensive alignment, switching to an attacking-style scheme that took advantage of that new speed. Finally, after all the bowl losses that saw Huskers often running in the secondary steps behind Miami and Florida State blazers, Nebraska had guys who could run with anyone.

The story of the turbo boost on defense actually began at the end of the 1990 season. That's when it was perceived that Nebraska football had hit bottom — or at least as low as you can get when you lose only three games, two of them to the co-national champs.

Late in the season, it had looked like that Husker team could be the one to break the school's national title drought. After breezing through an extremely light non-conference slate and a slew of Big Eight weaklings, the Huskers were 8-0, ranked second, and going into the fourth quarter at home led the ninth-ranked Colorado Buffaloes 12-0. Then the bottom dropped out. Colorado scored, and scored, and scored again. The Buffs put 27 points on the Blackshirts in a dreary, cold and rainy fourth quarter, the most in 101 years of Nebraska football. They left Lincoln with a 27-12 win and headed off to claim a share of a national title. A couple of weeks later, the Husker defense surrendered 45 points to an average, unranked Oklahoma team — the most ever allowed under Osborne. Then a month later in a bowl against Georgia Tech, the other co-national champ, the Blackshirts duplicated the ignominious feat, getting scorched again for 45. To be fair, an inept, turnover-prone offense had contributed to both defensive meltdowns. But it still wasn't pretty.

Nebraska finished the season ranked 24th, its lowest since 1968. It also finished out of the top 10 for the fourth straight year. That hadn't happened since before Bob Devaney. The pundits were wondering whether Nebraska's days as a football power were over. And Nebraskans, whose collective spirit tended to rise and fall with the Huskers, were howling. At Nebraska, the expectation was dominance. That was the monster Devaney and Osborne had created.

McBride had produced national Top 15 defenses most years in Lincoln, but that didn't stop calls of "McBride must go" from ringing across the state. "Maybe the college game is passing Tom Osborne's outdated offenses by, but I know it has run Charlie McBride's defense into the place where college defenses go to be buried," one fan wrote to The World-Herald. That was tame compared to the personal letters

McBride got, some of which called him a disgrace to the university. "My name was Chump," he recalled.

In the wake of the bowl loss, Osborne gathered his staff in South Stadium. He wasn't in any kind of panic mode. It wasn't as if they'd lost to a bunch of stiffs. And it wasn't Osborne's style to pound the table and demand changes, the way such a scene would play out in a lot of places. But it was clear the program had slipped. Morale within both the team and staff was low. Osborne's program seemed to be standing at a crossroads. "Nine and three ain't very well accepted right now," Osborne said. He decided it was time to internally re-examine every aspect of the program. It wasn't obvious from the outside, but they looked at recruiting, strength and conditioning, offensive and defensive schemes and everything in between. "Coach Osborne didn't stick his head in the sand," Ron Brown recalled. "It had a lot to do with setting a new trajectory for the program." Indeed, many changes did result from the review, from efforts to promote more team unity to the hiring of the team's first nutritionist. But none would prove more important than a decision to get faster on defense.

It had long been a tradition at Nebraska that the fastest players went to the offensive side of the ball. In fact, until the late 1980s, Nebraska rarely even specifically recruited defensive backs. They'd instead recruit six running backs and then move those who didn't make it into the rotation over to the defensive back-field. Supplemented by some walk-ons, they could usually do a pretty decent job. But the practice eventually was exposed. Probably what best symbolized Nebraska's historical lack of speed on defense had been that 1983 national championship game against Miami, when Nebraska coaches had two defensive backs switch jerseys to disguise who was covering whom. That game helped change the recruiting philo-sophy, the Huskers specifically going after cover guys. But as had been evidenced by the recent string of bowl losses, there still weren't enough fast defenders to go around. "In simple terms, we couldn't match up," George Darlington bluntly recalled. "We realized there was no way we were going to win a national championship unless we greatly improved the speed of our defensive football team."

A sportswriter around that time asked Osborne, "Why don't you just do like Miami and recruit more speed?" Osborne kind of laughed at the question, which suggested he hadn't figured out that speed was a desirable thing to have in a football player. Nebraska was already recruiting as many fast guys as it could. But Osborne also knew he and his staff were going to have to find a way to get more of them to come to Lincoln. So beginning with the recruiting class of 1991, the coaches elevated

"The free safety is now in the action more,
which is good. I like making the big hits."

— MIKE MINTER ON HIS MOVE TO FREE SAFETY IN 1994

speed as they looked at what skills and attributes players brought to the table. Osborne and his staff became very conscious of the times potential recruits had run for their school track teams. Regardless of how he looked on the field, could he go 10.5 in the 100? It helped broaden the pool of fast players they could go after. And a player's size, while still important, was downgraded. The Huskers would take a harder look at someone who was a little undersized if he could run. Players who would have been considered safeties before were now recruited as linebackers, while guys who would have been linebackers were now defensive ends.

Due to those recruiting changes and the shifting around of many players who were already on the roster, the average weight of Nebraska's starting linebackers dropped between 1991 and 1994 from around 230 pounds to under 220. The average for defensive backs dropped even more, from about 195 to under 180. But they were also that much faster. Ed Stewart was typical of Nebraska's new look on D. He had been recruited as a good safety prospect. But after moving to linebacker, the Chicago native blossomed into an All-American who, as McBride liked to say, blitzed so hard he peeled the skin off his eyeballs.

The focus on speed caused Nebraska to redraw its recruiting map, with starting defenders now less likely to come from within Nebraska. Recruiting for Osborne always started at home. He was always partial to the Nebraska kids and would grant a scholarship to any he felt could eventually play Division I football. The reality, though, was that within a 500-mile radius of Lincoln, there were only a handful of guys who could go 4.4 in the 40.

It meant Nebraska would have to increasingly use its longtime national recruiting cachet to go into populated urban areas around the country for offensive skill players and defenders. Florida, for example, was producing more than 200 scholarship football players a year, and they were pretty much all burners. Florida State and Miami had their pick. Nebraska needed to get its share. "You'd better have a lot of speed on the field," Osborne said of a 1992 recruiting class that would include Florida's Tommie Frazier, track speedster Riley Washington out of California and 1994's fastest Husker, Mike Minter.

The 1994 Huskers, as usual, featured a lot of home-grown talent, Nebraskans particularly filling most of the "non-skilled" positions on offense. In that Texas Tech game, three offensive line starters, the fullback, tight end and a receiver all hailed from Nebraska. But on defense, Connealy was the only starter from in-state. An injury and a lineup change would increase that number to three later in the season. That was still below the typical four to five in-state guys wearing Blackshirts in seasons past.

However, beyond player size or geography, an apparent change in Osborne's past practice on recruiting players known as Prop 48s also played a huge role in reshaping the defense. In 1986, the NCAA passed Proposition 48, requiring any high school athlete wanting to accept a Division I college scholarship to achieve a minimum college entrance exam score and minimum GPA in a core set of college prep classes. Those who didn't qualify could still come, but they'd have to pay their own way to school, sit out a year and lose a year of eligibility. If they then made the grades, they could be put on scholarship the next year as sophomores. A few conferences wouldn't allow member schools to accept these so-called Prop 48s. But the Big Eight Conference had no such rule, leaving it to individual institutions to decide whether they'd admit them.

Nebraska nonetheless initially did not take many Prop 48s. The school had enrolled only five true Prop 48s as of 1990 — an average of one a year — and four of them had not been major contributors. Two other high-profile players, standout tight end Johnny Mitchell and running back Derek Brown, had come to Nebraska around that time through a kind of Prop 48 loophole that allowed them to avoid losing that first year of eligibility.

But Osborne and Nebraska took seven true Prop 48s in the fall of 1991, each sitting out and losing a year of eligibility, and five more the next fall. Eight of those 12 players played on the defensive side of the ball, and they included some real difference-makers. The 1994 defense would include four starters who initially came to Nebraska in 1991 or 1992 as Prop 48s: Barron Miles, Christian Peter, Dwayne Harris and Tyrone Williams. The 1995 defense also had four Prop 48 starters, as returners Peter and Williams were joined by 1992 Prop 48 Jared Tomich and 1993's Michael Booker. Jamel Williams, a standout reserve on the 1995 defense, also was a 1993 Prop 48.

Osborne years later could recall no conscious decision of, "Hey, let's take a bunch of Prop 48s." In some cases, players were recruited with the expectation that they would meet standards, only to fall just short. Peter had been one such player, actually practicing with the Huskers his freshman year before it was realized that one of his core high school classes wasn't accepted. Others might just miss by a point or two on the standardized test, a rigid requirement the NCAA loosened years later. But Osborne said the sudden increase in Prop 48s likely was tied to the Huskers' concerted effort to get faster. "Those are kids who had speed," he said after he was read a list of Prop 48s from that era.

Osborne certainly saw no shame in accepting Prop 48 athletes. Back then and later, he argued that the ability to accept them was the best thing academically for both the schools and the players. Any who didn't qualify under Prop 48 could still travel another route to big-time football, attending a junior college and then transferring after one or two years. "Go to a JC, and we'll bring you back," schools would tell players. That's how many top programs, particularly those in states like California, Texas and Kansas that had lots of JC's, ultimately got non-qualifiers to campus.

Osborne made a good case that a player who came to Lincoln and showed he could do college work during his freshman year was better prepared, a much better academic risk and much more likely to graduate than a player coming out of a two-year school. Often such schools' academics were not very rigorous. Osborne knew of cases where players were able to pass 40 hours of credits in a single year at a JC, a ridiculous figure that suggested lower standards. Prop 48s also fit with the Nebraska mind-set, an academic version of the walk-on. If you show you are willing to come in and work hard on the books, we'll take a chance on you and work with you. "We did very well with those guys," Osborne would say years later of the Prop 48s. He was talking in terms of academics, not football, though the latter was certainly true, too.

Nebraska had some natural advantages in recruiting against other schools to get the best of the Prop 48s. It had relatively low tuition, making it easier for players to scrape together the money for that first year. In addition, Nebraska had an academic support program that was considered a model nationally, able to help Prop 48s and any other athletes obtain the tutoring and study skills needed to succeed in college.

After 1992, Nebraska took just two Prop 48s a year, and much to Osborne's chagrin, the school couldn't take any after 1996. That's when the Big Eight merged with four former Southwest Conference schools to form the Big 12, which by rule barred accepting non-qualifiers. Still, the big Prop 48 classes Nebraska enrolled in 1991 and 1992 clearly proved to be critical building blocks for the championship defenses to come.

Regardless of how the speed got to Lincoln, McBride soon found ways to take advantage of it. Since Devaney days, Nebraska had run with a five-man defensive front, with a nose guard flanked by two tackles and two ends, and then two

"You have to have the attitude that nobody can beat you, no matter how big they are. It's the attitude factor."

— BARRON MILES

linebackers behind. The 5-2 was effective against the ground-pounding attacks that were typical in the classic old Big Eight days, and it continued to be Nebraska's primary formation into the 1990s. The only time McBride tended to vary from it would be during some obvious passing downs, when one of the interior linemen would be pulled in favor of an extra "nickel" defensive back.

In the 1992 season, McBride began experimenting with a 4-3 formation on passing downs, featuring four down linemen and three linebackers. The Huskers used it nearly the whole game against Colorado and blasted the Buffs, as former stand-up linebackers Trev Alberts and Travis Hill stirred up trouble from their new rush-end positions. Then a few weeks later, the Husker coaches went to the 4-3 when Oklahoma was shredding the Blackshirts on the ground. Nothing else was working. Osborne and McBride were surprised to learn their specialty pass defense was just as effective in stopping the run. While the Sooners had gained 142 yards in the first quarter, they got only 91 the rest of the game. "It was weird," Osborne said afterward. But he and McBride weren't going to argue with success. They switched to the 4-3 full-time beginning in the 1993 season.

Now instead of reading and reacting as they did in the old 5-2, Nebraska's defenders were getting after people, with an aggressive, attacking style. If you're going to screw up, McBride would tell his players, screw up going 100 miles an hour. If there are 11 flying to the ball that way, that would cover up for a lot of mistakes. The players loved the new scheme because it was so simple. The defensive ends got upfield and after quarterbacks. The tackles created havoc inside, eating up blockers and wrecking the running game. Linebackers kept quarterbacks guessing, sometimes blitzing, other times dropping into pass coverage. And the defensive backs, who were supposed to cover their guys all over the field without any help, made it all go. This defense wasn't designed to bend but not break. The idea was to hit the offense with so many sacks and tackles for losses that they'd have trouble digging out of the hole. "We had two defensive tackles who played over the guards and nine guys who could run like the wind," Darlington said.

By the end of that 1993 season, the Orange Bowl game against Florida State offered proof that Nebraska's speed gap had largely been closed. The Blackshirts nearly shut down a Seminole attack that had been averaging almost 550 yards and 43 points a game, holding them to a lone, questionable touchdown. Kevin Steele, who would go on to coach with Bobby Bowden at FSU years later, said Bowden and other Seminole coaches told him they'd been totally unprepared for the way Nebraska ran. Unable to hold a late lead against Florida State in the end, the 1993 defense lacked a little something extra. But it wasn't because it wasn't fast enough.

Now this 1994 defense was even faster, and with its new speed, the image of the Blackshirts was transformed. The black practice jersey had been a point of pride for the defense dating back to the Devaney days. An assistant coach looking for a practice-jersey color that would set apart the first-team defense just happened to walk out of a Lincoln sporting goods store with a pile of black ones. A tradition was born. It was always a big day when a defensive player walked into the locker room and saw a black jersey hanging in his locker the first time. But now the Blackshirts were fast becoming their own brand. Nebraskans could walk into stores and buy black T-shirts and sweatshirts emblazoned with skulls and crossbones, the Blackshirts' visual signature. Red would always be the Huskers' color, but thanks to the Blackshirts, black was now part of the game-day palette in Memorial Stadium, too. The Blackshirts by 1994 were gaining a name far beyond Lincoln, too — as one of the most fearsome defenses in all of college football. They were also developing a little attitude. After an intrasquad scrimmage earlier that spring, Brown, the receivers coach, had tried to razz cornerback Miles about how the No. 1 offense had fared against the No. 1 defense. "You had to chase our running backs today," Brown said. "Yeah," Miles allowed in return. "Sideways."

Miles was one of a handful of players who epitomized Nebraska's new look on defense. Undersized didn't even begin to describe Miles. He came to Lincoln at 5-foot-9 and barely 140 pounds. He had good speed at 4.6 in the 40 but was one of those rare guys who was faster on the field than on a stopwatch. The Huskers recruited Miles after Frank Solich — a former pint-sized Nebraska star himself — watched him play in the New Jersey state championship game. Miles' team got clobbered. But several times, even after the game was out of hand, Miles had chased down opposing ball carriers. After the game, he had a bloody nose and was missing a tooth, but the Husker coaches loved his never-quit attitude.

Still, he faced some funny looks when he arrived in Lincoln in the fall of 1991. When the diminutive newcomer told teammates he indeed was not a water boy but a cornerback, they gave him looks that he interpreted to say, "Man, you don't have a chance." Miles had to sit out that first year as a Prop 48, unable to achieve the required standardized test score. And during his sophomore year in Lincoln, he learned the likely reason why. His math professor couldn't understand why Miles couldn't pass a test, even though he clearly knew the material. He figured out that Miles had dyslexia and a related attention-deficit disorder. While everyone else was able to concentrate on their test, all Miles could hear was the tick-tick-tick of the clock in his head. That professor started giving him his tests alone in a quiet room. Miles was glad to learn he really wasn't just a dumb jock. The academic support program — a key in drawing Miles to Lincoln in the first place — was able to find ways to help him cope. In the end, Miles would prove an academic success story, finishing his degree in early childhood education in four years. Osborne, who met with all his players each year to set goals both on the field and in the classroom, had insisted Miles do all he could to finish the degree before heading off to the pros. Life would make it hard to come back later. "Let's go do it," Osborne had said. And Miles did.

Because of Miles' size, most teams would try to pick on him, particularly matching up their tallest receivers against him. It was a mistake, a lesson they would usually learn the hard way. Osborne would later call Miles one of the most gifted athletes ever to play for him. And inch for inch, no Nebraska defender ever made more big plays. An explosive leaper, the now 165-pounder could outjump athletes half a foot taller. "He knew people were coming after him, and he didn't shy away from it," teammate Tony Veland recalled. "He always played big." Miles had intangibles, too, including great instincts and a complete lack of fear. Osborne considered a punt Miles blocked for a touchdown the previous year against Oklahoma State one of the single greatest plays he'd seen in a lifetime of football. Miles had caught the ball right off the punter's foot, keeping his eyes wide open the whole time.

Above all, Miles loved to play, one of those guys who always had a smile on his face. Now as the Huskers looked to get back to Miami, no one wanted redemption more than Miles. He had made a critical late hit out of bounds to aid Florida State's drive for the winning field goal. Miles had a sick feeling in his stomach as the bus pulled away from the Orange Bowl that night. But he also was making plans to come back to Miami. "I couldn't wait for the next season," he recalled. "I already knew what was going to happen."

It speaks to the melting pot that was Nebraska football that while the smallest member of the defense was a black guy from New Jersey's inner city, one of the biggest was a white, boot-stomping son of Nebraska's Sand Hills. Connealy, a 6-5, 275-pound defensive tackle, was in many ways the quintessential Nebraska lineman. Connealy had grown up hardened and tough on a ranch near Hyannis, Nebraska, pop. 336. "He had that farm-boy strength from picking up bales of hay from the time he was old enough to work," recalled Jason Peter, Connealy's backup that year. "And he wanted nothing more than to win for Nebraska. He was Nebraska." Despite having played eight-man football, Connealy was a starter by his sophomore year. But like a lot of the in-state kids, it was based as much on his determination and

"This defense is a blast to play. You are making big plays and going 100 mph and not sitting there reading people and getting blasted. You make things happen."

— TERRY CONNEALY ON THE 4-3

drive as his physical tools. "Connealy!" McBride would yell. "If you got any slower your heart would stop."

Connealy was also the Blackshirts' emotional leader. Around the practice field and in the locker room, he was about the nicest guy you could find. He'd offer tips to the scout-team players, explaining how he'd just beaten them. But come game day, he turned into a psychopath. After Osborne gave his pre-game speech and left the locker room, the four captains would take over, each saying a few words. They'd generally save the most fiery talker for last, and on the 1994 team, that was Connealy. He'd get up in front of the team, big goose bumps rising from his neck and arms, and go absolutely nuts. He'd start screaming and slobbering, punching people, kicking chalkboards and uttering words that would have made Osborne turn white. Connealy didn't just want to win. He wanted the Huskers to dominate.

Connealy was pretty much setting the tone for how the entire Nebraska defense was playing this year. The Blackshirts followed their smothering defensive performance against West Virginia with a solid one against Texas Tech. In fact, the biggest defensive concern afterward was an injury — one that was also a major blow to the team's defensive speed. In the second half, sophomore free safety Minter was trying to wrestle a Red Raider out of bounds when his foot planted into the turf and his leg twisted awkwardly. He had to be carried back to the sidelines, and within minutes team orthopedist Dr. Pat Clare gave the preliminary diagnosis: Minter had blown out his knee, a torn anterior cruciate ligament. His season was over. He sat on the bench and put a towel over his face, inconsolable.

The soft-spoken kid the Huskers had been able to pull out of his native Oklahoma had the fastest electronic 40-yard dash time on the team. But more than that, he was the quarterback of the defense. On the first day of fall camp a year earlier, Minter had left Darlington speechless by not only lining himself up correctly, but the other defensive backs, too. It was no surprise that McBride entrusted the mechanical engineering major to get the defense into the right coverage on the field. "There are several guys we can't afford to lose," Osborne said after the game. "Mike definitely is one of them." Indeed, not having Minter out there the rest of the season figured to be a huge loss to the Nebraska defense.

It would be almost like the offense losing Tommie Frazier.

The Pipeline

The new video replay boards in Memorial Stadium were made for plays like this. Taking a handoff on a counter sweep, Lawrence Phillips juked, ran by, bulled over and dragged UCLA defenders, finally hauled down after a gain of 60 yards. It was such an impressive run that even the Huskers' running backs coach couldn't resist looking up at the boards to take another look. "I told myself I wasn't going to watch replays," Frank Solich said. "But I had to sneak a peek at that one."

Nebraska's 1994 home opener will be best remembered for the debut of Husker-Vision. The tingly strains of the Alan Parsons Project song "Sirius" pulsed through the stadium, and both players and fans for the first time experienced the emotional rush of the "tunnel walk." A stirring new tradition was born. Fans also for the first time watched replays on new 17-by-23-foot video screens installed in two corners of the stadium — a first for a college football stadium. There were plenty of big plays to show that day, too, as the Huskers thrashed UCLA 49-21.

It was another scary-good performance for the offense, which treated the 12th-ranked Bruins like McNeese State. The Huskers rolled to 484 yards on the ground — the most UCLA had given up in half a century. Phillips ran for 175 and had another highlight-reel play when he tipped an errant pitch into the air, pulled it in with one hand and waltzed into the end zone.

But as great a back as Phillips was, what truly made the Husker offense go that day — and during the entire 1994 season — were the brawny guys on the fringes of those video images who were cutting down, bowling over and pulverizing the defense. Afterward, UCLA players marveled at the physicality and athleticism of the Husker

"I'm not going to say we're the best offensive line in college football. But we try to be."

— TACKLE ROB ZATECHKA, RIGHT, COMBINING ON A PANCAKE
WITH AARON GRAHAM AND JOEL WILKS

offensive line. "They were trying to cut everybody," a Bruin linebacker said. "I can't believe how far down the field their line was."

Even at a school with a celebrated history of great offensive linemen, many coaches and observers knew coming into the 1994 campaign that this Nebraska line was a special group. They'd been featured on the back cover of the media guide and dubbed "The Pipeline." And while the term pancake — an offensive lineman knocking an opponent on his back — had been around Nebraska football for a while, this was also the group that made it part of the state's common vernacular. Over the course of the season, Zach Wiegert, Brenden Stai, Aaron Graham, Joel Wilks and Rob Zatechka would serve up more pancakes than Aunt Jemima, tallying them weekly on a board in the offensive line meeting room. Averaging 6-4½ and 295 pounds, they were bigger than a lot of NFL lines. While Nebraska had a true star in Tommie Frazier and a budding one in Phillips, even they would have told you the foundation of this offense was the big guys up front.

Nebraska may have been the only place in the country where offensive linemen enjoyed celebrity status. And no one enjoyed the attention more than Wiegert, a senior right tackle. Like many Husker linemen, Wiegert had not been highly recruited. He'd been so dominant against his lightweight competition at Class C-1 Fremont Bergan High School that no one knew how good he was. But he was freak-ishly athletic for a big man, and Nebraska coaches finally offered him a scholarship after seeing the 250-pounder lead the fast break on Bergan's basketball team.

On the scout team as a redshirt freshman, he had a reputation for being lazy on the field and a goof-off away from it. Coach Jack Pierce, an assistant who ran the scout team, told him he'd better do a better job the following year. "Jack, I'm not going to be on the scout team next year," Wiegert replied. He was right. Not only did Wiegert leapfrog up the depth chart the next fall to become a rare sophomore line starter, he made All-Big Eight as well. By his junior year he was an All-American, with pro scouts marveling at his physical skills. Watching a 6-5, 300-pounder dunk a basketball with two hands was a frightening thing. Wiegert might screw up sometimes, but he'd quickly shake it off. Nothing bothered him, and he played with an intensity that was contagious. Teammates said he was confident in his abilities, a nice way of saying he was arrogant, but he'd back it up. By the end of 1994, he wouldn't give up a single sack or be called once for holding. There's a reason he won the school's seventh Outland as the nation's best interior lineman.

Wiegert had a bookend on the left side in Zatechka, who at 6-5, 315 was actually a little bigger. Doak Ostergard, an assistant trainer who would develop close relationships with many of the players, remembers seeing the big-framed Zatechka and Wiegert walking down the hall together shortly after reporting as freshmen in 1990. That'll work, he thought. Now a senior, Zatechka wasn't as mobile as Wiegert but was a powerful straight-ahead guy, and he didn't make mental mistakes. In fact, when it came to both body and brain, Zatechka had won the genetic lottery. The Lincoln native and future physician was one of the smartest guys on the team, running up a perfect 4.0 GPA while getting his biology degree. Belying the notion of a dumb offensive lineman, his favorite class was endocrinology. With his smarts, he was particularly good at playing the angles, knowing just how much he'd need to chip a defender to keep him out of a play.

Stai, a 6-5, 300-pounder, was the strongest and most physically dominant of the group, a barrel-chested Californian who line coach Milt Tenopir liked to say was stronger than mustard gas. If he got his hands on you, it was over. No one could consistently beat him one-on-one. And the bigger the game, the bigger he played. "When I hear a coach say, 'Impose your will on them,' I think of Brenden Stai," teammate Matt Vrzal recalled. By the end of the 1994 season, Stai would join Wiegert on many All-America teams.

Graham, a freckle-faced native of Denton, Texas, came to Lincoln in 1991 with a chip on his shoulder, having been overlooked by his home-state schools. And he came in with Texas-sized talk. He told one roommate, quarterback Brook Berringer, he wouldn't make the third string at Denton High. He looked at another roomie, tight end Mark Gilman of Kalispell, Montana, and said he didn't even know what to think of him. Do they even play football in Montana? "He talked about how good he was," recalled Phil Ellis, who roomed with and became a close friend of Graham. "Being from Texas, he was pretty full of himself." Over time, though, Graham would also become one of the most well-liked and respected guys on the team.

Graham also arrived in Lincoln with a heavy heart, having lost his mother to leukemia just weeks earlier. He grew from it, and it inspired him to be a better football player. He found added meaning in the old practice clichés like, "Play every day as if it's your last," and "Leave everything on the field." And that's the way he played. At 280 pounds, the junior wasn't the biggest guy on the line, but nobody fired off the ball more quickly. He was heady, steady and reliable. Despite the revolving door at quarterback the Huskers would see in 1994, they would suffer only a handful of bad exchanges. He was a year away from being an All-American himself.

Wilks, a senior from Tom Osborne's hometown of Hastings, followed in the long tradition of home-state walk-ons who went on to start on Nebraska's offensive line. He was the least-celebrated of this group, the only one who would not go on to play in the NFL. God just didn't bless him with that kind of body. Generously listed in the program at 280 pounds, the player his teammates called "Buddha" had to work his tail off daily to develop the size and strength to play at Nebraska. He'd drink a quart of those muscle-building protein drinks every day during meetings. And even within the circle of gargantuan men he ran with, his appetite was legendary. At lunchtime, he'd practically set up residence at the Huskers' training table. His teammates joked that by the time lunch was over, half the team had eaten with Wilks.

But teammates say that anything Wilks lacked in size he made up for with inner drive and an angry streak as wide as Nebraska — one that few outside the program knew the quiet man possessed. His goal, said backup guard Matt Hoskinson, was to hurt you and make you cry. "He was truly the meanest guy on the team; there's no other way to describe him," Hoskinson recalled. "It sounds like I'm knocking him, but I loved his attitude." It was an attitude that served Wilks and the Huskers well. While his linemates would grab the honors and the headlines that year, no member of the Pipeline would pile up more pancakes than Wilks. It spoke volumes for how the overachiever put everything he had into every snap. As Tenopir later put it, "There was a heart in those Nebraska kids that was hard to measure."

The Pipeline was a close-knit group, making its own nerdy fashion statement each week to show it. The line mates wore high socks and pulled them up over their calves, a fashion not seen since the 1970s. It definitely was not cool. But it was an old-school look for guys who shared an old-school mentality. If you wanted to get physical, that was fine with them.

Old school also described Tenopir, a true rock of the Nebraska football program. "Uncle Milty" liked to call himself a walk-on, having originally taken a job as a

"By the time the first Husker came onto the field, the crowd already was in full cry."

— THE WORLD-HERALD'S REPORT ON THE HOME OPENER WITH UCLA, WHICH FEATURED THE FIRST "TUNNEL WALK" ON HUSKERVISION

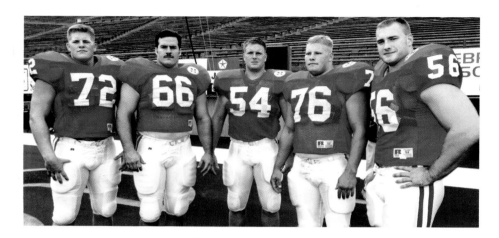

"We're just the O-Line. That's good enough."

— LINE COACH MILT TENOPIR, WHO SAID
ZACH WIEGERT (72), BRENDEN STAI (66), AARON GRAHAM (54),
JOEL WILKS (76) AND ROB ZATECHKA (56) DIDN'T NEED A NICKNAME

graduate assistant during Osborne's second year. He was now second only to George Darlington in longevity among Osborne's assistants. And as offensive line coach for a team that loved to run the ball, the Harvard, Nebraska, native figured he had one of the best football coaching jobs in America. Over the years, he would get to coach some of the best to ever play the college game, including 14 All-Americans and Outland winners Dave Rimington, Dean Steinkuhler, Will Shields, Wiegert and Aaron Taylor. If you did what you were told, he'd have you ready to play. His players always knew they were set for game day when they'd hear Tenopir utter his pat phrase, "The hay is in the barn." Tenopir loved his players, especially the Nebraska natives, but was demanding, too. "The only thing that Coach Tenopir wanted from you," recalled Vrzal, "was to be perfect every play."

Though Nebraska was known for its physical line play, Tenopir was quick to point out that option football was not simply smash-mouth football. What made the Nebraska option go was not just muscle but the intricate brutality of its blocking schemes. Husker linemen would at times double-team defenders at the point of attack and at other times crisscross and pull. They'd get up the field on the back side of plays and get down on all fours, making it tough for defenders to pursue across the field. They'd trap, with one lineman allowing the defender in front of him to penetrate inside before he would be blindsided by one of the other guys. Defensive linemen had a hard time knowing where the next crushing block would come from. Those who played for Tenopir say he was underrated as a tactician. He worked closely with Osborne to come up with blocking schemes week to week. From his bird's-eye perch in the press box on game day, he'd change them in the middle of the game if they weren't working.

While the Nebraska offensive lines benefited from great coaching, the game's most impressive weight room and unlimited food supplies, its greatest advantage may have been its practicing against the Nebraska defense. One day a week, Osborne would have coaches take the linemen on both sides down into the Pit during group work and run the No. 1's against the No. 1's at full tilt. Come game day, it was rare that the members of the Pipeline would line up against opponents any tougher than they'd seen in practice.

Now three games into the 1994 season, Nebraska clearly had the nation's best running attack, and the Pipeline was putting on a clinic. In fact, Osborne would use one play from that year's Texas Tech game as a future tutorial on what a dominant offensive line looks like. On the play, Phillips had been almost 10 yards past the line of scrimmage before anyone was close enough to lay a hand on him. Osborne showed up at the offensive line meeting room one day a year or so later and showed the play, pausing it at the moment of total destruction. "Fellas, that's how an offensive line blocks." That was all he said. He turned and left the room. Tenopir just smiled.

The Huskers followed that performance with the even more dominating one against UCLA. A Bruin linebacker noted that the scout player simulating Frazier's play during the week hadn't had Frazier's elusiveness, then added with a smile, "And he didn't have Tommie's linemen." The ABC broadcast team was so impressed by the line play that day Wiegert was named the Chevrolet Player of the Game. "Hey, where's my new Blazer?" he joked with sideline reporter Lynn Swann.

Wiegert's quip reflected the depth of good feelings surrounding these Huskers. They really had it rolling now. But though it wasn't visible on the field that day or up on those replay boards, major trouble was quietly lurking — misfortune that would ultimately put an even bigger load on the broad shoulders of Nebraska's Pipeline.

"We understand this is also a business.
The only difference is that No. 15
won't be calling the signals."

— CENTER AARON GRAHAM,
AFTER HEARING ABOUT TOMMIE FRAZIER'S BLOOD CLOT

Medical Drama

Tommie Frazier thought it was just a bruise. In the days leading up to the UCLA game, his leg started bugging him, some stiffness behind the knee. It still didn't stop him from passing for two touchdowns and running for another against the Bruins. By Monday, the leg was so tender and painful that Frazier couldn't make it through practice. He rode to the locker room on the back of an equipment cart.

Massaging loosened things up, and Frazier seemed improved Tuesday. But by Thursday he was limping around even more noticeably than before. That suggested this was something more than a bruise, possibly the result of a muscle strain or tear in his calf. He gingerly made it through the Friday walk-through before Saturday's game against the University of the Pacific.

Frazier awoke in severe pain the next morning at the East Campus hotel where the Huskers stayed the night before games. It was the first time Tom Osborne began to feel his quarterback had something really serious going on. The training staff again went to work massaging Frazier's calf. The coaches wanted to hold him out. This was Pacific, after all, an undermanned team coming to Lincoln to take a beating for a half-million-dollar paycheck. The junior wanted to play, and he moved well enough during pre-game warm-ups that Osborne and quarterbacks coach Turner Gill gave him the start. But they remained cautious. So when the Huskers quickly jumped out to a 14-0 lead after just nine offensive snaps, Frazier was pulled.

Frazier finished the game with just 5 yards rushing and 26 through the air, completing one of two passes — not the kind of numbers that were going to wow Heisman voters. Asked afterward whether he'd been able to make much progress in his game while seeing such limited duty, Frazier offered, "I completed 50 percent of my passes." It brought laughter to all the reporters gathered around him. Frazier's accuracy — the quarterback having completed just 48 percent of his throws through the first two games — had been one of the few nitpicks about the Huskers' early-season offensive performance. But soon, no one was laughing when it came to Frazier.

"Coach, my leg is killing me." Those were the words Frazier spoke to Kevin Steele when he called the Husker coach at home on Sunday, Sept. 25. Steele was concerned enough he drove across town to Frazier's apartment. Frazier's leg had unusual swelling around the knee. They called the trainers, and Dr. Pat Clare, the athletic department's orthopedic surgeon, met up with Frazier in the South Stadium training room. Clare immediately saw the rope-like thickening in the back of Frazier's leg from his thigh to his calf. I know what that is, he thought. "We've got to go to the hospital," he told the stunned Frazier. Before Frazier knew it, the quarterback found himself in a flimsy gown and lying in a hospital bed, an IV in his leg.

At Bryan Memorial Hospital that night, a dye test confirmed Clare's diagnosis: Frazier had a blood clot. And that night, Clare called a neighbor and fellow doctor he wanted to take over Frazier's care: Dr. Deepak Gangahar. Within just over a week, the Lincoln surgeon would become a household name in Nebraska.

Gangahar, a fourth-generation physician, grew up in a small town in Punjab state, in northern India. Like many doctors from his country, he came to the United States to complete his training. In 1978, he got a chance to come to Lincoln to join a cardiac practice, and he quickly fell in love with the city's small-town feel. He also quickly fell for Cornhusker football, mesmerized by the spectacle when he attended his first game in 1979. He'd never seen anything like it growing up in India.

One day in February 1985, Gangahar's wife couldn't understand why he was so sullen. He finally confided to her: The next day, he was scheduled to perform double bypass surgery on Tom Osborne. Woody Varner, the former University of Nebraska chancellor who was a friend of both men, joked to Gangahar that if anything went wrong, he'd probably have to move to Oklahoma. Gangahar, a modest professional with a delightful personality, said he'd probably need to flee the country altogether. But the surgery went well, and Gangahar enjoyed the chance to meet the quiet, disciplined coach who followed all of the doctor's health prescriptions to the letter.

Besides being a cardiac surgeon, Gangahar was also certified in vascular (circulatory system) and thoracic (lung) surgery. His vascular expertise led Clare to ask him to see Frazier. Little did either man know that within a week, Gangahar would be seeing another Husker quarterback under his lung-care specialty.

Gangahar could see Frazier's clot was a pretty serious one. There are two types of vein systems in the body: superficial veins near the surface of the skin, and deep, higher-volume veins closer to the bone that carry blood back to the lungs to be oxygenated. Frazier's clot was in a superficial vein, but it was close to the juncture where the vein fed into the deep vein system. If a clot were to form in the deep system and then break loose, it could migrate to the lungs, and that could be fatal.

Clots occur frequently in the elderly and people sick with cancer or heart disease, but this one was a bit of a medical mystery. Frazier was a strong and healthy young athlete, and there was no history of clots in his family. He also tested negative for any medical conditions that could lead to clotting. It seemed likely to Gangahar that the clot formed as a result of vein damage Frazier suffered when taking a blow to the leg. Husker coaches never did figure out when. The clot was now being treated with clot-dissolving drugs that were applied intravenously directly to the affected vein. Gangahar told Osborne Monday that Frazier would definitely be out for this weekend's game against Wyoming. Beyond that, the prognosis was unclear.

News of Frazier's hospitalization broke Monday morning, with Osborne telling reporters by the end of the day that the situation was serious. "It's not a done deal he'll miss the rest of the season," Osborne said after practice. "It could happen."

With Nebraska gunning for a national title, Frazier's health could not have been bigger news. There were front-page graphics illustrating Frazier's leg vein and the insidious clot, and interviews with national experts on the malady. Reporters and photographers surrounded Frazier as he gingerly walked out of the hospital on Wednesday afternoon, September 28, accompanied by a critical care nurse and his girlfriend. A typical Nebraskan's first thought upon hearing news of the clot was not, "I hope he'll be alright," but, "How long will he be out?" Tom Shatel, the columnist for The World-Herald, that week admonished fans for being more concerned about what it all meant to the Huskers' national title hopes than to a young man's health. "You could almost feel the state of hysteria grip Omaha and move west like a black cloud," he wrote. But given how badly fans ached for a title and Frazier's critical role on the team, the reaction was not a surprising one.

The day after Frazier was released, Frazier, Osborne, Gangahar and team doctors met to plot a strategy for his return. With how uncommon blood clots were for any 20-year-old, let alone an elite athlete, the group didn't have a lot to go on. Even with the clot now dissolved, Frazier remained on the anti-coagulant coumadin. Playing while on the blood thinner was out of the question. If Frazier were to suffer an internal injury, the inability to control the bleeding could put his life in danger.

In the end, the group decided Frazier would stay on the drugs for about two weeks. If there were no signs the clot had reformed, he could go off the drugs. That could possibly get Frazier back on the field in time for the October 15 game against unbeaten Kansas State — a showdown that was already beginning to loom large on the schedule.

Gill told a dispirited Frazier that week to keep his head up, not to worry about football. Right now, he just needed to focus on getting healthy again. "We need to put football aside," Gill said. "Then we'll see what football has in store."

Meeting before practice the day after Frazier was hospitalized, Gill expressed confidence that backup quarterback Brook Berringer was ready to lead the offense. "You're the man," Gill told the junior from Goodland, Kansas. But it's not like there were a lot of other choices for the Huskers to fall back on. Berringer was not only No. 2 on the depth chart, but he was the only other scholarship quarterback on the entire Husker roster.

With the pounding the quarterback takes in the option game, Osborne always knew the Huskers were just one play away from turning to the backup. But due to a variety of circumstances, quarterback was easily the team's thinnest position. Another scholarship quarterback who had come in with Frazier in the 1992 recruiting class transferred after it became clear Frazier had locked down the job. A recruiting gamble by Osborne the next year backfired. Osborne had told Scott Frost, a highly touted in-state player from Wood River, that Nebraska wouldn't take any other quarterback in the 1993 class if Frost would sign. When Frost committed to Stanford just before signing day, Osborne had no time to line up another. Tony Veland, who had emerged as the starter in the 1992 preseason before being sidelined by a serious injury, was switched to safety after his return in an effort to get his talents on the field. Now due to Mike Minter's injury, he was a starter there. The Omaha Benson grad would take some practice snaps as a precaution, but moving him back to quarterback was impractical now.

The next two quarterbacks behind Berringer were both in-state walk-ons who could easily have been confused for student managers. The player behind those two actually was a student manager, asked to suit up for the scout team because of the lack of quarterback depth. "It certainly is the most disturbing quarterback situation I have had," Osborne said — unaware that things were about to get even worse.

The Huskers' new starting quarterback could not have been more different from the guy he was replacing. One was a black player from inner-city Florida who competed in the state's biggest class in front of tens of thousands of fans. The other was white, hailed from a town of 5,000 in sparse, western Kansas and loved country music and the outdoors. Their experience behind center with the Huskers also set them apart. In his 23 starts, Frazier had amassed a total of 41 touchdowns and over 3,500 yards on the ground and through the air. In three years of mop-up duty, Berringer had rushed 24 times for 81 yards while throwing for 354 yards and five touchdowns. There's an old adage in football that the backup quarterback is the most popular player on the team, fans often intrigued by the next guy. At Nebraska this season, that was not the case.

While concerned about his quarterback situation, Osborne believed Berringer had the skills to succeed. Osborne had first noticed the lanky Kansan during a Husker summer camp in 1990. Berringer looked more like a classic drop-back passer than an option quarterback, but Osborne liked him. Standing tall in the pocket at 6-foot-4, he had a strong arm that could rocket a ball 70 yards downfield. And while he wasn't a dynamic runner in the mold of a Tommie Frazier, he had good straight-away speed, timed at 4.6 in the 40. He could run the option. His statistics his senior year at Goodland wouldn't wow anyone, totaling about 1,100 yards by air and ground with a team that went 5-4. But Osborne thought he was a potential gem when he signed for the Huskers in early 1991. Berringer, who had actually been born in Scottsbluff, Nebraska, loved the thought of being a Husker.

Berringer redshirted his first year at Nebraska, which put him in the same class as Frazier when the touted freshman came in and played right away. In the two years sitting behind Frazier on the depth chart, Berringer easily could have gone the route of others and left in search of playing time elsewhere. "I'm sure there were times Brook wondered if he'd ever get a shot with Frazier here," Ron Brown recalled. But thankfully, for whatever reason, he'd stuck it out.

Berringer's closest friends on the team knew football was no better than the second-biggest passion in his life — definitely below hunting and very possibly below flying. His relationship with airplanes was born out of tragedy in his youth. Berringer was only 7 when his father died of cancer. It was his father who had instilled in young Brook his love for the outdoors, teaching him to hunt pheasant. Brook treasured their memories together. Brook's Uncle Willie, his dad's identical twin brother, then took the boy under his wing. Uncle Willie was a commercial pilot, which seemed to Brook about the greatest job in the world. Berringer soon became fascinated with planes, and by the time he was in high school was looking to get his pilot's license.

Now with Berringer at the controls of the Nebraska offense, the whole state was counting on him to keep the Husker season aloft. Going into their October 1 clash with Wyoming, the Huskers rallied around their new quarterback. "Play your game," Barron Miles told Berringer. "Don't try to be Tommie." Frazier also had words of advice for Berringer, the same the coaches had given him in his first start as a freshman two years before. You don't have to be a one-man show, he told him. Lean on the other 10 guys you have out there. But neither Frazier, Osborne nor any of the Huskers knew what kind of leader Berringer would be. He was far more laid-back on the field than Frazier, not nearly as vocal. In the heat of battle, would Berringer be able to take charge? And when he needed to make a play, could he deliver? "We really didn't know how he'd react," Osborne later conceded. The Huskers would soon find out.

Despite being 40-point underdogs, Wyoming came to play that day. With Frazier reclining on a trainer's table on the sideline, his leg propped up under a towel, the visitors truly believed they had a chance to win. And the Cowboys were a hard-hitting bunch. Huskers of that era would recall only a couple of games where Nebraska actually got physically beaten up a bit. One was a trip to Arizona State in 1996. The other was Wyoming in its 1994 trip to Lincoln. The game turned into an unexpected dogfight. While it wasn't totally Berringer's fault, the offense was stuck in the mud, the Huskers generating just 13 yards in its first three possessions. With the backup quarterback in, Wyoming correctly guessed the Huskers would rely on Phillips, holding the I-back to just 9 yards on his first five carries. When Osborne had Berringer throw to try to loosen up the defense, the Cowboys intercepted to set up a score. With the Blackshirts also knocked back on their heels by Wyoming, the Huskers found themselves trailing 21-7 late in the second quarter. The visitors' sideline was as high as the Rockies, and a hush fell over Memorial Stadium. Potential disaster loomed.

On the sidelines, Osborne took the measure of his quarterback. He'd noticed that even as the Huskers fell behind, Berringer didn't panic. And even after throwing the critical interception, Berringer got mad but never got down. Osborne was seeing what the rest of college football would find in coming weeks: the kid from Goodland was one cool customer.

Just two minutes before halftime, the Huskers were on their own 36. It was time for a two-minute drill. Berringer huddled up with his teammates and took charge, confidently telling them exactly what they were going to do. Then setting up in the shotgun, he proceeded to hit on seven straight passes, adroitly leading the Huskers down to the Wyoming 5.

Then Berringer rolled right on a pass-run bootleg, a play Osborne liked to run inside of 15 yards. The quarterback saw an opening right in front of him and sprinted for the corner of the end zone. As he stretched for the pylon, he was clobbered by two Cowboy defenders, one hitting him head-on and the other putting a helmet into his ribs. That still couldn't keep the determined Berringer out of the end zone. He initially appeared stunned by the big shot he'd taken, and he may well have stayed down on the turf had two happy teammates not hauled him up to his feet. The quarterback jogged back to the bench, excited but also short of breath. He assumed he'd gotten the wind knocked out of him.

The touchdown — the first rushing score of Berringer's career — was huge. It came with just 12 seconds left in the half and pulled the Huskers within a single score. But more than that, Berringer had left a strong impression on his teammates with his grit and poise. As offensive lineman Rob Zatechka would put it after the game, "He personally took away their momentum."

Despite trailing 21-14, the Husker locker room at halftime was a calm place, really not a lot different from if the Huskers had been leading 40-0. Osborne was not one to panic, part of what made him such a great Saturday coach. And the Nebraska players and coaches had all been in this position before. Just the previous year, the Huskers had similarly trailed an inferior Kansas team at the half. Osborne had simply made his adjustments and urged the players to pick it up in the second half. As Frazier had walked through the tunnel back onto the field in Lawrence that day, he'd told Osborne: "Coach, we're gonna get this done!" The unflappable coach looked at him and calmly replied, "Well, you might try to get started pretty quick."

Though this was a different day with a different quarterback, the story was the same. By the time the Huskers reached the locker room, Milt Tenopir would have already drawn up each of Nebraska's formations on a board along with how the defense was lining up against it. The coaches would look at each diagram and discuss which of Nebraska's plays out of that formation would work best against that defensive look. "We can go 32 or 38 Option," Osborne would say. "Do you see that?" Then Osborne would sit down with his quarterback and go over all the adjustments. It was really pretty simple.

Berringer came out in the second half with the new plan and the same quiet confidence. He led Nebraska on three scoring drives in the third quarter, capping two of them himself with runs of 24 and 11 yards. Nebraska was on top, though it wouldn't secure the 42-32 victory until the Cowboys fumbled away a late punt at

"Hopefully, to my teammates
I showed poise and leadership and
that I can play with some pain."

— BROOK BERRINGER, AFTER SUFFERING A COLLAPSED LUNG
ON A TOUCHDOWN SCRAMBLE AGAINST WYOMING

their own 8 to set up NU's final score.

There were smiles and shoulder slaps in the locker room afterward, and Osborne expressed pride in how Berringer had played. Berringer for the first time went to the post-game press conference, fielding questions as if he'd been doing it all year. He dismissed all the negative talk about the Huskers during the week. "A lot of people said Nebraska can't win a national championship with Brook Berringer," he said. "I don't think that was true today."

Right after that, he headed to the training room. He had been hurting some during the second half, and his teammates had told him his breathing didn't sound right. Now he was feeling chest pain. The medical staff checked him over. When they listened to his chest, it seemed something was amiss. They feared he had a heart problem. At that point, Berringer became the second Husker quarterback in a week to land at Bryan Hospital under Gangahar's care. His heart, much to everyone's relief, checked out OK. But X-rays revealed he had a partially deflated left lung. That hit just before halftime had apparently caused the injury, and he'd played the whole second half with it. A teammate would later ask him why he hadn't come out when he was hurting. "We had to win the game, man," Berringer said. "I had to be in there."

It was an unusual injury for football. When it came to Nebraska's quarterbacks, that seemed to be par for the course. Berringer stayed in the hospital overnight for observation. Gangahar decided the leak was small enough that it should heal on its own. But it would make his status questionable for the next weekend's game against Oklahoma State.

Come Monday, both Berringer and Frazier were largely spectators as the Huskers returned to practice. Nebraska didn't have a waiver wire it could use to bring in another quarterback. Osborne told reporters that if Berringer could not go on Saturday, the starter would be Matt Turman, a walk-on out of Wahoo who was taking most of the snaps with the No. 1 offense that day.

In all his years in Lincoln, Osborne had never turned to his No. 3 quarterback to make plays with a game on the line. Fortunately, with both Berringer and Frazier appearing to be on the mend, that didn't seem real likely here.

But the situation at quarterback was now almost ridiculous. The way things were going, odds were you'd have as good a chance of running into a Nebraska quarterback at Bryan Hospital as in South Stadium.

Double Jeopardy

Tommie Frazier headed back to Bryan on Tuesday morning, October 4, for a routine checkup on his leg. He'd been feeling pretty well, not experiencing the stiffness of the previous week. He had every expectation that he'd get the doctor's OK and soon be back on the practice field. Instead, Frazier was once again hit with a rude, blind-side blitz. Dr. Deepak Gangahar discovered the clot had re-formed and actually was even worse. It was bigger, and it was now jutting into the deeper vein system. And most disturbingly, it had re-formed while Frazier was taking the anti-coagulants. Frazier was in disbelief when the doctors delivered the news. They asked if he wanted to call anyone. He phoned Kevin Steele. The coach was speechless. It sounded to Frazier as if the phone had gone dead.

Steele and Tom Osborne both came to the hospital to meet with Frazier and the doctors. The gravity of the situation was evident on all the faces there. It felt as if all the air had been sucked out of the room. Frazier would now need surgery to tie off the smaller vein so that it would no longer threaten to feed clots into the deeper vein system. After the surgery, he needed to stay on blood thinners for three to six months. Frazier's season was in all likelihood now over — and possibly his career. "No more playing games," Gangahar told Frazier and Osborne. "We cannot let that happen." It appeared blood clots had now been able to do what no defense ever could: shut down Tommie Frazier.

At his regular post-practice meeting with reporters, Osborne went over a litany

> "It has been difficult to recruit a so-called top quarterback the last couple of years, because they realize that Tommie is probably going to be the starter the next couple of years."
>
> — TOM OSBORNE

of minor bumps and bruises that had kept players out of drills, including a sore knee that recently had sidelined Barron Miles. The coach mentioned that Brook Berringer was back at practice but not yet taking hits. Then he dropped the bomb-shell: Tommie's blood clot is back. "He certainly isn't going to play anytime soon," Osborne said. "Quite likely, from all appearances, he won't play this year."

Osborne told his team about Frazier's condition in a hushed meeting in the South Stadium auditorium. It's just another thing we'll have to deal with, he said. We'll be all right. The team's season goal, to win a national championship, was up there on the wall in the room. Osborne told his players there was no reason they couldn't still reach all their goals. Still, it was devastating news. He had always said adversity is what builds character. "But I think we've had all the character-building we can stand for one season," reserve running back Damon Benning quipped to a reporter later that evening.

Benning went to visit Frazier in the hospital that night and found the quarterback doing well. "Better than I was," Benning would later recall. When Benning asked Frazier questions about his condition and prognosis, the quarterback had no answers. But Frazier also refused to accept defeat. "I'll be back," he repeatedly told Benning — although exactly when that could happen was far from clear to anyone.

The next day, Wednesday, Gangahar held what was surely the most heavily watched medical press conference in the state's history. Gangahar showed X-ray images of the clot and told reporters it was his recommendation that Frazier not play again this year. It was unfair, Gangahar said, but that was the reality. "You're talking about going from a Heisman Trophy to now his whole career is in jeopardy," Gangahar said.

And around the country, Nebraska was being written off as a title contender. Frazier was the heart of this team. The ESPN college football talking heads all said they saw no way Nebraska could compete without Frazier. How could a quarterback who until a week ago had never seen more than mop-up duty replace a Heisman candidate? In fact, in the wake of the close call against Wyoming, Nebraska was no longer No. 1 in either of the two major polls.

But Osborne wasn't writing off the Huskers. Football has always been a game of injuries and attrition. This was a little more disappointing than if Frazier had been hurt on the field. This was harder to understand. But the players didn't need to understand it. They just needed to avoid thinking that the loss of one player made them that much less a team. As long as we don't fall into that trap, Osborne believed, we've got a good chance.

Two players in particular would have a lot to say about what kind of team Nebraska would have going forward, beginning with this week's game against Oklahoma State.

The obvious one was Berringer. It was a judgment call, but Gangahar decided — in consultation with Berringer, his family and Osborne — to clear the quarterback to play against the Cowboys. Berringer's injury had come despite the fact he'd been wearing a flak jacket to protect his ribs. He was now being fitted with an even sturdier one that made him feel like a character in the movie "RoboCop." As a precaution, Gangahar would also be with Berringer on the sideline throughout the game, toting a sterile bag with all the equipment he would need to reinflate the lung.

The other key player was Lawrence Phillips. Osborne had given Phillips, Benning and junior Clinton Childs a lot of carries through the first five games to provide them the opportunity to step up in the place of Calvin Jones, the 1993 starter who had left early for the NFL draft. Phillips had clearly emerged, running for over 100 yards in all five games. Now he was going to need to show he could carry the load.

Osborne repeatedly called Phillips' number against OSU. In the first half, he tallied over 100 yards and scored Nebraska's lone touchdown. But the Huskers went into the halftime break holding a narrow 9-3 lead over the unranked Pokes, a team Nebraska had not lost to since 1961. The score did nothing to assure Husker fans that life was going to be just fine without Frazier.

At halftime, while the Huskers headed to the locker room, Gangahar and Berringer climbed into an ambulance. It had been prearranged before the game that Berringer would get a halftime lung X-ray at the student health clinic two blocks from the stadium. It was just precautionary. But doctor and quarterback already had a pretty good idea something was wrong. Berringer had taken a blow and landed on his back. Gangahar could tell Berringer was in distress, in pain and breathing rapidly. Gangahar put his stethoscope to Berringer's left lung and didn't hear a thing.

The X-ray showed that the lung had nearly totally collapsed this time (NU reports to the press at the time termed it only a 10 percent to 15 percent collapse). Using just a local anesthetic, Gangahar made a small incision and passed a catheter between Berringer's ribs into his chest cavity. He created a vacuum inside Berringer's chest and the lung quickly reinflated. Berringer's breathing almost immediately returned to normal. Gangahar then placed a surprising call to Osborne in the Husker locker room, telling the coach of the collapse and how he'd reinflated the lung.

"Can he play?" Osborne asked. "Absolutely not," Gangahar said. "He will not play." Osborne accepted and trusted Gangahar's assessment. There were now just six minutes left before the second half was to start. With one quarterback already in the hospital, and another soon headed there to join him, Osborne nodded to Matt Turman, who was about to go down in Husker history.

Ron Brown would never forget the team's reaction when Osborne announced in the locker room that Turman would be quarterbacking the second half. His teammates roared in support of the popular little underdog. "Let's do it!" It spoke volumes to how much the players on this team believed in each other. "We'll just win with Matt then," Miles said later, recalling the team's mind-set. "We're going to get there, and if Matt has to take us there, that's what we're doing."

At 5-foot-9 and 165 pounds, Matt Turman could barely see over the line of scrimmage, and he wasn't particularly fast. A year earlier, Osborne, a distant relative of Turman, had famously said in assessment of his No. 3 quarterback, "He's not the worst." Osborne would later explain he meant it as a compliment, an intentional understatement, though many fans didn't read it that way.

But one thing about Turman that could not be understated was his will. Turman had grown up down the road from Lincoln in Wahoo dreaming of one day playing quarterback at Nebraska, just like his idol, Turner Gill. He'd passed up chances to play at smaller schools. After initially walking on as a receiver, he talked Nebraska's coaches into letting him switch to quarterback. And now before 76,000 fans at Memorial Stadium, his dream was real.

Turman received final instructions from his former idol and led the Nebraska offense onto the field. Gill and the other coaches told him to take a deep breath and just play the way he had in practice the past two years. Center Aaron Graham almost had tears in his eyes as he watched Turman come into the huddle the first time. When Graham thought about how hard Turman had worked to get to this moment, it made him want to play that much harder.

Graham, Osborne and the other Huskers also knew Turman had the ability to get the job done. Around the practice field, Turman had always seemed to lead a charmed existence, often amazing teammates with how the bounces seemed to go his way. If Turman threw a ball out there, he just knew the receiver was going to catch it. And it seemed he always would, sometimes in spectacular fashion.

Turman even had that same touch during his brief game experience. In mop-up duty the previous year, Turman had one rushing attempt and threw one pass — both going for touchdowns. As Benning would later put it, if Turman had jumped off a building, he'd just know there would be a feather bed down at the bottom waiting for him. "He had that kind of karma," Benning recalled.

The coaches didn't ask Turman to jump off any buildings or to be superhuman. And he wasn't. He carried the ball just six times for six yards and completed one of his four passes. But he showed poise in directing the Huskers on scoring drives of 59, 50 and 58 yards to open the second half, ending any hopes for an OSU upset. All those reps he'd taken in practice helped him avoid the drive-killing mistake. The pressure didn't faze him at all. And he had a team that was rallying completely around him. The Husker sideline would be giddy with excitement whenever Turman, who was barely visible to the defense when standing under center, made a play. It might be a four-yard run, but by the reaction you would have thought he'd just gone 60 for a score. "Look at Matt! Look at Matt!"

In the second half, it was Phillips again who carried the load offensively, consistently getting yards after contact. By the end of the game, Phillips had toted the ball 33 times — one of the biggest totals in school history — racking up 221 yards and three touchdowns.

Miles and the Blackshirts also stepped it up. The Nebraska defense had been struggling since Mike Minter's injury, surrendering 414 yards and 21 points to UCLA and 380 yards and 22 points to Wyoming. But when it became clear Berringer wasn't returning, Charlie McBride huddled his players. "It's ours now!" he exclaimed, breathing fire. "We've got to do it!" The response: The Blackshirts in the second half yielded just 24 yards and not a single point, closing out the 32-3 win.

After the game, Turman's teammates pounded on the day's hero, so happy for him. This had been his moment. In two more years in Lincoln, he'd never have a brighter one. The World-Herald's Tom Shatel dubbed him the "Turmanator." His story also quickly drew comparisons to "Rudy," the 1970s movie about a walk-on at Notre Dame. Indeed, the Huskers' season had become something out of a Hollywood script. You just didn't know who central casting was going to send up next.

Osborne afterward was able to joke about it all, saying he'd be having open auditions for quarterback on Monday. "Where do we go from here, I don't know," Osborne told reporters. "I guess to Manhattan, Kansas."

Indeed, jokes aside, next up for the Huskers was a trip to play Kansas State, followed two weeks later by a visit from a dynamic Colorado team that would be awfully hard to outscore. Both were ranked and rolling unbeaten midway through the season.

Berringer, like Frazier, spent that night at Bryan Hospital. It was only for observation, but his status for the game in Manhattan was iffy, at best. At least publicly, though, the Husker players expressed confidence everything was OK. We have a ton of talent on this team, Wiegert said. "I don't care who the quarterback is. I don't care if it's Rudy."

The way things were going, it could well be.

"I've never known him not to show up ready."

— FRANK SOLICH, AFTER LAWRENCE PHILLIPS
RAN FOR 221 YARDS AGAINST OKLAHOMA STATE

Just What The Doctor Ordered

I t was Friday night in Manhattan, Kansas, at the Huskers' team hotel. The players had just watched their traditional night-before-the-game movie and been sent off to bed. Tom Osborne sat down on a couch outside a meeting room with Charlie McBride and George Darlington. "Fellas, it's going to be almost impossible for us to score many points," Osborne told his defensive coaches, looking a little pale in the face. "Your guys are going to have to play well for us to win."

The unusual apprehension in Osborne's words spoke to the challenge his team faced the next day. Nebraska was in for an epic struggle against a very good Wildcats team. True to Osborne's words, this game would demand a great performance from the defense. To win, Nebraska also would need heroic efforts from Lawrence Phillips and the Pipeline. And on a wet, gloomy day in Kansas' Flint Hills, all delivered. Osborne later remembered it as one of the most monumental single efforts he'd seen from a football team.

Late in the week, Osborne had decided Turman would get the start in Manhattan. That was the result of some complicated calculus involving Brook Berringer and his family and the doctors, particularly Deepak Gangahar. Berringer's lung condition was not life-threatening. But if he did play, the worst-case scenario was that he'd take a hit and further damage it, perhaps causing him to miss the rest of the season. Conversely, if he were held out and given the chance to heal, he would in all likelihood put the issue completely behind him.

For his part, Berringer wanted to take the risk and play, and his mother supported his desire. But Gangahar was concerned. By this time he had spent two games on

> "The only reason Matt's starting —
> because I like him, and he's a relative. Also maybe
> because he doesn't have a collapsed lung."
>
> — JOKING TOM OSBORNE, WHOSE SISTER-IN-LAW MARRIED A TURMAN RELATIVE

the Nebraska sideline, first with Tommie Frazier at the Wyoming game, and then with Berringer against OSU. He'd gotten his first up-close look at this sport, and it had been eye-opening. He couldn't believe how big these guys were and how they hit. "My gosh, those are monsters," he thought. "They look like giants from a different planet." He thought it best for Berringer to sit out. "Ninety-nine percent, I would like you not to play," he told him. And largely based on that recommendation, Osborne decided not to play Berringer. He would dress and be on the sidelines, but if at all possible, they would keep him off the field.

It was the first time in Osborne's 33 years at Nebraska that the team's top two quarterbacks were ruled out. And if Turman should somehow end up hurt, the next quarterback to play would be Clester Johnson, a backup wingback who hadn't played the position since high school. Osborne had joked that Johnson had a repertoire of eight plays, and in reality it was not all that far from the truth. It led to a lot of edgy meetings in South Stadium in the week leading up to the game.

On game day, purple-clad fans lined up in the rain hours before the made-for-TV 11 a.m. kickoff. The student section was filled by 9 a.m. And as the Huskers put on their pads and game faces in the locker room underneath and headed out for warm-ups, an overflow crowd of more than 42,000 was turning Wagner Field into a cauldron of sound. A fired-up Mike Ekeler, a Blair, Nebraska, native and KSU special-teams demon who would later coach at Nebraska, barked toward the Husker half of the field, war stripes painted in eye black on his face. "He looked like the devil," McBride said later. The Huskers were in hostile territory.

Kansas State's home football field was not normally considered a college football house of horrors, unless that was perhaps a reference to the quality of play of the home team. Nebraska had beaten KSU 25 straight times, blowouts the Husker coaches over the years came to count on to get their walk-ons on the field. If Nebraska football represented, as the patch on NU jerseys proudly proclaimed, "A Winning Tradition," the tradition at Kansas State was exactly the opposite. From 1955 to 1988, the doormat Mildcats produced only two winning seasons. Their record between 1985 and 1988 was an astonishing 3-40-1. Any win was cause for celebration in Manhattan.

But that was before the arrival of Bill Snyder, who had the greatest reversal of fortune in college football history well under way. The previous year, the miracle worker had taken KSU to just its second bowl game in school history. Now he had this team ranked as high as 13th in the polls.

The Wildcats were led by quarterback Chad May, who had torched the Nebraska defense for a Big Eight-record 489 yards in Lincoln the year before. May made headlines coming into the game, saying he once again was going to pick the Blackshirts apart. The tenacious Wildcat defense ranked sixth in the nation. The game against No. 2 Nebraska was being quite simply billed as the biggest game in Kansas State football history. The previous week, Wildcat fans had actually torn down the goalposts in Lawrence after beating hated in-state rival Kansas. This week, it was the goalposts in their home stadium that were now endangered.

As anxious as Osborne was going in, it didn't help that he also happened to see Turman's first pass attempt during warm-ups. The rain-slickened ball slipped out of the quarterback's stubby fingers and actually flew backward behind him. "Oh, boy, here we go," Ron Brown told Turner Gill after they, too, had witnessed it. Not only would Nebraska limit running of the option to protect the health of its only real quarterback, but any passes held the potential for disaster.

Osborne also knew Snyder was no dummy, and neither was his defensive coordinator — an up-and-coming young coach named Bob Stoops. They surely knew that Nebraska was going to throw out the playbook and rely almost exclusively on its I-backs. Almost from the start, the Wildcats began putting eight or nine guys in the tackle box, more than enough to put a helmet on every Nebraska blocker.

That's a look the Huskers would normally exploit by going to their bread-and-butter option, stringing out the defense and finding a soft spot. However, with the option largely unavailable, the Huskers had little choice but to play into the Wildcats' hands and run it up the middle. The only way the Huskers could move the ball that day would be if every player on the line beat the guy in front of him. More than any other game, this one was going to be decided by the hand-to-hand combat in the trenches.

That was just fine with Zach Wiegert and Co. Schemes aside, they had the most fun when they were firing straight off the ball. "They think it's a neat deal to pound around on somebody," Milt Tenopir put it later that day. They just pulled up their socks, relishing the chance to carry this team on their backs. Aaron Graham would recount the line's message to Turman before kickoff: "Listen, man, your job this week is to get the snap and hand off the football." The Pipeline would handle the rest.

And that's just what Osborne had Turman do, over and over and over again. Lawrence Phillips either carried the ball or caught a short pass behind the line of scrimmage on 17 of Nebraska's first 18 plays. In fact, many of those runs were the same play call, a simple isolation handoff to the I-back going up the middle. Of the 61 snaps the Huskers took that day, the offense ran that one iso play about 20 times. When Phillips did find a crease in the line, he didn't get far. The Wildcat safeties knew what was coming and practically used him for tackling practice.

But late in the first quarter the Huskers took advantage after a sack of May and a short KSU punt gave NU great field position. The line fought like gladiators, and Phillips got the ball on six straight plays, battling for every yard: first for seven, then eight, then six, then two, then three. Then with Nebraska putting an extra back in to help lead into the hole, Phillips bowled the final two yards into the end zone to put NU up 7-0. There'd been nothing subtle about it at all.

Defensively, it seemed Nebraska was just hanging on by a fingernail against the dangerous May. KSU joined the long line of teams trying to pick on the undersized Miles, and in this game he was living on the edge. On several occasions, he came flying in at the last second to just tip away passes as receivers ran downfield. At the start of the second quarter, May finally hit one when another Husker defender busted a coverage, pulling the Wildcats within 7-6. But athletic linebacker Troy Dumas put his 36-inch vertical jump to good use in leaping high to block the extra point. He helped preserve the Husker lead again just before halftime, picking off a pass from May after the Wildcats had driven deep into Husker territory. McBride's strategy going in had been to show blitz on almost every play but then usually have his defenders drop back into coverage. This time linebacker Ed Stewart came hard up the middle, and a rushed and confused May threw the ball right to Dumas, the only guy in the area. "We screwed him up a little," Stewart said later. The pick was the first May had thrown in his last 186 passes.

Late in the half, the Nebraska offense was struggling, and Berringer was pacing the sidelines like a cat. He felt his arm could make a difference here. So when the Huskers took over facing a possible two-minute drill, Berringer and Osborne approached Gangahar on the sideline. With Nebraska facing this obvious passing situation, could Berringer go in? They talked about it. Gangahar repeated he did not want Berringer to get hit. "I'll do my best to get rid of the ball before they get to me," Berringer said. Based on those words, Gangahar consented to him taking the field.

The two-minute drill was unsuccessful, but it whetted Berringer's appetite to play. He felt he'd shown he could go out there and avoid contact. And with the Huskers clinging to their one-point lead at halftime, he badly wanted to be out there. There were more discussions in the locker room. Gangahar, too, was encouraged by how

"He probably played as well in a game
as any corner I have ever seen here
in my 21 years at Nebraska."

— SECONDARY COACH GEORGE DARLINGTON,
ON BARRON MILES' PLAY AGAINST KANSAS STATE

Berringer handled the two-minute drill but kept repeating his caveat: I don't want you hit. In the end, Osborne, Berringer and Gangahar decided the quarterback would play. Gangahar would watch Berringer closely, and Osborne said he'd do as much as he could to limit the quarterback's chances of contact.

Osborne and some of his assistants years later would say they thought that Gangahar's time on the Husker sideline in the first half had played into his decision to clear Berringer to play. He had gotten caught up in the game and wanted to see Nebraska win. "It's kind of hard if you're in the locker room and standing on the sideline not to feel somewhat attached and feel somehow you want to see this work out," Osborne recalled. Gangahar said he never forgot that his first obligation was to Berringer and his health. But he added, "It would be unfair for me to say I was not caught up in the drama. I was very emotional. I was charged up."

It was a good thing for the Huskers. Because as Berringer returned to the field in the second half and joined the Nebraska huddle, someone else was missing: Lawrence Phillips. Late in the second quarter when Turman threw low on a screen pass, a KSU safety slammed his helmet into Phillips' hand. He doubled over in pain on the sidelines, and his thumb immediately began to hugely swell up. Osborne took a look and could see it was serious. So while the Huskers went to the locker room to game-plan the second half, their main offensive weapon headed to a local hospital for an X-ray. It turned out to be a bad sprain, but it was the thumb on Phillips' left hand, the one he usually carried the ball in. The trainers first tried to splint it, but it was too bulky for him to grip the ball. So instead Phillips just had the trainers tape it up the best they could. By the second possession of the second half, Phillips was back out on the field, often toting the ball in his off arm. Despite the pain and swelling, he insisted on being out there. "He may have been the toughest I-back we ever had," Tenopir recalled.

Osborne followed the doctor's orders, calling plays with an eye toward protecting Berringer. The quarterback didn't once carry on the option. During his 34 snaps, he would take hits twice on pass plays. On one, Berringer just couldn't help himself and scrambled for nine yards before being drilled; on the other he took a sack. Whenever Berringer came off, Gangahar would question the quarterback: Are you hurting? No. Are you short of breath? No. Gangahar listened to the lung. It sounded good.

It remained a 7-6 game headed to the fourth quarter. Then, as happened so often over the years to an upstart bent on an upset, the Huskers' physical play finally started to wear down Kansas State. The holes were getting bigger and bigger as the game wore on. Berringer led the Huskers on a grinding 11-play drive early in the final period. Phillips broke off the longest run of the day, a 17-yard burst behind big blocks from Wiegert and Brenden Stai. And then with all the attention on Phillips, fullback Jeff Makovicka completed the 75-yard march by going 15 on a trap, raising both arms in exultation after high-stepping into the end zone.

On Nebraska's next possession, Berringer used his arm to help clinch the game. Rolling out, the quarterback found wingback Abdul Muhammad racing down the field. The big 34-yard gain accounted for two-thirds of all the passing yards Nebraska gained that day, setting up a field goal that iced the 17-6 win. The Wildcats one day would end their long losing streak to Nebraska. But not this day. And not against this courageous Nebraska team. Berringer afterward was ecstatic, beaming in the locker room. Gangahar didn't need to be a doctor to know the fragile quarterback had come through just fine. The Huskers would have to be careful with Berringer the following week against Missouri, too, but this largely marked the end of concerns about Berringer's lung.

Tenopir went into the locker room and hugged each of his linemen, who were spent but excited. "Fellas, you guys won that sucker today," he told them. They had certainly had more dominating performances before. But none more gritty. The linemen weren't the only ones to come through this gut-check. Phillips, despite his painful thumb, battered his way to 126 yards on 31 carries, 4.1 bruising yards per attempt. It was his seventh straight 100-yard game.

Then there were the Blackshirts. They held KSU to -7 yards on the ground. And while May had come into the game a 65 percent passer, the now-former Heisman candidate was harassed into 22-of-48 throwing and sacked six times for over 50 yards in losses. "Nebraska is still Nebraska," Stewart happily proclaimed afterward, "and Kansas State is still Kansas State."

No one on the unit stood out more than Miles. May had just kept throwing at the Husker corner in the second half, so many times with only inches separating Miles from being either the hero or the goat. But Miles in the end knocked down a school-record six passes, and ABC's broadcasters named him the player of the game. "Why'd you keep throwing at me?" Miles asked May years later when they met as pros.

May also got a little extracurricular treatment from the Blackshirts, later accusing an unknown Husker of gouging a thumb into his eye during a pileup. Osborne said the coaches never were able to pinpoint the offender, and years later questions to

"I just carried the ball in my right hand
instead of my left."

— LAWRENCE PHILLIPS, ASKED HOW HE DEALT WITH HIS SPRAINED THUMB

Husker defenders would mostly be greeted with smiles and few words. Most have pointed the finger at the hard-wired Christian Peter. The feisty 300-pound defensive tackle from New Jersey had called May a baby for his complaints, and he'd also made it clear he wasn't happy with the way May had run his mouth the week before the game. "Do I believe it could have been Christian? Of course," McBride said. But Grant Wistrom years later said he had strong suspicions as to the culprit, and he was pretty sure it wasn't Peter.

Regardless, even if the Blackshirts' actions weren't always noble, no one could argue with the results. They never allowed KSU past the Nebraska 44 in the second half. This was the kind of dominating defense Osborne had thought the Huskers could have all along — arriving just in time. The Blackshirts didn't boast a superstar like a Trev Alberts or Broderick Thomas, but they were playing together as well as any unit Osborne and McBride ever had.

In a fit of sour grapes, May after the game declared the Huskers eminently beatable. Great teams don't make mistakes. They execute every play. They are rock solid at every position. "I don't think they're a great team," he said. But May was neglecting some of the intangibles that also make great teams, traits that had been on display in Manhattan that day: rallying around each other, and playing with heart and fortitude.

As the buses carried the Huskers back up the two-lane highways between Manhattan and Lincoln, Osborne sat in his traditional seat at the front. To him, this felt like a transformational moment. His team wouldn't get a lot of style points for this win. But these Huskers were beginning to look a lot like the team from the previous year, the one that refused to lose — even if nobody else believed in them. Without Frazier, Nebraska clearly was no longer a 40-points-per-game offensive juggernaut. But playing like this, the team could still win it all.

"This gives us a chance to accomplish the goals we set at the beginning of the season," Osborne had told reporters right after the game. "We'll just have to do it a different way."

Brook's Team

The Nebraska offense took the field in an electric Memorial Stadium. It was No. 3 Nebraska against No. 2 Colorado, a de facto elimination game in the race for a national title. In the huddle, Brook Berringer could see I-back Damon Benning was looking a little flighty. Berringer clapped his hands. "Hey, 2-1, you with me?"

It was just the kind of cool confidence Berringer had been flashing ever since taking over the Big Red offense. Teammates would later recall the look in his eye that day against Colorado. As both a quarterback and a leader, he had come into his own. And he wasn't the only one feeling it. Since the Kansas State game, the entire team had been developing a kind of cockiness that just grew week to week. "They know what they want," Milt Tenopir told a group of NU boosters around that time, "and they know how to get there."

All the adversity they'd been through had only served to pull the players closer together. They now believed to their core there wasn't anything they couldn't overcome. Nothing got to them. They also knew deep inside that there had been a major shift in the college football universe. It was just that no one outside of Nebraska had figured it out yet. The fact that many still didn't believe in them only served to make them that much more determined. "We're fighting with our backs to the wall," Lawrence Phillips said, "and that's going to help us."

Despite the win over Kansas State, Nebraska had again dropped in the polls, falling to third in the AP survey behind Colorado. A subsequent 42-7 waxing of Missouri also apparently didn't impress. Penn State's Nittany Lions were now the national media darlings, top-ranked and with a high-powered offense led by quarterback

"Hey, he can get the job done, and he proved it today.
He's a pro-type quarterback."

— NEBRASKA TIGHT END MARK GILMAN ON BROOK BERRINGER

Kerry Collins and running back Ki-Jana Carter. And that was important. As a Big Ten school, Penn State was bound for the Rose Bowl. There was no way the Huskers could face off with the Lions at season's end. If Penn State continued to hold that spot, Nebraska could go undefeated and still see its national championship hopes fall to the opinions of the pollsters.

The outside skepticism was understandable. Not many teams could lose their star quarterback and still go undefeated. But while the outside world still couldn't get over what the Huskers had lost in Tommie Frazier, the focus within the team was on what they had. And Berringer was growing tired of answering the questions about whether he could replace Frazier. After helping lead the team to four wins, he didn't know what else he could do to answer the critics. "I suppose winning a national championship is the only way to do it," he told reporters the week of the Colorado game. "So I guess that's what we'll do."

It was big talk, especially considering the team headed to Lincoln that weekend. Undefeated Colorado featured an explosive offense averaging 500 yards and 40 points a game. Rashaan Salaam, running out of a one-back West Coast set, was leading the nation in rushing and scoring and was on his way to 2,000 yards and the Heisman Trophy. Throw in quarterback Kordell Stewart and receiver Michael Westbrook, and the Colorado attack was being compared to Nebraska's 1983 "Scoring Explosion" team of quarterback Turner Gill, Heisman-winning back Mike Rozier and dynamic receiver Irving Fryar. With a win over Nebraska, the Buffaloes thought they would be well-positioned for a run at a national title.

Colorado also seemed to have fate on its side. It had defeated Michigan in September on a last-second 64-yard Hail Mary pass from Stewart to Westbrook. It was typical of several games they'd won in recent years in dramatic fashion. That included the 1990 national championship team's famed "Fifth Down" game against Missouri, where officials who couldn't count gave the Buffs the extra down they needed to score the winning touchdown. That tendency to win big games and the fact Nebraska had lost 12 straight against Top 5 teams were enough to make Colorado the favorite of the Las Vegas odds-makers — only the sixth time during Tom Osborne's tenure that the Huskers were underdogs at home.

Osborne and the Huskers often downplayed talk of any rivalry with Colorado, despite the fact Coach Bill McCartney put the Nebraska game in red on the schedule every year and for a brief time had tilted the series in the Buffs' favor. But the Buffs this year had Nebraska's attention. CU added fuel to the fire when the team arrived in Lincoln. Some defensive players got off the plane carrying bolt-cutters, a symbol of how they planned to dismantle Nebraska's Pipeline.

Osborne told his players just before kickoff that they should be confident, regardless of what the odds-makers said. "You aren't the underdogs. You're at home." Indeed, Nebraska had not lost at home in three years — and wouldn't again for another four. Lincoln had become an awfully tough place to play. And the crowd of 76,131 who sold out Memorial Stadium for the 200th straight time — a record streak stretching back to the Kennedy administration — made the football cathedral about as loud as it had ever been.

The Buffs made the mistake of coming out of the locker room before the Huskers, apparently unaware of the new tunnel walk tradition. So as the Buffs stood around, they were a little taken aback as the old stadium started literally shaking. Kordell Stewart, who would play with Husker linebacker Troy Dumas in the NFL, later told Dumas he got the sense at that moment that the Buffs were in trouble. In the end, Stewart could have hit two Hail Marys and the Buffs been given six downs, and it still might not have mattered. That's how badly Nebraska took it to them on a gorgeous fall day in Lincoln.

The meticulous Osborne was legend for the countless hours he spent every year watching tape, looking for his opponents' tendencies. Contrary to his muted demeanor, Osborne was extremely competitive, and his preparation was where it showed through. He was also known for constantly dreaming up new plays, often doodling them on napkins over lunch or dinner. He and his coaching staff had cooked up a few surprises on both sides of the ball for McCartney. And his team had also been sneaking in some extra time all season drilling on the new plans. That strategy had been born years earlier, and against another rival. In his early years, Osborne had struggled mightily to beat Oklahoma, and he later decided a big reason was his defense's inability to prepare for Barry Switzer's wishbone running game. It was so different, Osborne realized, that there was no hope of stopping it if the Huskers only had the usual four days to prepare. So every Monday all season, no matter Nebraska's opponent that week, Osborne would have his defense spend 20 minutes working against the wishbone. By Switzer's last year in 1988, the Blackshirts had pretty much learned to throttle the attack, holding the Sooners to just three points and 137 yards. Now with Switzer gone and OU a fallen Big Eight power, Osborne had been employing the same extra-work strategy to prepare for the most formidable team on the year's schedule. This year, it was the Buffs.

Osborne had noticed on film that the Colorado linebackers really sold out on runs between the tackles. With as run-heavy as the Nebraska offense had been recently, he felt that would make the Buffs vulnerable to play-action passes on iso plays. Osborne put in some new wrinkles featuring the tight ends, and in Berringer, he knew he had a quarterback who could get them the ball.

The strategy paid dividends early. With Nebraska already ahead 7-0, Berringer led a 76-yard drive in which he four times connected with tight ends, most of them short routes just behind the linebackers. Eric Alford caught the last one for a touchdown, so wide open he wished he'd been covered a little so it didn't look so easy. Alford and fellow tight end Mark Gilman both had career days, catching nine balls between them.

Osborne also installed three brand-new running plays, including one that made it a rough day for Kerry Hicks, who anchored a stout Colorado defensive line. Osborne was concerned that with Colorado's 5-2 alignment, center Aaron Graham would often be one-on-one against the Buffs' talented All-Big Eight nose guard. On the new "Wham" play, the Husker wingback went in motion toward the middle of the field, got about an eight-yard running head start and at the snap headed straight at the unsuspecting Hicks, drilling him right in the ear-hole. For a football player, that's almost a dream shot. Nebraska's receivers always took their blocking role seriously, knowing they were the key to turning 10-yard runs into 50-yard runs. But Clester Johnson and the other wingbacks really relished this duty. After a while, it seemed to the Huskers that Hicks' head was on a swivel, as concerned about whether he was about to get blind-sided as he was about the play in front of him. Huskers years later would still chuckle at mention of the Wham.

Osborne also noticed during the game that Colorado was playing its defensive linemen wide to defend the Nebraska option. He told his tackles to simply make a head fake to the outside and then go right after the linebackers. The CU tackles, unblocked, would run themselves out of the play, opening up some massive holes

"This was a big step.
We've got a chance to get some things done."

— TOM OSBORNE AFTER BEATING COLORADO

for Husker fullbacks on straight-ahead dive plays. Just under half of Nebraska's 203 rushing yards that day came from the fullbacks.

On defense, the Huskers knew they couldn't shut down Salaam. But they wanted to contain him and force Stewart to take the game into his own hands. McBride had put in some new alignments and blitzes he was pretty sure would confuse Stewart. Nebraska had once recruited Stewart. George Darlington recalled one reason they'd passed on him — coincidentally, in favor of the less-talented Berringer — was because they weren't sure he had the football IQ they were seeking. During the pivotal first half, when the game was decided, Stewart and the hapless Buffaloes managed just 89 yards against the Blackshirts. "He was looking around a lot," linebacker Phil Ellis said after the game, "and he didn't like what he saw."

Late in the half, as Ellis and the Blackshirts ran off the field, they told their coaches how Stewart and his teammates were now arguing with each other. "Coach, we've got 'em! They're done!" Salaam finished with 134 hard-earned yards on 22 carries in the Huskers' 24-7 licking, afterward tipping his cap to the Blackshirts. "They don't have guys out there trash talking," he said. "They just play hard-nosed football."

The Huskers had been more dominant on the field than even the final score suggested, and the college football world took notice. The win ultimately helped vault the Huskers to No. 1 in both polls, the media poll right after the game and the coaches' poll a week later. It was Nebraska's first victory over a higher-ranked team in almost a decade, likely the reason jubilant Husker fans tore down the goalposts for what would be the last time during the Osborne era. From that point on, wins in big games would be expected. "We're on a mission," Berringer said. "And we are going to get it done no matter what it takes."

For Berringer, the Colorado game had been kind of a coming-out party. He was now creating a lot of believers, taking advantage of the opportunity fate had given him. He was playing so well some were even beginning to ask the unthinkable: Is this team better off without Frazier? Berringer had certainly proven himself as a thrower. During one three-game stretch, he completed 71 percent of his passes, and his 267 yards against Kansas was just 30 yards short of the school record. His quarterback rating was the highest in the Big Eight, even better than May's.

As a runner, Berringer was no Frazier, picking up about 4 yards per carry with his straight-ahead style, compared with Frazier's 7.5. But he ran well enough to keep defenses honest. He was moving the team in his own way. And his teammates

"It was a surprise. I was like,
'Is he sick or something?' I guess not.
T.O. knows what he's doing."

— ERIC ALFORD, ON TOM OSBORNE CALLING
SO MANY PASSES TO THE TIGHT ENDS

"I've come to a lot of games over the years,
and for a sustained period of time,
today was the loudest crowd I've ever heard."

— HUSKER FAN MIKE RUTLEDGE, ON THE FIELD AFTER THE GAME

enjoyed his uplifting energy. While Frazier and Berringer were both great leaders, Berringer's leadership was more positive and upbeat. Colorado's Heath Irwin admitted after the game the Buffs had come into Lincoln relishing the idea of facing Berringer rather than Frazier. "But, shoot, they didn't miss a beat," he said. "It didn't set them back at all, and it added a dimension because of the way he could throw the ball."

Berringer had always believed, if given the chance, that he could prove what he could do. Now whenever there were light-hearted suggestions from reporters that there could be a quarterback controversy at Nebraska the next year when Frazier returned, Berringer didn't back away from it at all. "I never set a goal to be a backup quarterback," he said. "I'll never be happy being No. 2."

With movie-star looks and a guy-next-door quality, Berringer was having the time of his life, enjoying all that came with being the starting quarterback at Nebraska. He was the center of attention each week when Husker players met with the press. He was being asked to speak to grade school groups. His mailbox was full. He couldn't go out to eat without someone asking him to sign something. "Welcome to the big time," Ron Brown told him over lunch one day. With the way the state and his teammates were rallying around him, this was clearly now Berringer's team.

Or was it? The day after Thanksgiving, as the Huskers wrapped up their 12-0 regular season and Orange Bowl berth with a 13-3 victory over Oklahoma, there was suddenly a familiar face standing on the sidelines next to Osborne, wearing an unfamiliar No. 17 jersey: Tommie Frazier.

Tommie Returns

As the wins and the excitement mounted for the 1994 Cornhuskers and their fans, the player who had been the face of the program had virtually disappeared. Tommie Frazier, of course, had always been a lone wolf. But once out of the hospital, he became a virtual recluse. He didn't go to practice. He was nowhere to be found most game days. Only the few people he allowed close to him knew the anguish he was going through. Why did this happen to me? And why now? On a football field, Frazier had always been the one who would take charge. This seemed to be the first thing he'd ever faced that was completely beyond his control.

While Frazier originally had kept a brave face over his blood-clot ordeal, there were some tough times in the weeks that followed. Frazier shed tears during the eight days he spent hospitalized at Bryan. When the clot had first reappeared, Tom Osborne summoned Frazier's mother from Florida, with the school receiving a special hardship from the NCAA to pay for the trip. She had never seen him so down. At one point, he told her he wanted to go home, thinking his career was over. His roommate, Husker receiver Aaron Davis, would recall Frazier going through a lot of anxiety, fear and frustration in those days. He felt all of his hard work to get to this point in his career had gone for naught.

Osborne and Kevin Steele found time to visit Frazier almost every day, trying to boost his spirits. Osborne told him to focus on his health and school. The coach would fill him in on how the team was doing at practice, even telling him who was getting into scraps. One time, Osborne asked Frazier if the coach could pray for him, and he did. Osborne prayed for all of his players, though he usually never told them about it.

> "I tried to deal with it the best I could. I tried to come to the media room. Sometimes it was just too hard."
>
> — TOMMIE FRAZIER, ON HIS MEDICAL PROBLEMS

Once out of the hospital, Frazier declined interview requests and was not seen often around South Stadium, choosing instead to focus on his recovery. He told reporters later he had wanted the focus to be on the guys who were playing. But that didn't tell the whole story of what was going on inside the head of the moody 20-year-old. He also didn't want to be anyone's sob story. He despised that. And he'd admit years later he just wasn't mentally prepared to be around the team. It hurt not being part of the Huskers' perfect season as it rolled on week after week.

Osborne could tell his quarterback was struggling and feeling left out. One day in late October, Osborne saw Frazier in Steele's office. "Maybe you might want to come around so your teammates can see you're doing well," Osborne said. He made it sound as if it was for his teammates' benefit, but Frazier knew what his coach was trying to do. And it turned into a key turning point in the quarterback's emotional recovery. After that, Frazier started showing up at some practices, even running around a little and throwing some balls. He found it did feel good to be around the guys again. One of the things that had also kept him going as the calendar turned from October to November was the thought that he could eventually get a do-over for this season. The athletic department had put in the paperwork to get him a medical hardship, allowing him to preserve his junior year of eligibility.

Even as things started to go well under Brook Berringer, rumors persisted around the program that Frazier would be coming back. Osborne insisted there was nothing to them. However, two events in the span of just a week's time in mid-November eventually would change everything.

On November 15, Frazier received a surprisingly good medical report. An ultrasound showed the vein was healing well. And most importantly, there was no sign at all of any clot residue. The vein was completely clean. The results were significant, making it appear unlikely a clot would now reform. Dr. Deepak Gangahar was now even more confident the clot had been caused by a one-time blow, rather than some type of serious illness. Gangahar attributed the quick recovery to the fact that Frazier was a young, world-class athlete. "It's definitely a faster recovery than the average person," Gangahar said. "But we're not talking about the average person, either." Frazier started dressing for practice more frequently and took more non-contact snaps, just to spell Berringer. The plan was still to hold Frazier out of games so he could get the medical redshirt.

Then on Tuesday, November 22, the NCAA informed Nebraska it was rejecting Frazier's hardship petition. The rule stated a player could get a hardship after an

"We told the doctor we wouldn't put
Tommie in unless Brook went down or
something really catastrophic happened."

— TOM OSBORNE, ON FRAZIER'S FIRST GAME BACK IN UNIFORM

injury if he had participated in no more than 20 percent of his team's games. That meant Frazier could have played in 2.4 games. Frazier played in just over three, counting the handful of snaps he took against Pacific. Nebraska contended the West Virginia game shouldn't count because it was like a preseason bowl, and bowls were exempt under the rule. But the argument didn't fly with the NCAA.

Osborne was distressed by the ruling, but Frazier took it well, not batting an eye. Perhaps it was because he had an inkling of how the ruling could now alter the course of history for him and the Huskers. Over the next 24 hours, it changed everyone's thinking when it came to his participation the rest of this season.

Frazier wanted to play. If he wasn't getting the hardship, he told Osborne, it didn't make any sense not to try. Osborne readily assented but needed to talk to the doctors first. Gangahar told Osborne he saw no risk in Frazier returning to the field, and by Wednesday night gave the go-ahead for him to travel with the team the next day to Oklahoma. Frazier was taken off the anti-coagulants that night, which would allow the drugs to clear his system in plenty of time for Friday's game. Thanksgiving night, Frazier was spotted by a World-Herald reporter smiling and laughing as he entered a meeting room at the team's hotel in Norman. Osborne confirmed that Frazier had been cleared, though he would only play in the event of injuries to both Berringer and Matt Turman.

Events had turned so quickly that the equipment staff didn't have a jersey for Frazier. His No. 15 road jersey had been damaged in the Texas Tech game, and since he was out by the next time NU played away from Lincoln, it had never been replaced. So Frazier wore No. 17 on the sideline that day.

Osborne half-jokingly admitted after the game that he looked over to No. 17 a couple of times as the offense struggled some against the Sooners. And addressing Frazier's status at length for the first time, he said Frazier would be able to play in the upcoming Orange Bowl against Miami, the national championship game. Nebraska suddenly had the makings of a quarterback controversy.

Both quarterbacks wanted to start in the bowl, and both could make a case for being the man. Berringer had led the team to victory in eight games, and the team had a chemistry going with him. "I would think you would stick with me, but you never know," Berringer said the day of the Oklahoma game. "I don't want to get into that too much."

Frazier admitted the Huskers had become Brook's team. However, he had lost his job only due to injury. It wasn't as if he had been beaten out. He should be given the chance to win his job back. The arguments about chemistry didn't make sense to Frazier. The team had played well under both quarterbacks. How was there a chemistry issue?

There was talk and speculation outside the program that the two quarterbacks simply didn't get along. Frazier years later said it was all overblown. Were they good friends? No. It wasn't like he would ask Berringer out for pizza or that Berringer would take him hunting. They had little in common, other than being quarterbacks at Nebraska. But there were tons of other guys on the team Frazier didn't hang out with, and that didn't mean he didn't like or get along with them. "When you have two people competing for the same job, people automatically assume you don't like each other, and that wasn't the case," he said. "I helped Brook, and he helped me." Frazier also denied any suggestion that he had resented the success Berringer had enjoyed during his absence. "I was happy to see him get his opportunity and make the most if it," Frazier said. "He kept the hopes and dreams alive for our team."

There was some disagreement within the team over who should quarterback the Huskers in Miami. Tight end Eric Alford was one of few players to publicly express an opinion, saying he thought the team should stick with Berringer. But Frazier heard lots of other buzz about it in the locker room, with opinions going both ways. There was certainly a potential for the quarterback situation to create dissension. But Osborne, Ron Brown and several players years later said there actually was very little acrimony, for a number of reasons. The Huskers were united in their goal. They believed in both Berringer and Frazier. The coaches planned to be transparent and fair in making the decision. More importantly, the players trusted Osborne and his judgment. As Ed Stewart later put it: "At the end of the day, whoever Dr. Tom thinks should be in there will be in there. Let's play ball."

Osborne decided the only fair approach was to have both quarterbacks settle it on the field. During bowl preparations, they'd be graded on every snap, every decision and every throw, just as they had during fall camp. This would not be an arbitrary call. The numbers would reveal who was playing better.

Osborne also told both players their performance in a final scrimmage down in Miami would be critical. So under high security at a local university in Miami on Christmas Eve, Frazier was tackled in live football for the first time in 13 weeks. The defense didn't hold back. He took hits on eight or nine options and pass plays, including some pretty good shots.

"It's not quite as big a deal as the perception of it is. We've got two capable quarterbacks who have run the team."

— BROOK BERRINGER, WHEN ASKED WHO WOULD START
AT QUARTERBACK IN THE ORANGE BOWL

For Frazier, it actually felt good to be hit again. And one play in particular showed he was ready to play. A defender came in clean on a pass rush and had a clear shot at Frazier. The quarterback eluded him without being touched and scrambled for a first down. "Uh-oh," one of the defenders was heard to say. "He's back." Frazier had put on a little weight while he was out — he'd actually play the bowl game at 225 pounds, 15 more than he carried at the start of the season. But the play showed Osborne, Frazier and the team that he had not lost his quickness.

Berringer, who received an equal number of snaps, had his moments, too. But he also turned the ball over twice on interceptions — one more than Frazier had that day. Turnovers were a bugaboo for Osborne. Largely because of them, Frazier narrowly graded out better.

Osborne announced his decision at media day five days later. Frazier would start, but Berringer would also play in the first half. Osborne also made one thing clear to both quarterbacks: In the end, he would do whatever he felt he needed to do to win the game.

There was immediately much second-guessing in the media about whether it was wise for Osborne to trust his team's championship hopes to a quarterback who had not taken a snap in a game since September. Others questioned whether having two quarterbacks in the mix during the game would be a distraction or hurt the team's preparation. But those weren't issues inside the team. "The media made a way bigger deal out of it than the players," Husker fullback Cory Schlesinger recalled. "With Brook we'd throw more, and with Tommie we'd run more. To us, it really didn't make a difference."

Indeed, the pundits were ignoring the upside of the Huskers' quarterback situation. Nebraska now had two capable, experienced signal-callers in whom the team had complete confidence. And each would bring his own strengths to the table, giving Nebraska a unique one-two punch against an imposing Miami defense. "Why not use both weapons instead of just one?" Tony Veland recalled thinking.

As it turned out, were it not for the combined talents of both quarterbacks, Osborne and the Huskers may very well have fallen short yet again.

"This ain't no ordinary team.
And this ain't no ordinary defense.
We come to play ball. They better strap
it on real tight, because we're coming."

— WARREN SAPP OF MIAMI

Hurricane Warning

Warren Sapp recoiled in mock horror when he learned Tommie Frazier would be leading the Huskers in the Orange Bowl on Jan. 1. "Oooooh, we're shaking." Sapp's sidekick, Rohan Marley, took the trash talk to another level, seeming to suggest that the Hurricanes could soon be sending the Nebraska quarterback back to the hospital. "I hope they know what they're doing," he said. "I'd hate to see him go back to the doctors after the game."

It was typical stuff from Miami's Hurricanes. The trash-talking, cheap-shotting, taunting, rule-flaunting renegades reveled in their reputation as college football's bad boys. "They were a low-class outfit," George Darlington recalled. "It was part of their mystique."

The fact that the Hurricanes could often back up their big talk only served to make their act all the more infuriating. Tom Osborne and the Huskers unwittingly had helped create this monster during that crushing loss after the 1983 season. Fueled by the rich talent the school began harvesting out of its inner-city Miami backyard, the Hurricanes created a dynasty, proceeding to win three more national championships by 1991. This Miami bunch was a step down from those teams of the past, but not a big one. They'd lost only once, an early-season setback against Washington. They'd rebounded to impressively beat Florida State, the team many had expected to repeat as national champs. Miami had also won 62 of its last 63 games in the Orange Bowl, their home stadium. They hadn't lost a night game at home since 1977. Cocksure and intimidating, the 'Canes had most teams beaten as soon as they stepped off the bus.

And in recent years, of course, the Hurricanes had owned Osborne's Cornhuskers. In the Orange Bowls after the 1988 and 1991 seasons, Miami had held Nebraska to just three total points and the two lowest offensive yardage outputs of Osborne's entire tenure. Now both Osborne and Miami Coach Dennis Erickson agreed that this fierce Miami defense — ranked first nationally in both scoring defense and total defense — was likely the school's best ever. The third-ranked Hurricanes also had much to play for, with an outside chance to claim another national championship if the bowl results fell out right. The Hurricanes were more than capable of

making it another long, cold winter on the Plains for Osborne's Huskers and their fans.

The anchor of the Miami defense was Sapp, a 6-3, 280-pound defensive tackle with a nonstop motor and nonstop mouth. Amazingly quick for his size, he'd racked up 10½ sacks, 20 tackles for loss and 84 total tackles during the season, all despite often being double- and triple-teamed. He said he wasn't bothered by all the extra attention. "Come on, join the party," joked Sapp, who won the Lombardi Award and finished sixth in Heisman voting. With Sapp swallowing up so many blockers, Hurricane linebacker Ray Lewis could be an absolute terror. A future NFL superstar, the vicious hitter had amassed more than 150 tackles in just 11 games. The Hurricanes just didn't give up big plays on the ground. All week long, Sapp, Lewis and their teammates talked of how they didn't think Nebraska and its touted line could run the option against Miami's speed. "Just chalk it up," Sapp said.

The Orange Bowl matchup between Nebraska and Miami was as much as anything a marriage of convenience. After having seen the Big Eight-champ Huskers flop on the field in Miami year after year, the Orange Bowl committee had wanted nothing to do with them this year. One member of the committee told Sports Illustrated in October that of its 200 members, perhaps only one wanted Nebraska to come back this year, and he was an NU alum. The committee had been rooting hard for Colorado when the Buffs came to Lincoln. And even after Nebraska thrashed Colorado, the Orange Bowl had continued to hope Nebraska would stumble in its remaining games, ready to take one-loss Colorado over a one-loss Nebraska team in a heartbeat. When Nebraska beat Oklahoma in Norman to finish its regular season 12-0, Darlington ran into a pair of Orange Bowl officials, who looked as if they'd just experienced a death in the family. "Fellas, whether you like it or not," he crowed, "you have us again."

At the same time, Osborne earlier in the season had actually lobbied Orange Bowl officials to try to avoid the familiar trap of having to play a Florida school in Florida.

"No one ever really lays a big hit on me anyway, because I try to adjust my body to the defender."

— TOMMIE FRAZIER, WHEN ASKED ABOUT HIS FIRST SCRIMMAGE
SINCE BEING SIDELINED

Howard Schnellenberger, coach of the '83 'Canes, had once told Osborne he figured playing in the Orange Bowl was worth 10 points to his team. But by the time this year's NU-Miami matchup had been set, Osborne and Nebraska's players made it clear they wanted nothing more than to once again play Miami in Miami. "I wouldn't have it any other way," Zach Wiegert said of the matchup. That's because the national championship in 1994 was coming down to a beauty contest between No. 1 Nebraska and No. 2 Penn State, with no chance for them to decide it on the field.

Osborne had actually tried to settle it that way, calling up old friend Joe Paterno one day late in the season to see if the Penn State coach would be willing to break the Big Ten's contract with the Rose Bowl. Osborne was sure there was another bowl that would salivate at the chance to put the two teams on the field. It seemed to Osborne that Paterno wanted to do it. But in the end he didn't see it as good form to try to break that contract, especially given that Penn State was the Big Ten's newest member. Osborne told Paterno he understood. It had been worth a try. (Coincidentally, Osborne in 2009 as athletic director at Nebraska would help shepherd the school into Big Ten membership.)

While the Huskers often dismissed the polls, they closely watched them — and that included Osborne. One writer caught Osborne doing a little scoreboard watching the day of the Colorado victory, the coach noting that Penn State was up big at the half and then speculating what that would mean in the polls. While Nebraska led going into the bowls, nearly a third of poll voters were putting the Nittany Lions No. 1 on their ballots. Now both teams were looking to make hay in their bowl games, with Penn State slated to play in the Rose against lackluster Pac-10 champ Oregon. As the Huskers saw it, if they beat the No. 3 team on its home field, then there was no way the voters could fail to vote the Huskers national champions.

Osborne, of course, was planning some surprises for the Hurricanes. Security had been higher than ever around Nebraska practices, partly to protect the secrecy of a

"I hope it won't go a half-hour. I have a reputation for speaking in a monotone and being boring."

— TOM OSBORNE, WHEN INTRODUCED AT A PRESS CONFERENCE AS BEING AVAILABLE FOR 30 MINUTES

Husker lineup change. Osborne and Milt Tenopir had agreed that guards Brenden Stai and Joel Wilks would swap places in the Nebraska offensive line, Stai moving to the left side directly across from Sapp. Wilks was a good player, but the stronger Stai was a better matchup against the powerful Hurricane. And Osborne had a few new schemes up his sleeve, too. He planned a series of new misdirection and reverse plays designed to use the aggressiveness of Sapp and Lewis against them.

And while much of the pregame hype had been about Sapp vs. that great NU offensive line, Charlie McBride and his defense — which ranked second in the nation in scoring only to Miami — thought they could make some hay against a fast but inconsistent Miami offense. Frank Costa, the Hurricanes' starting quarterback, would never be confused with Jim Kelly, Bernie Kosar or Vinny Testaverde, some of the stars who had preceded him under center in Coral Gables. McBride felt that if the Blackshirts could dial up some pressure on Costa, he'd struggle.

For the Husker players, there had been very little let-up since the Oklahoma game. Osborne went in concerned that the Hurricanes would be much better acclimated to Miami's 90 percent humidity, so conditioning would be key. Osborne and the coaches ran the players so much some worried whether their legs would recover in time. It was almost like fall camp all over again. Osborne even had the Huskers running on Christmas Day. As the Huskers sprinted down the field, Osborne reminded his players that Miami had taken the day off. "They're at the beach!" he called out. Throughout the week, Osborne drilled such messages into his players: They aren't hitting like this. They aren't working this hard. We will wear them down.

All the hard work was fine with most of the Huskers. In fact, true to their "Unfinished Business" motto, many players were treating this game as a business trip. For the seniors, this was their fourth trip to the Orange Bowl. They had been to the aquarium to see the dolphins. They'd been to the beach. They were tired of all the pre-bowl luncheons, dinners and community outings. They just wanted to get ready to play some football. When they weren't practicing, eating, sleeping or riding a bus between practice and the hotel, many spent their time just resting in their rooms or soaking their battered bodies in the hotel pool. The Huskers' media relations people at one point talked to Barron Miles in exasperation. You guys have to do something. "We'll do our talking on the field," he replied.

Finally, Miles agreed to attend a dinner that would feature representatives from both teams. Osborne himself talked him into it, convincing the senior he needed to show that Nebraska appreciated the city's hospitality. Miles went — and almost got into a fight. Sapp, Marley and other Hurricanes almost immediately started running their mouths. "It was just those guys being who they are," Miles recalled. Though Miles didn't back down, the confrontation never got physical and in the end didn't amount to a lot. But to Miles, the Hurricanes' bluster showed they had no idea what they were in for come New Year's Night.

"They thought they were going to bully us," Miles said. "They didn't know what the Florida State loss had done to our team. They didn't understand the dedication that had gone into this season. We were going to finish this off."

Bringing It Home

As Husker tight end Matt Shaw warmed up with his teammates on the west end of the Orange Bowl, he drank in the atmosphere and history of one of college football's classic venues. The hot and steamy stadium was filling up with a record crowd of almost 82,000 fans, including some 20,000 irrepressibly hopeful folks in red. Ahead of him, toward the open east end of the old horseshoe-shaped structure, stood the scoreboard flanked by its iconic stands of palms. Just above, running along the face of the upper deck, Shaw could see those familiar words: THE CITY OF MIAMI WELCOMES YOU TO THE ORANGE BOWL.

Of course, the Orange Bowl in recent years had not been such a hospitable place for Shaw and his senior teammates. They had already lost games on this field in each of their years playing in the Nebraska program. This was the same field where they'd all stood heartsick a year earlier after watching that potential game-winning kick go awry. But Shaw, Zach Wiegert, Barron Miles, Terry Connealy, Rob Zatechka and the other seniors were determined that this night would be different. Since the Orange Bowl loss their freshman year, when they hadn't scored a single point against another Miami team, they felt they had seen this program come full circle. Tonight, it was going to be their time.

After 365 days of work, sweat, pain and perseverance to get back to this place, it was now down to 60 minutes of football for a national championship. But for the Nebraska-born players like Shaw, this was the culmination of a lifetime of waiting, hoping and dreaming. Many of them had watched on TV as 10- to 12-year-olds as that two-point conversion pass at the end of the 1983 season fell to the turf. Matt Vrzal, a reserve offensive lineman from Grand Island, vividly remembered how his

> "We're back on top, where we belong. This is something we wanted for the whole state of Nebraska."
>
> — DEFENSIVE LINEMAN TERRY CONNEALY,
> WHOSE SACK OF FRANK COSTA SEALED THE ORANGE BOWL WIN

dad in frustration crushed a full can of beer in his hand, the suds flying all over. It was a young boy's first lesson in how much Big Red football meant in Nebraska. Shaw, a native of Lincoln, had actually been in the hostile and nasty Orange Bowl stands that night 11 years before. Red paint on his face, he'd stood in little-kid devastation when the undefeated Huskers' magical season crash-landed. It was one of the unhappiest memories of his youth. Little did Shaw know then that he would grow up to be a blue-collar walk-on in the Nebraska program with a chance to write a different ending against the Hurricanes he grew up so detesting.

There would be nine native Nebraskans in the Huskers' starting lineup this night, none more unheralded than Shaw. Despite starting nearly every game at tight end in 1994, Shaw had not caught a single pass. "We'll try to get you one," Tom Osborne would sheepishly tell him each week. But Shaw really didn't care. He knew he wasn't on the field because he had great hands or ran great routes. It was because he was a punishing blocker on the edge. Shaw, in effect, was the unrecognized sixth segment of the Pipeline. Unsung, no-name players like Shaw had always been integral to the success of Nebraska football, and this game would prove no exception. On this night, during each crucial fourth-quarter offensive snap that would long stick in the minds of Nebraska's fans, Shaw would be on the field, ferociously and anonymously laying himself on the line.

Shaw and his teammates wanted to win this game for the hundreds of thousands of Husker fans out there who longed for a return to the glory days. They wanted to win for the previous year's seniors, who had shown the way and were a big reason the Huskers were back here again. And above all, they wanted to win it for their coach. That was something they had talked about openly leading up to the game. Shaw believed it was love for Coach Osborne that had pulled the Huskers this far, through all the season's adversity. To be the team to finally give him a national championship would be an honor. There wasn't a Cornhusker on this field who was not prepared to give heart, body and soul to make that happen.

The Huskers filed back into the cramped visitors' locker room beneath the stands. Taped for battle, they huddled around their coach. Osborne had his final game notes scrawled on a piece of scratch paper, just a few words to remind him of his final talking points. He spoke of the opportunity the Huskers had before them. So many guys go through their whole career and never get a chance like this. He told them of the plan to rotate players into the lineup, part of the strategy of wearing out Miami in the fourth quarter. He talked about big plays. This game will probably hinge on three or four of them. Think about what you can do — a sack, a fumble recovery or a big block — to help the team get the job done. And he told them they should be confident. They were ready for this night. "I don't think we've ever had a team better prepared to handle this situation," he told them. "You're ready to play. There's no concern on my part as to how we're going to get the job done."

The desire to see Osborne finally win a national championship also made Nebraska the sentimental favorites in America's living rooms. Everyone loves an underdog, and after all those years of falling short, that was Osborne and the Huskers as they entered the field to their new tunnel walk music. But things didn't start out well for Nebraska. It appeared the Huskers and their fans were once again destined for Orange Bowl disappointment.

Despite the 98-day layoff, Tommie Frazier was his usual relaxed self. But he also came out sluggishly. The Huskers went three-and-out on their first possession, Frazier missing on a third-down pass. He did move the Huskers the next time, nearly 50 yards into Miami territory. But then he aggressively tried to make a play, and it cost him. Warren Sapp flew around the double-team of Brenden Stai and Aaron Graham and into Frazier's face. Backpedaling, the quarterback threw deep and off-balance into double coverage, and Miami intercepted at its own 3. Sapp was living up to his pre-game billing and bragging. In fact, despite having a fellow All-American across from him, for much of the game he'd be blowing up screen plays, dragging down runners by the scruff of the neck and talking smack. A couple of times after chasing ball carriers out of bounds, Huskers on the sideline would recall that Sapp gestured at Osborne, pointing his finger and shaking his head side to side.

The Blackshirts weren't faring much better. They allowed Miami to drive for a field goal the first time out. And then after the Frazier interception, the Hurricanes went a demoralizing 97 yards in just five plays, leaving Nebraska's fleet defense grasping at the sticky air. The score came on a 35-yard swing pass from Frank Costa to Trent Jones in which a slew of Huskers took poor angles and missed tackles. The Black-shirts headed to the bench in frustration. The two scores in two Miami possessions had been a blow to their confidence. There was also some bickering between the defensive backs and defensive line about getting more pressure on Costa. With Costa having time to throw, the secondary was struggling to hang with the Miami receivers one-on-one. But Miles refused to get down as he took a seat on the bench next to a trainer. "We're going to win this game," he vowed. "Wait and see." Those seemed like bold words at that point. Behind 10-0, this was looking an awful lot like those past New Year's nightmares where the Huskers were simply overmatched.

Immediately after the Frazier interception, Osborne told Brook Berringer to get warmed up. Osborne said later he wasn't down on Frazier. He had planned from the beginning that Berringer would quarterback the second quarter. But the gangly quarterback and his arm also provided a change of pace against a Miami defense that was clearly geared to stopping the option. On his second possession, when Nebraska took over on a short field, Berringer got the Husker offense on a roll. Lawrence Phillips gained seven on a sweep, and then Osborne took advantage of Ray Lewis' run pursuit by running a reverse to the speedy Riley Washington for nine. Then Berringer rolled right on play action and made eye contact with tight end Mark Gilman, who had gotten behind Lewis. Berringer lofted a perfect spiral that Gilman hauled in for a huge 19-yard score. The Husker sideline came to life.

After their shaky start, the Blackshirts settled down, too. And it was because they started bringing the heat on Costa. With NU down early, Osborne approached Charlie McBride on the sidelines. "Let's start blitzing them," Osborne told him. "I don't care if we lose by a hundred points. Let's put him on his back." McBride started bringing all three of his linebackers up to the line of scrimmage, sometimes sending them all after Costa. Grant Wistrom and Ed Stewart blew up flanker screens, a play that had been killing Nebraska earlier. Troy Dumas sacked Costa on a delayed blitz. While Costa had burned the Blackshirts for more than 100 yards in the first quarter, he hit only 3 of 11 passes for 23 yards in the second. But such numbers weren't the only indicator that the Blackshirts were getting a handle on the Hurricanes.

McBride had a meticulous way of preparing for game day. He would painstakingly write out a cheat sheet with the defensive calls he planned to use against various formations and in various situations. It was a work of art. He'd put it in a rain shield and clutch it in his hand, glancing at it from time to time during the game. He may never have even realized it, but whenever he saw a game was in hand, he'd fold the sheet up and stick it in his back pocket. Well, late in the second quarter, linebackers coach Kevin Steele glanced over and was surprised to see McBride fold up and pocket his cheat sheet. Miami still was ahead. But McBride was now dialed in. He knew exactly what the Blackshirts needed to do. "It was a good feeling," Steele recalled.

The Huskers went into halftime trailing 10-7 but feeling much better about their play. The quarterbacks were quickly told that Berringer would stay under center in the second half, on the strength of the touchdown drive he'd led. But Turner Gill also told Frazier to stay mentally ready. You might get another chance, he said. Osborne came into the locker room with a bit of spring in his step. He actually liked what he'd been seeing. There were times that Osborne's unmatched ability to intuit the flow of a game made it seem he had some superhuman power to see the future. He proceeded on this night to give a halftime speech so prophetic it would have been almost impossible to believe had the whole thing not been captured by a Husker-Vision camera.

As his players huddled around him on benches and knees, Osborne expressed confidence that the Huskers would wear Miami down in the second half. They'll probably get a little rejuvenated in the third quarter, he said. But if the Huskers kept playing physical football, their superior depth and conditioning would show through. "So just keep hammering them," he said bluntly. "The fourth quarter, we'll get to do what we want to do."

Then he predicted Miami's cheap-shotting ways were finally going to cost them. He had seen how chippy things had gotten during the first half. Twice after kicks in the first half Nebraska and Miami players had skirmishes, including one in which both players were flagged for offsetting personal fouls. Osborne figured a blowup was coming. If the Hurricanes mouth off, he told his team, just play harder. And if they do cheap-shot you, keep your hands to yourself. "I'll promise you this, if you guys will get your hands down, they're going to get a critical penalty at a time that's going to kill them," he said. "So I don't want anybody being a banty rooster. The thing you can do that will hurt those guys the most is to get a penalty walked off."

Then the coach known for his dispassionate locker room speeches actually became a little animated. "Listen, fellas, we're going for the national championship, and we've got 30 minutes to get it done," he said with a bit of urgency in his voice. "Let's get it done, OK. No excuses. This time we get it done."

It took only minutes in the second half for one of Osborne's first predictions to come true. The 'Canes did come out fresh and moved 78 yards down the field with a short passing game. On the last play, Jonathan Harris took a pass in the flat and ran right through the entire Husker secondary, which again was victimized by bad tackling. After the kick, it was suddenly 17-7, matching the Huskers' biggest first-half deficit.

Then, on the Hurricanes' next possession, another Osborne prediction came to pass. And it would help provide the Huskers a game-changing boost of momentum. If most Huskers had to bet who among them would be most likely to draw a personal foul for retaliating, many would have put their money on Christian Peter. His short fuse and propensity to lash out were already well-documented, the tackle frequently in the middle of fights at practice. It was not uncommon for coaches to have to step in and settle him down. During practices leading up to the Miami game, Osborne decided to give the scout team pretty much free rein to do whatever they wanted to Peter. Facing the Hurricanes, Peter needed practice keeping his cool.

Miami was already backed up due in part to an excessive celebration penalty after the Harris touchdown — more typical dumb stuff from the Hurricanes. Then after a run play, Peter got in a scrum with Miami's center. Both players appeared to grab handfuls of jersey before Peter got spun to the ground with the Miami center on top of him. One replay appeared to show that Peter said or did something to provoke the Hurricane, because he suddenly and aggressively shoved Peter's head and shoulders into the turf. Per Osborne's instructions, Peter kept his hands down — as Milt Tenopir later described it, looking like Jesus on the cross. Flags went flying. The personal foul backed up the Hurricanes to their own 4.

Now Nebraska needed a big play, and Husker rush end Dwayne Harris delivered. McBride called a defense called Tornado Y Free Y. The middle linebacker stood over the guard as if he were going to blitz, but instead dropped back to cover the tight end. It was actually the safety who would be coming on this disguised blitz. The Miami tackle on the side of the blitzer suddenly saw he had two guys to block, and his hesitation allowed Harris to beat him to the inside. The Husker was in Costa's face before the quarterback had time to do anything. Harris grabbed the front of Costa's shoulder pads with one of his long arms and dragged him down in the back of the end zone. Costa fell right at the feet of an ecstatic Herbie Husker, Nebraska's corny-looking mascot. Harris sprung up and held up two fingers for the two-point safety. NU had pulled within 17-9. You could feel the momentum now shift to Nebraska. And were it not for some costly miscues on offense, the Huskers might have taken total control right then.

Late in the third period, Berringer had the Huskers moving again. He hit wide receiver Abdul Muhammad on three passes as the Huskers drove 57 yards deep into Hurricane territory. But Berringer then bobbled a snap and never got the ball to Clinton Childs on a handoff, and Miami recovered. The frustration showed on Osborne's face, just the kind of fundamental breakdown that would really get to him. The Huskers went into the final period still trailing by eight.

Then early in the fourth quarter, Nebraska caught a huge break. Miami's center snapped the ball over the punter's head, and a mad scramble ended with the punter illegally kicking the ball out of the end zone. Nebraska had the ball on the Miami 4.

That's when Osborne made a call that, had things not turned out differently in the end, might have been second-guessed across the state for decades to come. Instead of pounding Phillips into the middle, Osborne again had Berringer roll out. Under pressure, he tried to throw the ball out of the back of the end zone. Everyone was stunned to see a Miami defender leap high and bring it down. Interception.

The air went out of the north stands, where most of Nebraska's fans were sitting. The crushing interception had come in the east end zone — the same cursed ground where Nebraska championship dreams always have gone to die. It's where Gill's two-point conversion pass fell in 1984, the same place Byron Bennett's kick the previous year veered off into the stands. Husker fans in the Orange Bowl and watching on TV from Omaha to Alliance got that familiar feeling in the pit of the stomach. It was as if yet another title shot was floating away on a Biscayne Bay breeze. But that same breeze would carry in Tommie Frazier.

Even before Berringer returned to the sidelines, Osborne decided he was ready to make a critical move. "What do you think?" Osborne asked Gill, who already knew what the head coach was thinking. "It's about time for Tommie," Gill replied. "I think so," Osborne agreed.

Frazier, after getting the word from Gill, used a break in the action to begin rallying his team. Helmet in hand, he worked the Nebraska sideline, going eyeball to eyeball with anyone within reach. "We are going to win this game," Frazier said, fire flashing in his eyes. "You either believe it or you don't. If you don't, get off the sidelines!"

He was getting people jacked up. Fullback Cory Schlesinger, usually quiet, was about to come unglued. Defensive end Donta Jones looked like he was going to explode. The Blackshirts quickly got the Huskers back on track, holding Miami for the fourth straight possession. Entering the game for the first time since late in the first quarter, Frazier huddled up his team. If this had been a movie, Frazier would have heroically led his inspired teammates right down the field against Sapp and the Hurricanes as soon as he returned.

But on Frazier's first play, Sapp knifed into the backfield and took him down before he could even get going on the option, a five-yard loss. Sapp, continuing to show-boat, sprung to his feet and started dancing. Then he turned toward the Nebraska sideline and made a throat-slashing gesture. Osborne, who had made eye contact with Sapp, would years later say he thought the gesture was aimed directly at him. On third down, Frazier was stuffed again on the option. NBC color commentator

Cris Collinsworth said Nebraska couldn't afford to run any more options. Sapp and Miami are just too quick, he said. He predicted Berringer and his arm would soon be returning to the game.

With Frazier and the Huskers three and out, another unsung Husker hero took to the field. Darin Erstad was an All-American outfielder on the Nebraska baseball team who also just happened to possess the strongest kicking leg on campus. Doak Ostergard, an assistant trainer who worked with baseball players, too, had noticed how the ball just exploded off his foot when Erstad was screwing around with the baseball team one day. Ostergard unsuccessfully tried to convince Osborne and the staff to bring him in for the 1993 season. If things had gone differently, perhaps it would have been Erstad, not Bennett, lining up for that long field goal against Florida State on this same field a year earlier.

Regardless, Osborne did invite the North Dakota native to come out in 1994 to punt, kick off and serve as the specialist on long field-goal tries. In what would prove to be his only season of college football before going No. 1 in the 1995 amateur baseball draft, Erstad had been helping the Huskers win the field position battle weekly, depositing almost half his punts inside the opponents' 20-yard line. He'd also hit a couple of long field goals, 48 and 46 yards, with the second in a critical spot against Oklahoma. This time, Erstad dropped in a punt that the Huskers touched down at the Miami 4.

The kick proved critical, because the Blackshirts were now in complete control. Harris sacked Costa again to disrupt this possession. Throughout the second half, Costa was getting hit whenever he dropped back to pass. One time it would be Connealy driving him down, Costa coming up with a chunk of turf stuck in his face mask. Then it would be Harris or linebacker Dumas or reserve tackle Jason Pesterfield flattening him. Some of them were borderline late hits, though the refs never thought any merited a flag. After the game, Husker coaches on film would count 19 solid shots that the Blackshirts put on Costa. As the minutes ticked off, Costa's white jersey was stained green and brown, and he seemed to drag himself up a little more slowly each time. No one could have stood up to that kind of pounding, which by game's end had literally left Costa's body black and blue.

After the Blackshirts held yet again, a Miami punt set up Nebraska in great field position, at the Hurricane 40 with eight minutes to play. As the Nebraska offense again took the field, Sapp, who had played high school football against Frazier in south Florida, had some words for his old rival. As recounted by Frazier later,

"I was physically exhausted
in the fourth quarter. I wasn't injured,
but I was hurting an awful lot."

— FRANK COSTA

it was an exchange that would go down in Husker lore.

"Hey, Thomas, where you been?"

"It's not where I've been, it's where I'm going, fat ass."

Frazier and the Huskers indeed were ready to go places. The Huskers fighting in the trenches would always be the first to sense when a team was starting to crack. Just looking in the 'Canes' eyes, they'd already seen for a while now it was happening. "We're just going to kill 'em," Wiegert had told Pat Clare after the long third-quarter drive that ended with Berringer's fumble. But it wasn't until this point, 52 minutes into the game, that it would become obvious to everyone that Miami was running out of steam. This was where all that work from the heat of the Nebraska summer right through this past sweltering week in Miami really started to pay off. And this is where Osborne's final halftime prediction became reality. True to his words, the Huskers from this point did pretty much whatever they wanted to do.

"We're getting it done," Frazier told his teammates in the huddle. "We're scoring now." Phillips then got the Huskers started, and he really did it on his own. Frazier tossed him a pitch on the option, and it seemed he had nowhere to go. But the sophomore somehow ran through three defenders at the line of scrimmage, and when it appeared he was going to run out of bounds, he suddenly hit the brakes, dodged inside another defender at the sideline, and continued to charge downfield. He was finally dragged down at the Miami 15 after 25 yards — the longest run the Hurricanes had given up all year. That successful outside run also set up Osborne's next move.

Whenever Osborne watched his offense from the sideline, he'd always pay attention to what the opposing tackles were doing. If they were pursuing too hard to the outside to stop the option game, he'd look to call a fullback trap. The quarterback would deftly hide the ball in the belly of the fullback and then continue down the line with the I-back, who was also complicit in the deception. The "trap" part of the play would be executed by the offensive line. They'd try to lure one of the defensive tackles inside and then pull another lineman from the backside over to wall him off from the play, creating a hole in the tackle's original spot. Often the other defenders chasing the quarterback and I-back would run right past the fullback as the bowling ball known more for his crushing blocks rumbled down the field. The trap also tended to work best against undisciplined teams, which pretty much defined this Miami bunch.

Osborne decided it was time for a trap — one they had yet to run this game.

Rather than up the middle, the 32 Trap would be run to the right into the tight-end hole, trapping a defensive end. The play had worked well in practice leading up to the game, with Schlesinger running loose in the secondary nearly every time. As Frazier called the play in the huddle, Schlesinger thought to himself, "I'm going to get into the end zone here." Frazier reversed behind center, placed the ball in Schlesinger's gut and then went down the line selling the option. The pipeline went to work. Graham fired straight out and took the dangerous Lewis off his feet, while Stai got low and tripped up the mouthy Sapp. Wiegert and Joel Wilks crossed, Wiegert taking out the nose guard in front of Wilks while Wilks pulled on the trap. The trapped defensive end had already overcommitted deep into the backfield, so Wilks led Schlesinger into the hole, going after the strong-side linebacker.

Schlesinger was a classic Nebraska fullback, a human sledgehammer from the no-stoplight town of Duncan in northeast Nebraska. The senior's neck started at his ears and only got wider on its way down to his shoulders. His picture should have been there in the dictionary right next to the term "football player." And he loved nothing more than to lead the I-back into a hole, taking on a linebacker head-on and hitting him like an anvil. The guy his teammates called Joe Rockhead would go on from here to make a nice living in the NFL performing the same job for Hall-of-Fame runner Barry Sanders. It's as if he were born to do it. But Schlesinger would show everyone in the Orange Bowl he could run, too. As he took the ball from Frazier, he saw the play was working just as in practice. The sea parted right in front of him, and he followed Wilks' rear end into the hole. He almost ran up Wilks' back before bending the run around his teammate's block. He then hurdled a desperate, diving defender inside the 10 and rumbled into the end zone. He put the ball on his head and let it roll off, an impromptu celebration that teammates would later razz him about. As he turned, he saw the sea of red in the north stands going crazy.

Trailing 17-15, Osborne calmly called for a two-point conversion, going into the same east end zone where the 1984 play had failed. And tempting fate, he again dared to throw, sending in a run-pass option. Frazier rolled right, quickly saw he had no running room, and then zipped a pass to Eric Alford running open across the back of the end zone. Alford clutched the ball to his chest. Osborne showed no reaction, but there was suddenly bedlam in every living room in Nebraska.

As Miles and the Blackshirts once again took the field, he was confident that Nebraska wasn't done scoring. It appeared to him on Schlesinger's run that the Miami defensive backs, tired of the pounding they'd been taking, wanted nothing to do with tackling the fullback. Miles had seen this dynamic late in games before.

"We were swarming to the ball until the
end of the game. And then, all of a sudden,
we didn't make some tackles. At the end,
they made the plays and we didn't."

— WARREN SAPP

He was equally confident that he and the Blackshirts were going to force another three-and-out. And thanks to a little luck, they did. Miles batted down a second-down pass, the final pass breakup in a career that would see him finish as the Huskers' all-time leader. After getting burned a couple times early, he was now besting Miami's taller receivers regularly, at times flying high to swat balls away. Then on third down, Costa dropped back again. Tyrone Williams, the other corner, appeared to blow his assignment, hanging in the middle of the field while a 'Cane receiver streaked all alone down the sideline, 20 yards behind the defense. It had 6 points written all over it. But Costa got decked by Harris yet again and rushed his throw. The ball sailed beyond the receiver's grasp, harmlessly bouncing on the turf. Wow, that was close, Miles thought. Sometimes you have to have a little luck to win a national title. Maybe fate was finally with Tom Osborne and Nebraska.

Barely a minute had clicked off the clock when Frazier and the offense again trotted out to the field opposite a Miami defense that was now visibly sagging. The Huskers had decent field position at their own 42. If we really want to win this game, Frazier told his teammates, let's do it now.

Soon facing a crucial third and 4 near midfield, Osborne showed he didn't share Collinsworth's thoughts on the option game. He called for a sprint option to the right, a play in which Frazier and the I-back would simply try to get to the edge as quickly as possible. Frazier this time got the defensive end caught in no-man's land between Frazier and Phillips. Running on fresh legs, Frazier ducked the run inside the Hurricane, and Lewis also over-pursued to the outside. Tight end Shaw came off the ball and took out the other linebacker on that side. Suddenly Frazier was loose in the Miami secondary, looking for the first time that night like the magical Tommie Frazier of old. He was finally dragged down inside the Miami 30 after a 25-yard gain, springing up and churning his legs in excitement.

A minute later, Frazier and the Huskers once again found themselves facing a decisive third and 3 from the Miami 20. They were already in field-goal range, but no one on the Nebraska sideline was thinking field goal at this point. They all remembered last year, when the inability to punch in a late touchdown, instead settling for a field goal, had doomed them on this same field. Osborne told the team it was critical to pick up this one.

Miami called a timeout as the Huskers went to the line. And anyone reading the body language on the field at that moment would have seen where this thing was headed. The Huskers stood together by the sideline with their helmets on,

"Everything just busted open for me
on both runs. I don't think they knew
I had the ball either time."

— CORY SCHLESINGER, ON HIS TWO FOURTH-QUARTER TOUCHDOWNS

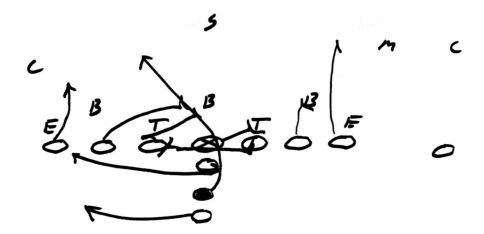

36 Trap: The winning touchdown in the Orange Bowl

— DRAWN BY TOM OSBORNE IN 2012

looking like boxers anticipating the next bell. Sapp and the rest of the Hurricanes were littered across the field, helmets off, down on one knee, gasping for air. They were indeed sapped.

As Osborne discussed the next critical call with Tenopir in the headset, the head coach made it clear who he entrusted with his team's hopes here. "I want the ball in Tommie's hands."

They agreed to another sprint option to the right, and once again Frazier delivered. This play was blocked differently than the one three plays earlier, the plan calling for Shaw to hook the defensive end to isolate the safety on Frazier and Phillips. But the end fouled the play, floating outside and not allowing Shaw to get his hooks into him. No matter. When that happened, Shaw was trained to change his tack, instead shoving the defender even further to the outside. Frazier in an instant read Shaw's block, planted his foot in the turf and cut his run up the field. Wiegert got an angle and pushed aside a fast-closing Lewis, causing him to barely miss the quarterback. It all allowed Frazier to gain a critical six yards down to the Miami 14. It was Frazier doing what he did best, unflinchingly making plays when it mattered most. While he would gain only a net 31 yards on the ground, complete only three passes and not have a direct hand in a single Husker TD, there was no question at the end that Frazier was once again the Orange Bowl MVP.

The Hurricanes were on the ropes and staggering. There suddenly wasn't much talk coming from the Miami side of the line. With the option now working, Osborne figured it set up a perfect moment for another trap. The 36 Trap he called was a staple of the Husker arsenal, going right up the gut. And as it happened — proving to Husker fans there is a football god — Sapp would be the intended trap victim. In fact, he would be the perfect foil for this play.

The play called for Stai to drop back as if going into pass protection to get Sapp going upfield. But Osborne, hoping to take advantage of Sapp's aggressiveness, really wanted his lineman to sell it. Osborne sent in both the play and instructions for Stai to throw a big head fake at Sapp, similar to the tactic used against Colorado weeks earlier. "Tight left 36 Trap, and tell Stai to head bob," Osborne told receiver Reggie Baul, the messenger on this play.

Osborne calmly chomped on his gum as the play unfolded. He couldn't have drawn it up better. Stai threw a big head-and-shoulder fake, and Sapp went charging up the field. Wilks was the trapper, but Sapp so badly ran himself out of the play that Wilks hardly had to touch him. Center Graham down-blocked on the nose guard, and in a fraction of a second, a hole big enough to drive an SUV through had opened in the Miami front. Schlesinger ran by Frazier's right hip, took the ball and came through. With Sapp taking himself out of the picture, Stai went downfield and teamed with Zatechka to wipe out Lewis, while Wiegert and Shaw released to take out the other two 'backers. Muhammad chopped down the only defensive back in the neighborhood. Schlesinger cut to the left around Zatechka and Stai. And then completing a play that would happily play on a loop through the heads of Husker fans for years to come, he tumbled into the end zone. He was immediately engulfed by Shaw, Muhammad and the rest of his ecstatic teammates.

"Smile, Tom," Collinsworth said as the NBC cameras broadcast an image of Osborne on the sideline in which he showed about as much emotion as a face on Mount Rushmore. But the Huskers had their first lead of the game. With the extra point, it was 24-17 Nebraska. The Huskers now were just 2:46 away from giving Osborne his first national championship. But that was more than double the 1:16 it took for them to cough up the lead against Florida State 12 months earlier. The entire state of Nebraska was wheezing with anxiety and excitement.

Connealy and the Blackshirts trotted onto the field. The senior defensive tackle from tiny Hyannis was about to have his signature moment as a Husker. Knowing Costa would be forced to throw, he and his line mates were going to really be able to tee off now. And while both he and Peter were known for their inside bull rushes, Connealy, at that critical moment, decided it might be a good time to pull out a little spin move.

McBride absolutely hated such flashy stunts. "Dammit, if you guys are going to do that crap, you'd better make a play," he'd say. If it didn't work, you typically wouldn't be in the game much longer. But Connealy figured he was down to his last snaps as a Husker anyway. If he was ever going to pull off a spin, this would be his last chance. And he'd been setting the guard up for this move the whole game — hell, for his whole career. "Well, now or never," he thought.

With Miami facing second down from its own 23, Connealy spun like a crazed 275-pound ballerina at the snap and surprised even himself with how quickly he got around the guard. Now charging up the middle against a retreating, defenseless Costa, Connealy engulfed the bruised and battered quarterback and drove him into the ground. Five years of hard work, much of it in obscurity, culminated in one shining moment in the Orange Bowl. Connealy got up screaming and pumping his arms as he stood over the crumpled Costa, an image that would become one of the most iconic in Husker history.

On the next play, the D-linemen vowed to all meet at the quarterback. Costa dropped back, and, sure enough, it was like he was looking at a Husker team photo. Harris, Connealy and Jones all ran right through a beaten Miami line and gang-tackled Costa inside the 10. That loss brought the Hurricanes' net offensive production in the fourth quarter against the Blackshirts to an astounding -35 yards.

As Miami lined up on fourth down with barely a minute left, Miles looked over the Hurricane formation. He figured they were going to run the same play where Costa had, luckily, overthrown the receiver on the last possession, except this time to Miles' side. He had it covered. Costa instead made a desperation heave to the other side that hung up in the air like a punt. There was a jump ball between Williams and the Miami receiver, and when the ball deflected out, strong safety Kareem Moss came down with the ball in his hands.

This was the crowning moment for Osborne and the Huskers. Frazier would still need to take a couple of knees to run out the clock. The poll voters would still need to have their say the next day. But everyone on the field, everyone on the sidelines and every Big Red fan in the stands and watching on TV knew: The Huskers, at long last, were national champions.

Miles, who had been born the very day Nebraska won its last national title — on Jan. 1, 1972 — had helped the Huskers win another on his 23rd birthday. He threw up his arms and then raised an index finger to the sky as he chased across the field after his teammates. All along the Nebraska sideline, players violently hugged each other and whooped it up. Some turned toward the north stadium crowd and pumped their fists, cameras flashing all around the stadium. Then after Frazier took the final snap and raised both arms over his head, the happy Huskers stormed the field. Connealy couldn't help thinking about all that hard work the Huskers had put in during the summer, 1:16 on the clock. After how painfully close they had been last year, how incredible this was now. "It's my best day on earth," he said.

For Shaw, the reception-less wonder at tight end who'd delivered a critical block on nearly every pivotal play of the final minutes, this was like every emotion he ever had rolled into one. The walk-on knew he would never play another down of organized football in his life. But how could you top this? His home-state Huskers finally were champs again. It was like an out-of-body experience, a feeling he knew he'd never have again. He hugged a tearful Graham, a moment that would later grace the cover of a special edition of Sports Illustrated. "It had taken a lot of blood, sweat and tears to get to that moment," Shaw said of the image years later. "It was kind of surreal."

And Osborne, of course, offered up almost no emotion at all, at least none that you could see. He smiled just a little as one of the refs congratulated him on the sideline during the game's final moments. He looked more irritated than anything when he was doused with a cooler of ice water as he headed to midfield. He was quickly engulfed by a mob of cameras and reporters. "It's enjoyable," he flatly told a reporter from NBC. "Put it that way."

But unmistakably, this title did mean a lot to him. More than anything, Osborne was proud of this team's character. Of all the teams he coached, he'd never seen one with more spirit and resolve. He loved how whenever this team was in a tough spot, someone had always been there to step up, giving it his all. When the defense struggled early in the season, the offense simply went out and outscored people. And when the offense struggled to find a new identity with Frazier out, the defense played lights out. "Unfinished Business" had not just been a bunch of rhetoric. This team had gotten the job done, and it was largely because they simply believed in each other. Osborne would have better collections of players, but perhaps no better team.

The seniors on this team in particular would always have a warm place in Osborne's heart. They were hardly the most naturally talented group. But he'd always take character, work ethic and loyalty over talent or any other quality you could find in a team. Those were the true pillars of a champion. "This team couldn't have been a better reflection of those things," he said later. Osborne would never have said it, but the players on this team had really been a mirror reflection of their coach: consistent, focused and resilient.

To the people in Nebraska, the 1994 Huskers would transcend sports, becoming more than just a football team. They'd inspired the state and infused it with an unmatched feeling of joy. That it had taken a generation of heartbreak to get here just made it all the sweeter now. While there was much more yet to come for Osborne and the Huskers, no future accomplishment would be savored more than this one.

And with the way it happened, there was enough poetic justice to write an epic verse. Beating Miami. In Miami. Led at the end by the quarterback who'd been written off. The winning touchdown scored by a hard-headed Nebraska kid. Into that haunted east end zone. On one of the most basic plays in Tom Osborne's stale old playbook.

Osborne trotted into the tunnel to a huge, adoring ovation from Nebraska's fans. In the bowels of the Orange Bowl, he ran into his wife, Nancy, and they shared a special moment. After more than three decades together in football, he'd never seen her so excited after a game.

Nancy Osborne had for all those years dutifully played the role of coach's wife. Given the expectations at Nebraska and her husband's ways, that was not always easy. While he put in 100-hour weeks preparing his teams season after season, she at times single-handedly raised their three children. Even when he was there, he often wasn't there, his head lost in X's and O's. As he once put it, "It was like I was in a foreign country six months of the year." And she'd sit in the stands with the fans and hear all the negative things they said about her husband. She'd ignore them, rarely telling him about it. Sometimes after the Huskers lost a big game, the kids would face so much flak at school they didn't want to go. She'd prop them up and get them out the door. Now, after all she had endured standing by her man, this one may have meant more to her than even to him. "I wasn't probably as effervescent as she was," Osborne would recall of the moment years later. "But it was good to see how happy she was."

"I don't think I've ever been around a group
of players who had one consistent goal
and stayed on track the way they did."

— TOM OSBORNE

The Husker locker room was a special place, alive with chaos, electricity and love. The room was filled with about as much testosterone as you'd find anywhere. But these men weren't afraid to profess their love for each other. That tone was set by Osborne. Christian Peter even came in and planted a kiss on his coach's cheek. Osborne briefly thanked the players for their effort and season-long dedication. He hugged coaches and players. Bob Devaney came in and congratulated Osborne, and Kevin Steele realized he was witnessing a piece of college football history.

At Osborne's suggestion, the players ran back out into the stadium to celebrate with and thank their fans — the people whose passion truly made Nebraska football go. Osborne rode uncomfortably back to the field on the shoulders of Moss and Jon Vedral. It wasn't exactly Osborne's style to parade around that way, but it was something the players wanted to do. In fact, the low-key Osborne was in general about as comfortable with public celebrations as he'd be walking into a go-go club.

The team buses in the early morning hours of Jan. 2 pulled up in front of the Sheraton Bal Harbour. The lobby was a mosh pit, a wall-to-wall mass of red-clad humanity ready to celebrate with the victors. Energized and excited, most coaches and players happily waded on in. Maybe most head coaches would have, too. Osborne looked for a way out. He and Jack Stark, the team psychologist, went around the back of the bus, found their way to a side door and located an elevator. "Jack, I feel like I've been dragged through a door," he said as they started up. And indeed, Osborne looked exhausted. But also as if a huge weight had been lifted off his shoulders.

The celebration in Miami and across Nebraska would go on throughout the morning. Given the pent-up emotions, there was no telling when it would end. But the man whose patience, compassion, diligence and care made it possible headed for bed. He briefly talked to Nancy. He called to check on Ron Brown's wife, who was seven months pregnant and had left the game at halftime. And then he went to sleep.

Osborne always said football was a process, and what happened this wonderful night did nothing to change that. There were recruits to go see this week. There was a whole new team to assemble. And it wasn't too soon to start breaking down some tape of next season's opponents. After all, the 1995 opener loomed out there, now just 241 days away.

Back to Back

"Like I've said before, all we can control is how well we play. And that's what we're going to focus on."

— TOM OSBORNE BEFORE THE 1995 SEASON

Lawrence Phillips

awrence Phillips fell back hard on his heels as soon as he took the handoff, a hard-charging Oklahoma State Cowboy aiming to corral him in the backfield. What followed was a sequence that showed why the junior I-back from West Covina, California, was starting the 1995 season on everyone's Heisman watch list. Phillips cut hard to the right, causing the Cowboy to slip and fall right on his backside, then just as quickly darted left through a little crease in the line. Accelerating like a sports car going from zero to 100, he then left everyone in his wake, streaking untouched 80 yards for a touchdown. Phillips followed that run minutes later with a 27-yard TD jaunt, and Nebraska's 64-21 rout was on.

The Cornhuskers in 1995 once again opened their season on a big stage, playing a nationally televised Thursday night game on ESPN. On a 99-degree night in Stillwater, the second-ranked Huskers were as merciless as the heat, offering no sign of a letdown from 1994. A revamped Pipeline paved the way as Phillips, Tommie Frazier and the offense rolled up more than 500 yards on the ground. Meanwhile, the Blackshirts looked much like the unit that was smothering every team it faced at the end of 1994.

It wouldn't have been surprising for the Huskers to take a step back in 1995. They returned only eight starters from that title-winning team. And teams are often not quite as hungry a year after winning it all, something that should have been particularly true given how driven the 1994 squad had been. But the Nebraska Way really didn't leave a lot of room for letdowns. Under Tom Osborne, it was always on to the next practice and next game, all part of that never-ending drive to get better. A championship didn't change that. In fact, when the Huskers reported for winter conditioning just days after the crystal Sears Trophy had been secured, assistant

> "I had a few good runs. But you have to have
> 30 runs to know how well you really played."
>
> — LAWRENCE PHILLIPS AFTER OKLAHOMA STATE GAME

strength coach Bryan Bailey told players they weren't national champions anymore. They were the defending national champions. And come next fall, they would be getting everyone's best shot.

Practices now were no less competitive and hard-nosed than before. All the new starters stepping in already had lots of reps in the Osborne system. And the players certainly weren't letting up on each other. Among Husker teams of that era, a unique code of peer leadership and internal accountability had developed among the players. Missing a "voluntary" off-season workout wasn't tolerated. The coaches couldn't require you to be there, but your teammates could. And just showing up wasn't enough. You'd better come ready to work. Dog it and you could be in for a major ass-chewing — or worse. Team leaders also demanded a certain ruggedness, always looking for ways to toughen you up. Make a good play in practice and an upperclassman might give you an ear-ringing slap upside the head — not so much for the good play, but because it was an excuse to rock you in the head. Such treatment could sometimes make the Husker locker room a tough place. You might walk in one day and get your head shaved, a ritual that showed you'd truly arrived as a player. But by 1995, the Huskers' internal code was well established, with respected leaders like Frazier, Christian Peter and Aaron Graham there to crack the whip. They knew from personal experience how fine the line was between a championship season and a major disappointment. "I just don't think we were allowed to feel complacent," recalled Grant Wistrom, who that fall was a sophomore moving into a starting role at rush end.

If 1994's motto was Unfinished Business, this year's was Business as Usual. The Huskers were now on a quest for back-to-back national championships, seeking to become the first team to win undisputed titles in consecutive years since Oklahoma in 1955 and '56. As Osborne put it years later, "The expectation among the players just got to be that we ought to be on top." These Huskers would pay whatever price was necessary to get to Tempe, Arizona, and the Fiesta Bowl come January 2. The 1995 season would be the first for the Bowl Alliance, an agreement among most major conferences and bowls to match up the No. 1 and No. 2 teams at season's end. It was intended to avoid the kind of beauty contest that Penn State and Nebraska engaged in the year before. As far as the Huskers were concerned, if anybody else wanted to lay claim to the title, they were going to have to go through Nebraska. "Looking back on my four years here, I've never felt as confident as I do now," Graham told his teammates that fall. "The way I look at it, someone's going to have to come and take it from us."

With the return of a healthy Frazier and the bruising Phillips, Nebraska came into the season with two potential Heisman winners in its starting backfield. Kind of lost in all the medical drama the previous year was that Phillips had put together one of the finest seasons ever by a Nebraska running back. His 1,722 rushing yards were the second-highest single season total in school history, trailing only Heisman winner Mike Rozier. It was the most ever by a Big Eight sophomore. I-back at Nebraska was one of the marquee positions in all of college football. Still, Osborne was already saying the 20-year-old Phillips was about as good as any the Huskers had ever had. Phillips had finished eighth in the 1994 Heisman voting, and he was actually the only Top 10 finisher who was back playing college ball in 1995. By all appearances, come season's end, everyone in America was going to know Phillips' name.

The 6-foot, 218-pounder had everything the great backs possess. Speed. Size. Quickness. Power. Vision. The moves. He could make you miss, even in a tight hole. Or he could simply run you over. He had an unusual ability to cut on a dime without having to regather himself. And it took him only a couple of steps to reach full speed. Football people said it was jaw-dropping to see him blast right by you, to think that a man that big could run that fast. And Phillips was a warrior, possessing a mental and physical toughness that was extraordinary even among those who played the bruising game. Phillips was once asked what it would take to get him off the field. "It would have to be a situation where I can't walk," he replied, "or a situation where I might die."

But the football field wasn't the only place Phillips could be explosive. As everyone would come to see, a deep anger smoldered inside him. When properly channeled in football, the emotion served him well, the fuel that made him such a fierce competitor. In other settings, it would often prove his undoing. The anger was rooted in a past the quiet junior was reluctant to talk about, Phillips stiff-arming anyone who would get too close to it. But if you were looking for why Phillips ran so angry, so hard and with a toughness rarely seen in college football, you'd find it on the streets of south-central L.A. he once had freely roamed.

Born in Little Rock, Arkansas, Phillips moved to Los Angeles with his mother at age 3. His father was out of his life at a very early age. When Phillips was about 12, he didn't care for the latest man in his mother's life, and it became a frequent source of conflict at home. Friends say he felt his mother was choosing the boyfriend over him. So Phillips just left. He was often away for days at a time, sleeping wherever — at a friend's house or sometimes in cars. School became just a place to drop in.

"Lawrence truly enjoys the game —
you can see it in his practice habits."

— FRANK SOLICH ON LAWRENCE PHILLIPS

And he sometimes ran with a bad crowd, the boy frequently coming home in the company of police officers. His juvenile record — parts of which would not become available until more than a decade after his years in Nebraska — showed arrests for attempted robbery and theft. Phillips' mother told authorities she'd lost control of her son. After truant officers discovered he had been out of school at one point for 2½ months, Phillips was made a ward of Los Angeles County. Friends said Phillips would never forget the time on his own and the hurt from his youth, and it impacted his life profoundly.

The boy ended up in MacLaren Hall, Los Angeles County's shelter for abused and neglected children. That's where Barbara Thomas found him one day when she went looking for a boy to fill an open slot in a group home she ran. "You don't want him. He's a serious, serious behavior problem," one staffer told Thomas. That's exactly what I want, Thomas replied. She felt she could work with the tough-looking boy. So in the summer of 1987, Phillips moved into the Tina Mac group home in West Covina, an east Los Angeles suburb just south of the smog-shrouded San Gabriel Mountains.

When the rebellious Phillips first walked into Tina Mac's, he headed for the recreation room and boldly lit up a Newport. There would be volatile times in the months ahead. Phillips became upset when one of the other residents damaged his tennis shoes. So Phillips took the boy's clothes outside to the barbecue pit and set them on fire. When Thomas asked the boys who was responsible, Phillips was quick to confess. She appreciated his honesty, which she thought showed Phillips had a good heart. But the incident also revealed a fiery temper. Months later, he was kicked out of school for fighting, forcing him to finish the eighth grade at an alternative school. Other boys in the home feared Phillips and stayed out of his way. "They say when someone hits you you're supposed to turn the other cheek," Thomas said in the summer of 1995. "He couldn't do that. He would try to kill that person."

But after Phillips had spent two years with little discipline in his life, Thomas wasn't expecting overnight miracles. She worked to get through to the boy. And in what became a fortuitous stroke, she introduced him to football. As it turned out, opponents on the football field found Phillips just as elusive as the truant officers did.

He went on to play at West Covina High School, first on the freshman team and then starting at linebacker on the varsity as a sophomore. But Phillips wasn't happy at West Covina. He was frustrated by the football team's losing record and thought he should have been starting at running back. His school attendance continued to be spotty, making it always a question whether he would be academically eligible to play. Conflicts with teachers were common. One of Phillips' final acts before leaving the school after his sophomore year was to throw an egg at the principal.

That fall, he showed up in the office of Ty Pagone, an assistant principal and former football coach at nearby Baldwin Park High School. Phillips wanted to play for the L.A. high school football power. Pagone knew a little about Phillips. He told him the chance to play was there, but he'd be on a short leash. He continued to live at the group home but became eligible to play at Baldwin Park by claiming a relative's residence as his own.

With Phillips starting at tailback and rushing for nearly 1,200 yards, Baldwin Park rolled to a state championship in 1991. That initially got the college recruiters excited. But many were scared off when they learned of Phillips' academic record. For Phillips to accept a college scholarship under Prop 48, NCAA rules required him to have a C average in 11 core classes, including English, math, social studies and science. Entering his junior year, Phillips had not passed any. If he was going to accept a Division I scholarship, he'd have to essentially cram four years of core classes into two. Which is just what Phillips set out to do.

He arrived at school each day at 6:45 a.m. to take one extra class. He stayed an hour late at the end for another. He was up to the challenge. Testing had shown he was intellectually gifted. The main hurdle was maintaining the commitment, leading Pagone and head football coach Tony Zane sometimes to drive to the group home and drag Phillips out of bed. The boy who years earlier refused to even go to school was now in class every day, with a purpose. And for all the behavioral problems he had at West Covina, Baldwin Park officials say Phillips was practically a model student. His algebra teacher described him as earnest and respectful, a nice kid who would come in over lunch to ask her for extra help.

Nebraska never backed off in its interest in Phillips, and it intensified when he ran for 1,700 yards his senior year and was rated one of the nation's best backs. While the potential recruit was coming out of a group home, he by all appearances was there due to abandonment, not any serious juvenile delinquency. And officials at Tina Mac's and Baldwin Park were all now praising Phillips' attitude, demeanor and relationship with fellow students. "I talked to people from the janitor on up, and they didn't have a bad thing to say about Lawrence Phillips," recalled George Darlington, Phillips' primary recruiter for Nebraska. "He was a player we'd recruit 100 times out of 100 coming out of high school."

In later years, Darlington and Osborne would often cite such things when questioned whether Nebraska had overlooked obvious warning signs in bringing Phillips to campus. Osborne would never have any second thoughts about recruiting Phillips. "When you have a guy from that background, you understand it's not necessarily going to be smooth sailing," he said nearly two decades later, "but it's not as if he'd been to prison or had a drug problem. The coaches were so positive about him." Ron Brown said Phillips by all appearances was a real-life Horatio Alger story, a kid who through hard work and determination had pulled himself up despite an impoverishment of love and support. Why would anyone slam a door on him now? With all the references he had out of high school, Brown said, who wouldn't have said, "This guy has overcome all these things. Let's give him a chance."

Osborne made his official home visit to the young prospect in early 1993, flying out west to California to meet with Phillips at Pagone's home. The coach talked about Nebraska's academic support program, its winning tradition and history of great I-backs. Phillips had only one question.

"Who wears No. 1?" — his jersey number at Baldwin Park.

"You will," Osborne replied.

Phillips in turn traveled to Lincoln and enjoyed his campus visit, impressed with how players could walk right in and talk to Osborne. Phillips' personality meshed with the Huskers' reserved head coach, and the whole place felt like a big family — the one he never had. He liked the winning football, too. But Southern Cal, Washington State, Arizona State and Illinois were also in the mix, and the hometown Trojans in particular made a major push. Head coach John Robinson came calling with Charles White, one of USC's Heisman Trophy winners. Robinson told Phillips he wanted to bring both the national championship and Heisman back home to L.A.

In the end, Nebraska may have won out because of just how far it is from south-central L.A. Phillips wondered how he would handle returning to his old neighborhood for college. With a big smile on his face, Phillips told Pagone just before signing day he was going to Nebraska. It was a chance for him to get away from some negative things in his life. Moving to Lincoln, though, proved a major cultural adjustment. That wasn't unusual for black players, who would often come from nearly all-black neighborhoods and find themselves in a school and town that was nearly all white. "It was so different even going from north Omaha down to Lincoln," recalled fellow I-back Clinton Childs, referring to the predominantly black neighborhood where he grew up. "You can only imagine what it was like to bring Lawrence from West Covina." Paul Koch, an assistant strength coach, remembers Phillips walking into Nebraska's cavernous weight facility the first time looking both wide-eyed and a little scared. Phillips initially kept to himself. During his first month in Lincoln, he ran up a $300 phone bill calling his friends and coaches back home in California.

But when it came to football, Phillips arrived ready to play. Doak Ostergard, an assistant trainer, saw the freshman for the first time when he showed up that fall to go through physical testing. "Holy moly," he thought as one of the most amazing physical specimens he'd ever seen lined up to run the 40. Phillips clocked in at 4.74, not bad for a guy running his first electronically timed dash. It compared favorably with some of Nebraska's fastest freshmen ever, including Calvin Jones, then the team's starter at I-back. Still, Ostergard could see from the look on Phillips' face he wasn't happy at all. He lined up to run it a second time and stumbled for a few steps coming out of his start. And then it was like he was shot from a cannon. He went 4.57, the fastest of any of the 35 newcomers. This freshman was both talented and driven.

During his first major scrimmage a couple of weeks later, Phillips ripped off two TD runs of over 50 yards. Though they came against the No. 4 defense, the runs had him dreaming of Big Red glory. "I was wishing it was a home game for the Nebraska Cornhuskers," he said, "but I guess I'll have to wait a couple of years for that."

A couple of years?

"Well, maybe a year," he replied.

In the end, the unassuming freshman would have seen the field in the season opener that fall had it not been for the sudden return of an old problem: He got into a fight with a teammate. Scraps in practice were not uncommon, usually just punished with a trip up the stadium stairs. But Osborne years later would recall that this fight took place in the locker room, with Phillips clearly the aggressor. Phillips got upset at something the player said, a confrontation ensued, and Phillips punched him. Osborne decided the fight was serious enough to merit a one-game suspension. It was the first sign in Lincoln that Phillips' adolescent volatility was not completely behind him.

Phillips made his debut the following week against Texas Tech, and he made it look easy, running for 80 yards on 14 carries. Wearing the Huskers' No. 1 jersey, he reached the end zone on his last carry, a 30-yarder. The following week marked Phillips' big personal homecoming, a game against UCLA in front of family and friends in Pasadena's Rose Bowl. After starting I-back Damon Benning fumbled twice in the first half, Phillips entered and ran for 137 yards and a touchdown in the Huskers' 14-13 win. What stood out in Brown's memory years later, even more than Phillips' on-field performance that day, was what happened after he fumbled early in the second half. Brown made a point of going over to give the freshman a reassuring pat on the shoulder. Phillips burst into tears, feeling he'd let the whole team down. "From that moment on, I felt a compassion for that kid," Brown said. "I didn't see a hard street kid from L.A. I saw a sensitive baby boy in an overgrown body."

Phillips continued to shine for those refuse-to-lose Huskers that year, mostly in a backup role. But it seemed Phillips' past was always looming out there, just on the periphery of his life. And at inopportune times, it would come back to haunt him. As the Huskers were preparing late that year for their national championship battle with Florida State, Phillips suddenly failed to show up for practice. Darlington and Osborne would eventually learn why. Phillips' mother had moved to Lincoln to follow her son's career, and then moved to Omaha with a boyfriend. The man allegedly beat her. After hearing of it, Phillips drove to Omaha that day to help remove her from the situation.

Phillips showed up back at practice on Monday, and Osborne immediately suspended him from the bowl game. Phillips had a good reason for missing practice, but he hadn't cleared it with coaches. Husker team captains were concerned. One reason Phillips had been playing so much as a freshman was because the Huskers had been banged up at running back. With a championship at stake, they wanted Phillips to play. The captains convinced Osborne to limit the suspension to the first half of the Orange Bowl, which would make Phillips available if he was needed in the second half.

Phillips indeed would be called on in relief, and the Seminoles had no answer for him. He ran for 64 yards and a touchdown to help the Huskers rally before they fell just short. It wasn't disclosed at the time that Phillips had been suspended for the first half. Some Huskers on the '93 team would always be left to wonder whether it would have made a difference had Phillips been available the whole game.

During the 1994 season, Phillips came into his own, ripping off 11 straight 100-yard games for the national champions, despite playing through ankle, groin, toe and thumb injuries. He'd essentially gutted out the game against Kansas State

"Our plan was to make a statement about
being No. 1 or No. 2 so we can go
to Phoenix and play in the Fiesta Bowl."

— LAWRENCE PHILLIPS, ASKED IF HIS PERFORMANCE AGAINST
OKLAHOMA STATE 'MADE A STATEMENT' IN THE HEISMAN RACE

with one arm. During one three-game stretch while the Huskers were unsettled at quarterback, the workhorse was called on to tote the ball 96 times. And his toughness became legend. Around that time, while he was still nursing his painful thumb, Phillips grabbed reserve linebacker Jay Foreman in practice one day and told him to hit him on his hand as hard as he could in an effort to strip the ball. "That's the way it's going to be in the game," he said. "I have to be ready."

As 1995 rolled around, there were great expectations for Phillips. Not that the hype was getting to him. When he played well, he'd be the first to defer credit to the offensive line. He wasn't one to pound his chest or dance in the end zone. He didn't mouth off or cheap shot. He just played football. And all he wanted to do was win. Teammates said Phillips was always willing to give his all for the team. Few worked more tenaciously on the field or in the weight room. Even when just running through a play in practice, Phillips would bust out and sprint 50 yards downfield — always ready to break a long one. And a prima donna he was not. "With Lawrence, you didn't get any 'You'd better not hit me because I'm the star player,'" defensive tackle Jason Peter recalled. "He didn't avoid contact in practice. Lawrence was looking to hit someone." Years later, former Huskers would frequently use the same two words to describe Phillips: Great teammate. The trouble he would later see didn't change that. It was hard for teammates not to like and respect someone who played the way he did. "Just an excellent team guy," said Ed Stewart, who played on the '94 Huskers. "A standup guy," echoed Barron Miles. "It was a pleasure to play with him."

Teammates could see the young man was growing more mature and confident. And off the field, it seemed Phillips had mostly adjusted to life in Nebraska. While protective of his past, even when talking to Osborne and his coaches, Phillips had several good friends on the team. He often played video games with Frazier, the competitive back always insisting on a rematch when he lost. "I loved him," Frazier said years later. "I don't have any negative thing to say about him. People go through things in their lives they can't handle. We all have demons in our closet."

And Phillips developed a close friendship with Childs and his family. Sometimes Childs would get out of school on Friday and travel to Omaha, only to find Phillips already on the couch laughing and joking with Childs' mom. The no-nonsense Linda Childs loved Lawrence, and the feeling was mutual. In 1996 when Phillips learned she had cancer, the then-St. Louis Rams running back within hours was on a flight to Omaha to offer support. "I've been around Lawrence too much and seen him do good by too many people to even come close to classifying him as a bad person,"

Childs recalled. Another thing people don't know about Phillips is that he was a good student, Childs said, with no problems in the classroom. "If you look back at his childhood, fending for himself at such a young age, to accomplish what he did was huge," Childs said. "It speaks volumes to the person he is inside."

But problems with Phillips' temper continued to flare up, at times publicly. In the spring of 1994, he was charged with a misdemeanor after grabbing a 21-year-old man and pulling him away from another person. The charge was dropped after Phillips entered a pretrial diversion program, agreeing to pay $400 to replace the victim's damaged necklace (he never did complete all the program's legal requirements). Two months before the start of the 1995 season, Phillips was arrested and fined for disturbing the peace after police came to break up a loud party. Phillips complied with requests to leave but then went outside to his car and blared his stereo so loudly that officers 100 feet away said they couldn't hear themselves speak. Several teammates would later say they believed alcohol was a big factor in those scrapes.

There were other incidents of anger around the program that never made headlines. As Osborne would put it at one point in 1995, "There are occasions — maybe every three, four or five months — where something may happen where he becomes a little bit explosive." But no incident going into the 1995 season had been serious enough to make Osborne think, "We can't have this guy around anymore." Phillips acknowledged the problems with his temper in a preseason interview with Sports Illustrated, saying he was working on controlling it. "I'm learning to stay out of situations where I could get into trouble."

Anger wasn't the only source of Phillips' troubles at the start of the 1995 season. He was facing scrutiny from the NCAA for possible rules violations. Phillips was questioned about a lunch bought for him by the recruiter for an agent, the running back later repaying $20 for the meal. There were also questions about the car Phillips was driving — a 1995 Mustang convertible worth $20,000. Tina McElhannon, the co-owner of the West Covina group home, said she had leased the car for Phillips and was also providing him with airfare and $500 a month in spending money.

At the heart of the issue was whether Phillips was receiving special benefits based on his athletic ability. Nebraska officials looked into it and decided the arrangement was legal, a conclusion with which the NCAA ultimately concurred. Though it was fishy on its face, the group home owners were not Nebraska boosters and had acted as his legal guardians since before he was recruited by Nebraska. As long as they were truly the ones funding the car and other payments, it was OK. Still, the strain of the NCAA scrutiny wore on Phillips, Osborne said, becoming a stressor that may have contributed to subsequent events. The back didn't learn he'd be eligible to play until two days before that 1995 opener against Oklahoma State.

But Phillips wasted no time getting his Heisman run started that night against the Cowboys, scoring three times and totaling 153 yards on just 12 carries. Still the consummate team player, Phillips downplayed any Heisman talk. This was all about another run for a title. "The goal is to get to Phoenix," he said. "Our plan tonight was to start getting some respect (from poll voters) so we can get there."

A number of those voters had been up in the press box during the game. There, they could pick up a copy of the Huskers' preseason media guide. On the cover of the thick, glossy book was a photo-illustration of a camera with Heisman hopeful Phillips staring out from the lens, along with a theme for the Husker season ahead: Staying Focused.

As events would transpire over the next 10 days, that cover image would become, all at the same time, eerie, prescient and incongruous.

A Great Team

Christian Peter had assumed Terry Connealy's role as the madman who would get the Huskers jacked up just before kickoff. Except Peter was more of a showman. That's why he approached team psychologist Jack Stark on the eve of Nebraska's big September 9 game against Michigan State in East Lansing with a simple request: Can you get me a Spartans helmet? His idea was to smash it with a sledgehammer in the locker room before the Huskers took the field. Stark actually tried to get a helmet but was not surprised when the equipment manager for Michigan State wasn't willing to part with one. "That's a $300 piece of equipment," the manager said incredulously. So Stark went instead to the campus bookstore and returned with a white plastic bag that held several items bearing Spartan logos, including a clock and a Christmas ornament. That'll do, Peter told him. And the senior defensive tackle proceeded to deliver one of the most unique and bizarre pre-game speeches in Husker history.

Per tradition, Peter and the other captains got in front of the team after Tom Osborne had left the locker room and headed out to the field. Peter had been a big fan of professional wrestling growing up, even though his parents always told him it was a waste of time. And in these moments he would take on the persona of his hero Ric Flair, with his "To be the man you've got to beat the man" swagger. Michigan State was where Bob Devaney had first cut his coaching teeth, and the Husker coaching legend was on the trip. In fact, he had just spoken to the team and remained in the locker room now. Peter seized on that. There's no way we're going to let Bob Devaney down. And then, angry, red-faced and cursing like a sailor, Peter started railing about how the Huskers were going to destroy the Spartans.

Peter pulled the Spartan clock out of the bag. Fellow captain Phil Ellis held it up and

"You've got to go in day in and day out
and lead by example."

— CHRISTIAN PETER, AFTER BEING ELECTED 1995 CO-CAPTAIN

Peter obliterated it with a single smash from his fist. The Huskers were hooting and hollering, but Peter was just getting started. He took out the Christmas bulb and crushed it into his own forehead. Such ornaments, of course, are made of glass, and Peter's reckless act caused blood to flow down his face. "This dude is crazy," Tommie Frazier thought. But the blood didn't stop Peter from continuing to rage on about what the Huskers were going to do to the Spartans. Then Peter picked up an old wooden chair and hurled it across the room — in the direction of Devaney. The old coach flinched and ducked as it flew over his head and smashed into the wall above him, breaking into about a dozen pieces. "It wasn't well-planned," Ellis allowed years later.

But Peter's antics had the intended effect. The Huskers were bonkers by the time the bloodied, maniacal Peter led the charge out to the field. As Grant Wistrom would later put it: "There wasn't anyone in that room that wasn't ready to run through a brick wall and rip someone's heart out." Which is pretty much what the Huskers proceeded to do. Three hours later, the Spartans had been left in much the same shape as the clock, ornament and chair, not to mention Peter's forehead. It was a 50-10 demolition.

The NU offense was overpowering that day, clicking in midseason form. Frazier discovered early on that there wasn't any play that Nebraska could run that wouldn't work. And even after Frazier went out in the first half with a thigh bruise, the Huskers didn't skip a beat. Brook Berringer, who during the preseason had lost a close battle with Frazier for the starting job, led the Huskers to scores on six of the next seven drives. Both Nebraska's 552 rushing yards and 666 total yards were the most Michigan State had given up in 99 years of football. "Potential disasters don't seem to register with this team," Lawrence Phillips said afterward in reference to Frazier's injury. "We always get it together."

Phillips was once again the star, running for 206 yards and scoring four touchdowns despite a gimpy ankle. He had now scored seven TDs in just two games, averaging

"It's easy to wear your legs out with
the type of holes they were opening."

— CLINTON CHILDS ON THE OFFENSIVE LINE'S JOB AGAINST MICHIGAN STATE

11 yards every time he touched the ball. Osborne could see that Phillips, despite adding about 10 pounds in the past year, hadn't lost a step. On one play that would be particularly memorable for the coach, Phillips took a direct snap from center and rumbled 50 yards for a score. Michigan State Coach Nick Saban would later tell George Darlington there were two running backs in his career that he'd watched from the sideline and considered the best backs he'd ever seen. One was NFL standout Eric Dickerson. The other was Lawrence Phillips, rampaging on that memorable day in East Lansing.

The game was a track meet for the other Nebraska I-backs, too. Childs, a hard-nosed and physical runner who had been one of the best high school wrestlers in the country, picked up 83 yards on eight carries. Freshman Ahman Green, one of the nation's most highly prized recruits, got 74 on just four totes. And James Sims, a fifth-stringer who was among the fastest guys on the team, burst for an 80-yard score on his only carry. Throw in Damon Benning, who was hurt and left back in Lincoln, and the Huskers had a solid stable of backs behind Phillips, all from Omaha. Nebraska may never have been deeper at I-back. The 10 yards a carry the Huskers averaged against the Spartans may have been the most an Osborne team ever put up against a team that wasn't the likes of Pacific or Utah State.

Much of the credit for that production went to the Pipeline. After losing four starters from the previous year, including three who were now playing in the NFL, the offensive coaches had openly wondered how good the Huskers were going to be up front. Milt Tenopir assured Osborne things would be just fine. The new starters stepping up to join center Aaron Graham — Chris Dishman, Eric Anderson, Aaron Taylor and Steve Ott — had seen plenty of snaps as backups. "Our seconds played a lot of football last year," Tenopir reminded him. Now as Osborne watched the Pipeline viciously dismantle the Spartans' big and physical front, he could see the Huskers had not missed a beat there at all. The new line sure didn't look like much. When Phillips first huddled up with them, he thought to himself, "These guys are smaller." Indeed, the Pipeline had gone from tall, sculpted athletes to short, stocky guys with big guts. But the new starters were deceptively athletic. Taylor, a future Outland winner, had grown up playing soccer in Texas and had great feet. Anderson, a Lincoln native, had amazing, under-the-radar physical skills. And Dishman and Ott were both country-strong Nebraska kids who played with great passion. This group appeared more than capable of getting the job done.

The Blackshirts were once again smothering, with seven different players tackling Spartans behind the line. That included two sacks by Terrell Farley, a newcomer fresh out of junior college with freakish speed and instincts for the ball. Nine days earlier against OSU, Farley had intercepted a pass and returned it for a touchdown on one of his very first plays in a Husker uniform. Now he was a holy terror, making tackles sideline to sideline. And Osborne would put his defensive front up against any in the country. Sophomore Jason Peter was playing side by side at tackle with his brother Christian, the two fulfilling a dream they'd first talked about in high school. The tenacious duo was as immovable in the middle as a pair of goal posts. Charlie McBride's biggest concern was that they'd kill each other in practice, where they'd often get on each other. But the brothers with the matching shaved heads and Peterbilt truck tattoos on their left biceps were inseparable. Pretty much the only time they weren't together was when they were in class. And Grant Wistrom and Jared Tomich, the two new starters at defensive end, had unbelievable motors. This close-knit line would take Osborne's brand of physical football to a whole new level. In all, McBride had more playmakers on defense than he could even get on the field, 13 defenders on the two-deep ultimately playing in the NFL.

"A monster is being created," World-Herald columnist Tom Shatel wrote in summing up the Huskers that day from East Lansing. "It might be too early to make comparisons to 1994 and reservations to the Fiesta Bowl. Then again, after what happened Saturday, maybe not."

Even Osborne couldn't argue with those words. The measured coach was never one to puff up his teams or to look too far ahead. But even he had to admit after this one: We have a great team here. The Spartans would play in a bowl and in Tony Banks had a quarterback who would be the first signal-caller picked in the next NFL draft. And the Huskers had gone into their stadium and completely dismantled them. Two games into the season, Osborne could already see this was the deepest, most talented team he'd ever had. And it was playing with confidence, pride and a killer instinct. No environment fazed these road warriors. He wouldn't hesitate to take these guys anywhere.

When Osborne went to midfield to shake hands, he could tell that Saban — who a decade later would win national championships at LSU and Alabama — was taking the loss hard. "Nick, you really don't have as bad a team as you think," Osborne told him. "We are really pretty good this year."

With the early kickoff in East Lansing, the Huskers' team plane landed back in Lincoln by early evening. As usual, Osborne took to the intercom, reminding his players to stay out of trouble and come back Monday ready to work. After most

"It's a beautiful line.
I don't see much difference.
Except this one is quicker."

— WINGBACK CLESTER JOHNSON'S APPRAISAL OF,
LEFT TO RIGHT, ERIC ANDERSON, STEVE OTT, AARON GRAHAM,
AARON TAYLOR AND CHRIS DISHMAN

players had left the plane, Osborne noticed Phillips was still there, asleep in his seat. As Osborne gathered his things, the coach had a sudden impulse to consider inviting Phillips over to his home for dinner that night. Big and tough as Phillips was, Osborne had always sensed a loneliness and fragility in Phillips.

It was a poignant moment, one that perhaps could have altered the course of events to come. But Osborne decided against extending the invite, thinking Phillips might find it odd. The coach instead just congratulated him on his game and reminded him to get treatment for his bruised ankle in the morning. Phillips thanked him.

Osborne went to the HuskerVision studios at Memorial Stadium and recorded his weekly TV show. Then after working until 2 a.m. grading the tape from the game, he went to bed.

He didn't sleep long. At 5:30, he was awakened by a phone call from Turner Gill. The quarterbacks coach told Osborne that Phillips had just attacked a young woman. The police were now looking for him.

Osborne was both shocked and saddened. By the time he hung up, he later wrote in his 1996 autobiography, he knew that nothing could ever be the same for him, Lawrence Phillips or the entire Husker team. This season that had started with such an air of greatness was about to turn into a long and often joyless slog to the end.

"Obviously, this arrest has
generated a monumental amount
of interest by the news media."

— LINCOLN POLICE CHIEF TOM CASADY

A Brutal Attack

Scaling the building's outside balconies like Spider-Man, Lawrence Phillips reached the third-floor apartment of his teammate and slid open the unlocked glass door. The enraged Husker was looking for his former girlfriend. A young woman's security and his Heisman Trophy run were about to be brutally and violently laid to waste.

Lawrence Phillips had met Kate McEwen shortly after arriving on the Lincoln campus in the fall of 1993. Given his background, they weren't the likeliest of couples. A member of the Husker women's basketball team, she came from a large, white, upper middle-class Catholic family in Topeka, Kansas. But something clicked between them. They first started socializing together with other athletes and then drew close.

Phillips confided in her, telling her things about his past he didn't tell anyone else. It opened her eyes to a whole new world. She tried to help him make the difficult adjustment from L.A. group home to Lincoln. By the end of their freshman year, friends say, the relationship had evolved into romance. The couple would go to movies together or rent movies to watch in his apartment. On Sundays, she would join him to watch pro football. Tom Osborne believed the relationship may have been the first truly close one Phillips ever had.

One of the things Phillips had disclosed to McEwen was his lifelong battle to control his temper. She thought she could help him. But she also felt the brunt of that anger. She would later say he regularly beat and threatened her, seeking to keep her under his control.

Friends of McEwen said they twice during 1994 noticed bruises, one on her neck, the other on an arm. She said they were just basketball injuries. In a later civil lawsuit she filed against Phillips after he had left Nebraska for the NFL, she described an incident in October 1994 in which he shoved her head into a wall so hard it broke through the drywall, and then choked her and refused to let her leave. In April 1995, she alleged in the suit, he threatened to shoot her gangland-style in the knees, and the next month slashed her tires and threatened to kill her. Tommie Frazier never saw any violent interactions between Phillips and McEwen, but the relationship was at times a rocky one. "Sometimes he would yell at her," he recalled, "sometimes she would yell at him." McEwen several times broke off from Phillips only to go back to him, seemingly caught up in an emotional cycle of abuse and reconciliation. Friends said she still cared for Phillips and wanted to believe he could change.

The relationship ended again during the summer of 1995. Friends said McEwen became acquainted with Husker quarterback Scott Frost, a Wood River, Nebraska, native who had transferred to Nebraska from Stanford. He and some friends began socializing with a group of women that included McEwen. Frost never considered the two to be dating, though the relationship was moving in that direction. At one point after Frost learned Phillips and McEwen had been in a relationship, Frost asked a teammate and friend of Phillips about it. He was assured they were no longer dating. Frost never had the impression he was potentially stepping into some kind of love triangle.

Some of McEwen's friends said she remained open to possibly resuming her relationship with Phillips. Others said she just wanted to maintain a friendship with him. Regardless, the two clearly continued to have regular contact after their latest breakup. In her suit, McEwen alleged that on August 24 — a week before the Huskers' season opener against Oklahoma State — she agreed to give a drunken Phillips a ride home. He allegedly refused to let her leave and then sexually assaulted her. She never reported the incident to police.

Osborne later said he was never informed of any of the violence she alleged in her suit. But right around that time, he did become aware of how seriously troubled the relationship was. In late August, a friend of McEwen and the friend's father met with Osborne to express concerns about Phillips' threatening behavior. Osborne was alarmed by what he heard. He could not recall being told of specific incidents, but he was left with the impression there had been serious physical episodes. The young woman was in danger.

Osborne contacted McEwen, who acknowledged troubles and said she was frightened. He advised her to stay away from Phillips and gave her his phone number. He immediately sat down with Phillips and warned him to stay away from McEwen, telling him he was concerned about the direction the relationship appeared to be taking. Osborne also gave a pointed ultimatum: If there was any more trouble with McEwen, Phillips would be removed from the team. In addition, Osborne ordered the running back to undergo twice-a-week counseling with Jack Stark on how to develop more positive relationships. At the time, Osborne felt he had done as much as he could. In the end, no one heeded Osborne's admonitions. The two continued to see each other. Phillips still believed the couple had a future together. "I was pretty dumb," Osborne said years later. "I should have known when affairs of the heart are involved, people don't always do what they say they're going to do."

Frazier recalled that McEwen dropped off Phillips the day the Huskers flew to Michigan State, and she called him in East Lansing the night before the game. Ron Brown also recalled seeing McEwen pick up Phillips after the team returned Saturday evening. A friend of McEwen said she talked on the phone with Phillips that night. The friend said McEwen told her Phillips seemed to be changing. He was being nice and they were getting along great. But McEwen also spoke of her interest in Frost. "Be careful," the friend told her. As the friend later told a reporter, "I knew if Lawrence ever knew she was with Scott, he would go crazy."

Phillips later told Osborne he thought he earlier had set up a date with McEwen that night. Phillips instead spent the evening hanging out with some teammates at the home of a friend. They watched college football on TV, listened to music and relaxed. Phillips was drinking, which Frazier believed was likely a factor in what happened next. The account of what transpired is drawn from police reports and interviews with Osborne, Frost (the first he has granted on the subject), friends of McEwen and Husker players.

McEwen spent the evening out with a group of friends that included Frost's roommate. Frost did not go out with the group as they hit some Lincoln bars. But McEwen and the group did end up back at Frost's apartment around 2 a.m., and all but Frost and McEwen ultimately left. At 3 a.m., a life-changing phone call came in to the party Phillips was attending. Some past published reports have said Phillips was home in bed when he got the call, but according to Frazier that wasn't true. The caller informed Phillips where McEwen was at that moment. "That's when the night went downhill," Frazier said later.

Just who made that call was never made public, and more than a decade later it remained a secret to nearly everyone outside the Husker program. Those in a position to know seem intent to keep it that way. The most oft-told story — that the caller was a jealous woman seeking to drive a wedge between Phillips and McEwen — also is false, Frazier said. "It was a person — leave it at that," he said.

Osborne maintained years later he never was able to get Phillips or anyone else

"We were awakened by shouting. I heard
a girl saying for someone to leave her alone."

— NEIGHBOR WHO WITNESSED LAWRENCE PHILLIPS'
ASSAULT ON AN EX-GIRLFRIEND

to tell him who made the call. That made Osborne suspect it was a player. "There's probably a reluctance on the part of the players to rat on or inform on one of their teammates," he said. "I'm assuming it was one of the players on the team, but I don't know that." Had he known it was a player, Osborne said, he would have taken some type of disciplinary action. "Knowing Lawrence was a guy who was pretty volatile, whoever did that was playing with fire," he said. "That person was stirring something up that was not going to bode well for Lawrence, the girl or the team."

Phillips initially appeared more surprised than angered by the call. He just wanted to get to the bottom of it. Even after Phillips went to Frost's north Lincoln apartment building and saw McEwen's car, he was not immediately concerned. She had acquaintances in the building. Then the person who summoned Phillips showed him the mailbox in the apartment foyer with the name "Frost." That's the apartment where McEwen is, Phillips was told.

That lit the fuse, and Phillips went off. The incensed running back first rang or knocked on the door of Frost's apartment. McEwen had been sitting on the living-room floor watching TV while Frost slept in his bedroom. She immediately suspected it was Phillips. In a panic, she woke up Frost. "Someone is at the door," he recalled her saying. "I think it's Lawrence." Frost looked out the door but saw or heard no one.

Frost was on his way back toward his bedroom when the sliding glass door of the balcony suddenly opened right in front of him. It was Phillips. Menacingly, he stepped into the living room, and Frost moved toward him. "What are you doing?" Frost asked, hoping to try to soothe the situation. Phillips' only response was to throw Frost against a wall. In a rage he then went in pursuit of McEwen, who fled to the bathroom. She tried to shut and lock the door, but he got an arm inside and forced his way in. "Why did you lie to me!" Phillips screamed.

The rampaging running back then proceeded to rough McEwen up. Before she knew it, she was down on the bathroom floor feeling pain in her chest. She later told investigators she wasn't sure if he had hit her or shoved her down. Frost told police that when he pushed open the bathroom door, Phillips had McEwen down on the floor. He appeared to be hitting her, but he could not see for sure. Then taking McEwen by her head, neck and hair — "caveman style" as her attorney put it in her civil suit — Phillips started dragging McEwen out of the apartment.

Frost again stood in Phillips' way as he moved to the door with McEwen in tow.

Phillips again threw him aside. Frost rushed to the phone in the kitchen and dialed 911, the call coming in at 4:44. After the call, which lasted about 20 seconds, Frost left the apartment in pursuit of Phillips and McEwen. He found them on the stairs, Phillips dragging the young woman down by her hair.

At the bottom of the stairs in a foyer by the mailboxes, Frost again confronted Phillips, who was holding McEwen by the neck. Frost forced his way between them and was able to free her from Phillips' grasp. Another man who had heard the commotion was able to grab McEwen and pull her through the security door to safety and then into his girlfriend's apartment. That left Frost and Phillips alone, standing face to face. Frost, at 215 pounds and a tremendous athlete, was nearly Phillips' equal physically. Phillips said something threatening, to the effect of, "All right, it's on you now." There was a quick shoving confrontation between the two before Frost was able to dart back through the security door. Locked out, Phillips kicked the door and in raging frustration beat in the mailboxes, badly bloodying his hands. Soon the wail of police sirens could be heard, and Phillips fled.

At some point, either in the bathroom or while being dragged, McEwen had struck her head, cutting it. She had also suffered a bloodied lip, bruises and scrapes. She was transported to Lincoln General Hospital, where she required several stitches for her cut. Within hours, the university would have her under 24-hour protection.

Phillips wasn't seen or heard from for hours. Osborne was concerned about him, fearing what he might do to himself, given that he had now blown his chances both with McEwen and football. In his efforts that Sunday to find Phillips, Osborne reached out to the California group home owners to see if they had heard from him. Finally around 5 p.m., he got a phone call from Tina McElhannon, who had Phillips on another line. She appealed to Osborne, urging him to give Phillips another chance. Osborne advised Phillips to get an attorney and surrender to police, which he did three hours later.

Despite McElhannon's appeal, Osborne felt he had no choice but to dismiss Phillips from the team. Phillips had clearly violated his express order regarding McEwen. "This is it. He's gone," Osborne thought to himself. And Osborne's first public statement on the matter, released by the university at 10 p.m. Sunday night, was unequivocal: Phillips was off the team. "We will do everything we can to help him get his life back together," Osborne's written statement said, "but he is dismissed from the football team, effective immediately." The statement also said all players had previously been told "that abusive behavior such as this will not be tolerated."

The next morning in his regular conference call with Big Eight reporters, Osborne said he was comfortable with his decision. "It was very painful. I care very much about Lawrence. But this was something that needed to be done at this time, so we did it." However, when asked whether there was any chance Phillips could return, Osborne appeared to crack the door open just a bit with a "you never say never" response.

Hours later, Osborne received a standing ovation when he appeared at a booster luncheon in Lincoln. His decision was also publicly applauded by advocates for victims of domestic violence. But in his remarks to the boosters, Osborne opened the door for Phillips even wider. "Unfortunately, he will not play for quite a while, if at all," he said. His view was clearly evolving. In fact, by the end of the day, Osborne was no longer calling Phillips' removal from the team a dismissal, but "an indefinite suspension."

Osborne at the time never gave a clear and detailed account of when or why he had changed his mind. His sudden reversal caused quite a bit of confusion, especially given his clear original statement. The World-Herald on Tuesday published stories on both the front page and sports page regarding Phillips — one saying the star back was off the team, the other that he was suspended.

Years later, Osborne recalled a number of factors that had contributed to the softening of his stance. Most importantly, he had learned more from Phillips and others about the circumstances surrounding the incident. "I just knew more about the situation Monday than I did on Sunday," he recalled. Key, Osborne said, was a meeting he had in his office with Phillips that Monday morning. Until the meeting, he had not been aware there had been mutual contact between Phillips and McEwen. He also learned of the role of the person who led Phillips to Frost's apartment. It wasn't as if Phillips had set out in the night stalking McEwen. During the meeting, Osborne also asked Phillips what he later considered to be a key question: "Were you in control, or were you out of control?" Phillips said he had not been in control of his actions.

Phillips also denied during the meeting with Osborne that he had struck McEwen with his fist, as press accounts from police that morning indicated. The statements Frost and McEwen gave to police were not definitive on that but certainly suggested she had been struck (in her lawsuit against Phillips, McEwen would later say Phillips both beat and kicked her). Phillips additionally disputed that he'd dragged McEwen by her hair, although that was something Frost had clearly witnessed.

The conflicting accounts did give Osborne some pause, the coach trying to grasp just how severe the incident had been. He questioned whether it was really as bad as it was being made to sound in the press. Some press accounts were even suggesting the damage to the mailboxes had been caused by Phillips beating McEwen's head into them. To be sure, given how big and physical Phillips was, he certainly would have been capable of hurting McEwen more severely if he had wanted to. Regardless, even the most charitable reading of the witness accounts and of McEwen's injuries make it clear Phillips' acts were violent, egregious, traumatizing to the young woman and criminal.

Along with giving Osborne some new perspective, the meeting with Phillips also tugged at the coach's heartstrings — another critical factor in his change in thinking. As they spoke, Phillips broke down and cried. Osborne's eyes welled up, too. He could sense Phillips' anguish. "Lawrence had built an emotional wall around himself that was very hard to penetrate," Osborne later wrote in a 1996 autobiography, *On Solid Ground*. "I had never seen the person behind the wall until that moment." By the end of their conversation, Osborne held out for Phillips the possibility of returning to the team. "I always saw a certain amount of vulnerability in that kid," Osborne said in looking back years later. "Probably I was soft-hearted, and maybe I shouldn't have been."

Phillips' teammates were largely silent on the attack, but years later several would come to his defense. While not condoning what he had done, they said it was important to consider the circumstances. If you learned a person you cared about was in someone else's apartment, do you know how you'd react? "When that moment hits," Clinton Childs asked, "could you say you would turn and walk away?" They say the roots of his anger should also not be forgotten. Could you imagine if it was your child who had been shuffled around the way Lawrence was as a kid? Others said there were other extenuating circumstances that, if brought to light, would change public perceptions. They declined to elaborate. "That one will probably stay in the locker room for a while," said Matt Vrzal, a reserve lineman who in later years took a more prominent leadership role among 1990s-era players as president of the Letterman's Club. "We're protective of the program, we really are, because it's what we're conditioned to do."

In the end, Osborne decided that football was pretty much the only environment in which Phillips functioned well, the game bringing both meaning and structure to his life. Osborne also saw the game as the running back's potential salvation, the only hope for getting him to deal with his anger issues. If he didn't learn to control his rage, both Phillips and others would pay the price down the line.

The coach also figured if he cut Phillips loose, the young man would have no one to turn to but the pro football agents. They'd swoop in and offer him a quick buck and lots of promises — but no security or support to help him deal with his problems. "It was almost like a death sentence, like you were throwing him away," Osborne said later. "I just felt when a kid comes 2,000 miles away and essentially you are all he's got in the way of a support system, you should do everything you can to make sure the person has a decent chance to have a good life."

Osborne knew at the time that booting Phillips from the team would have made things much easier for both him and the university. But he said he could not have lived with himself if he had let others pressure him into doing something he didn't believe was right.

Rather than effectively banishing Phillips, Osborne instead required him to agree to undergo an evaluation for his anger. Stark, the team psychologist, helped arrange admission for Phillips in the Menninger Clinic, an internationally known psychiatric and treatment facility that just happened to be in McEwen's hometown of Topeka. It had become obvious to Stark that Phillips had been deeply hurt by the abandonment of his youth, in a more complex way than anyone had realized. He needed expert therapists who could get to the root of his anger. If Phillips completed any counseling and therapy program recommended at the clinic, kept out of trouble and also stayed on top of his studies, Osborne told him there was a possibility he could return. In the meantime, Phillips was suspended from all games, practices and team activities, including the training table. McEwen, as a member of the basketball team, still ate her meals there. Osborne sensed Phillips was reluctant to go to Menninger, knowing its doctors would be delving into his painful past. But he agreed to all of Osborne's conditions.

Osborne considered it a harsh and strict punishment. In fact, the players voiced their belief that it was too harsh. Osborne and Stark in 1991 had established the Unity Council. It was kind of a team senate, made up of two players from each position, that was intended to help the coach address issues surrounding the climate of the team. It gave players a forum to address little grievances, like unpopular food choices at the training table or a strength staff member who was being rude. But the Unity Council also had a chance to weigh in with Osborne on issues of discipline, providing some internal transparency to the process. Together, Osborne and the players years earlier had established a point system for discipline, with players assessed so many points for missing a practice or weightlifting session, skipping a class or committing other infractions.

The Unity Council recommended that Phillips be suspended for a single game, a punishment they felt was consistent under the point system for a player committing a misdemeanor. Phillips ultimately faced misdemeanor charges of assault and trespassing for the incident. But regardless of the point system, Osborne always had the final say in these matters. He decided that was insufficient, especially given his earlier admonition to Phillips. Osborne's decision to keep Phillips around would hardly resonate for many outside the program. It would prove highly unpopular around the country. And given the potential benefits to the Huskers' football fortunes, many would be justifiably skeptical. Coaches and players over the years have frequently argued that Nebraska didn't need Phillips to win a championship, and in hindsight everyone could look back at season's end and see that was true. But it's worth noting that at the time of the suspension, no one — not even Osborne — knew that was the case.

Brown is one who doesn't doubt Osborne's motives. Brown, like Osborne a devout Christian, often attended Bible study and devotional sessions with the coach. He later remembered praying and consulting with Osborne on the Phillips decision. "We all can have a secret agenda," Brown said. "But when you are with someone enough, you see the sincerity." Brown said it was a difficult decision for Osborne. But the coach looked within himself and decided in the end to err on the side of compassion. Given his moral makeup, it was probably the only decision Osborne could make. "I thought Tom came to the point where the easy thing to do would have been to kick him off," Brown recalled. "For him to keep Lawrence, it invited all kinds of trouble. Even if it meant we needed Lawrence to win a national champion-ship, it wasn't worth it, and he knew it. He knew we would be pretty good without Lawrence, and we already had won a national title. His conscience, based on his relationship with God, even though there were pros and cons, told him it was the right thing to do."

Milt Tenopir years later recalled talk during coaches' meetings of whether Phillips should return, but it was never about whether the team needed him. It always centered on Phillips' welfare. "Tom knew exactly what the public's perception would be, and he wasn't worried about that," Tenopir said. "There's no question in my mind he did it because it was what was best for Lawrence, not what was best for Nebraska."

Then-Nebraska athletic director Bill Byrne also trusted Osborne was making the decision for the right reasons and supported what the coach was trying to do. He said the timing of Phillips' arrest, coming in the midst of former NFL star O.J. Simpson's highly publicized trial in the slayings of his ex-wife and her boyfriend, had created a "toxic situation." Everyone was unfairly trying to paint the two episodes with the same brush. "I was very concerned about that," Byrne recalled. "Some of these people wanted (Phillips) neutered and tossed upon the trash heap of life. That was just not right."

Stark said that to fully comprehend how Osborne handled Phillips, you have to understand what a genuinely compassionate man Osborne was. It went far beyond his football players. Stark said he will never forget the time he went into the South Stadium offices early in the morning to take care of some things. Osborne was already there hard at work, so Stark didn't bother him. Soon after, a mentally disabled man came in, having walked more than a mile from his group home. He wanted to give Osborne a list of plays he'd worked up, hoping they would help the Huskers. Stark listened in amazement through his cracked office door as Osborne talked to the man for half an hour, in the end thanking him for coming by. It was particularly moving for Stark, who had a profoundly disabled son of his own. "You can learn a lot about a person," Stark said, "when you see how they act when no one is looking."

At Osborne's regular Tuesday weekly press conference two days after Phillips' arrest, the coach publicly laid out his plans for Phillips. He argued that suspending Phillips, keeping him in a structured environment, with the carrot that he could possibly return, was best for all involved. "What I'm concerned with is helping Lawrence and the young lady and the football team, six months to a year from now, have the best possible outcome," Osborne said.

But it was not a decision made in a vacuum. When Osborne spoke those words, joining the regular local media in Lincoln that day were reporters from ESPN, CNN, the Washington Post and USA Today. The next day, ABC News and the CBS news program "48 Hours" were on hand for his post-practice session with reporters. Lawrence Phillips had engulfed Osborne and Nebraska in a national media firestorm.

This had become more than just a story about the fall of a potential Heisman winner. Suddenly reporters and commentators across the country were questioning the character and motives of the man on whose moral foundation the entire Nebraska football program had been built.

The
Boys Town
Father Flanagan Award
for
Service to Youth

Tom and Nancy Osborne
May 4, 1995

Football's Father Flanagan

In May 1995, many in Nebraska were still walking on air in the wake of Nebraska's national championship. Lawrence Phillips was still months away from becoming a national media sensation. That's when Tom Osborne made a pilgrimage to Omaha to be honored at Boys Town, the world-famous home for boys. He and Nancy were to receive the institution's annual Father Flanagan Award for service to children. The award recognized the Osbornes for their TeamMates program, which matched Husker players as mentors to at-risk youth in Lincoln. The Osbornes had also set up an endowment to send graduates of the program to college. TeamMates would expand over the next decade to include hundreds of mentors and dozens of chapters all across the state.

In his remarks that night to the 550 boys and girls at Boys Town, Osborne talked about how tough things had gotten for young people. When he'd started recruiting in the '60s, single-parent families were a rarity. Now they were pretty much the rule. At the same time, kids were now growing up in a culture where moral absolutes no longer exist, violence is glorified, and dangerous temptations abound. "So we're taking young people who do not have as stable a background and thrusting them into an environment I believe is hostile," he said. "To be a young person today is a difficult proposition."

If the Rev. Edward J. Flanagan had been alive to hear Tom Osborne speak that night, he would have seen that he and the football coach really had a lot in common — and not because Osborne was running some kind of home for wayward boys in Lincoln. Two strong-willed Nebraskans, deeply religious, passionate in belief, including their belief that people can redeem themselves. You could even hear

> "One thing I'm thankful for is to have grown up and lived in a country where we're allowed to have dreams, and that's what this was with Tom and me."
>
> — NANCY OSBORNE ON THE TEAMMATES PROGRAM

an echo of Flanagan's famous credo — "There are no bad boys. There is only bad environment, bad training, bad example, bad thinking" — in Osborne's words in 1995 as he defended his decision to give Phillips another chance. "My experience with players and my background in psychology lead me to believe no one's all good and no one's all bad," Osborne said that fall. "And behavior has a reason, probably because of the experience the person had."

Much like Flanagan before him, Osborne also saw himself as a surrogate parent for the young men under his charge — including those who got into trouble. The same care and compassion he showed his players did not end when they slipped up. "I guess in some ways when someone's out of line, I feel a little like I would if it were one of my own children," he would say that fall. "I just can't walk away from whatever they do, good or bad."

These weren't new beliefs for Osborne. He'd certainly had players in trouble before. And just four years earlier, he'd stood by another running back who — under the influence of an undiagnosed mental illness — had brutally beaten a woman. Osborne had even taken the player into his home. But never before had he found his beliefs facing such scrutiny, skepticism and attack. Osborne's decision to open the door to Phillips — coming as the O.J. Simpson case had raised national awareness about domestic abuse — set off a conflagration of criticism. Phillips' arrest was already a major embarrassment for Osborne, the university and the entire state of Nebraska. Now it was widely believed Osborne was bringing Phillips back to preserve the Huskers' bid for a national championship. Almost overnight, Osborne went from being the sympathetic and honorable man everyone had been rooting for to a coach who would do anything, including coddle women-beating criminals, to win.

And Phillips wasn't the only Husker now thrown under a harsh light. Barely 24 hours before Phillips' attack on Kate McEwen, backup running back Damon Benning had been arrested by Lincoln police in another domestic disturbance. Benning in the end was completely exonerated. It was determined he had done little more than restrain a former girlfriend who tried to force her way into his apartment. But with the incident occurring the same weekend as the Phillips arrest, Benning's arrest further fueled the Phillips furor. Many national media outlets reported it as another case of a Nebraska running back attacking a woman. And most of the stories were also mentioning other Husker players who had run afoul of the law in recent years, including a pair of cases involving firearms. All the players involved were still on the team. One was now a team captain.

One serious case involved starting cornerback Tyrone Williams, who was still facing weapons and assault charges related to a January 1994 incident in which he fired two gunshots into an occupied car. Williams retrieved the .22-caliber handgun from his apartment after he and some teammates got into a conflict with some other men in Lincoln. Then he broke out the window of the car before firing two shots into the back. Never before could Osborne recall a Husker player committing a crime involving the firing of a gun. Williams' penalty: Osborne suspended him from the 1994 spring game and for the 1994 season opener. But he otherwise played on, starting 24 games for the 1994 and 1995 Huskers while his case was tied up in court. Williams was a legitimate lockdown cover corner, arguably more important to the team than Phillips.

Less than a month before the 1995 season opener, reserve receiver Riley Washington was charged with attempted murder in a shooting outside a Lincoln convenience store. Some Huskers and ex-Huskers had been feuding with some Lincoln men — a dispute several witnesses said was gang-related. Someone pulled a gun, and a man was shot in the chest. Police arrested Washington, who two years earlier had been convicted of a misdemeanor for having a loaded shotgun in his car back home in California. Washington spent almost two weeks in jail before being bailed out. He was formally arraigned just days after Phillips' arrest, adding to the uproar. While the junior from Chula Vista was initially suspended, Osborne weeks later allowed him to return to the team in the midst of the controversy. Washington maintained he was innocent, and Osborne believed him. Osborne several times noted the victim had been arrested on 55 misdemeanor charges, including four arrests for giving false information to police. But prosecutors didn't share Osborne's assessment, taking Washington to trial on two felonies. In the end, well after the 1995 season had ended, a jury would quickly acquit Washington after a trial rife with conflicting statements. A key piece of evidence was a convenience store videotape that showed Washington wearing a black T-shirt, not a red shirt as the victim had alleged.

Also under a harsh light was Christian Peter, a team captain who two years earlier had been convicted of third-degree sexual assault for groping a former Miss Nebraska in the crotch at a Lincoln bar. Subsequently, another woman just months before the start of the 1995 season filed a civil suit alleging Peter twice raped her in a university dorm during the fall of 1991. She did not report the alleged rapes to police until two years later. Peter denied the allegation, and prosecutors in 1993 decided there was insufficient evidence to charge Peter. The university ultimately financially settled the civil suit. Osborne punished Peter for the groping conviction and other indiscretions, but the defensive tackle never missed a game.

With Phillips' arrest, mug shot-like photos of Husker players became a staple of ESPN news reports. And Osborne himself became the focus of much of the coverage. The media love a scandal, and they felt they'd found one right in the middle of the nation's heartland, within a program run by a straight-arrow man who was now portrayed as having sold his soul to win a national title. A Newsday columnist suggested Osborne was putting his own twist on Father Flanagan's credo: that there was no such thing as a bad boy who could run 4.4 in the 40. "Pssst, Tom. Need a tailback? Maybe O.J. Simpson has some eligibility left," a Boston columnist wrote. "Nebraska football used to be something special. Not anymore."

Suddenly a program that took pride in doing things the right way — playing with class, graduating players, leading the country in academic All-Americans and never running seriously afoul of NCAA rules — was being likened to renegade outfits like Miami and Oklahoma. And a program long built on the discipline of its players was being portrayed as one where just about anything goes, including attacking and raping women.

To be sure, almost no big-time football program was immune to having players occasionally end up in handcuffs. These players were not to be confused with Boy Scouts. In most cases, the reason they got to campus had everything to do with their aggressiveness and ability to clobber people and little to do with brains or good works. "You don't win football games with choirboys," Osborne had said months before Phillips' arrest. "You've got to be tough to play." Arrests for fights and alcohol violations had been common on college campuses as long as college football had been played.

Beginning in the 1980s, though, a rash of arrests of football players accused of serious and violent offenses was seen across the country. Some of the most notorious cases came at Oklahoma, where coach Barry Switzer's players, according to one Sports Illustrated article, had "terrorized" the campus. Within a matter of months, a player shot and wounded a teammate after a fight, another was arrested on suspicion of selling cocaine, and, in the most serious incident, three players were accused of gang-raping two women in the football dorm. Those crimes and NCAA recruiting violations ultimately led to Switzer's ouster in 1989. Florida State, Alabama, Miami, Colorado, Notre Dame and Washington in recent years had all been plagued by bad headlines both before and after winning national championships. A Colorado newspaper had reported in 1989 that 25 percent of the players on the Buffaloes' roster had been arrested, mostly for minor violations. Nebraska had largely avoided serious criminal problems during the 1980s, but that certainly was no longer the case. Overall, though, it's difficult to say whether the Nebraska indiscretions were worse or less so than those at other big football schools.

Family trends like the ones Osborne had talked about at Boys Town no doubt contributed to the increased lawlessness among college athletes. Osborne said at the time only about a third of his players were coming from traditional two-parent homes where they received lots of support. All the top schools also were pulling players out of the nation's inner cities, which beginning in the 1980s had become infiltrated by violent, drug-dealing gangs originating in L.A. Even small and mid-sized cities like Omaha weren't immune to the culture of violence enveloping those communities. Many kids who were not in gangs were still influenced by them. It was far riskier in the 1990s to go into these tough places for players. But it didn't stop schools from doing it. Nebraska pulled a sizable number of players from inner cities, including a half-dozen Osborne said at the time had come from "really tough environments."

There's also no doubt that Nebraska's national championship had made it a lightning rod for media scrutiny. The same issues at say, Iowa State, would not have received nearly the attention. Few in the media outside Nebraska cared about Peter's 1993 arrest or Williams' in 1994 until Nebraska won that national title in January 1995. Osborne had been warned by Notre Dame Coach Lou Holtz, Alabama Coach Gene Stallings and Florida State's Bobby Bowden that every misstep would now be magnified. "With that trophy up there goes a lot of things," Osborne would say months later. "Sometimes you'd just as soon give the darn thing back."

But given the school's squeaky-clean reputation, even many Nebraska backers had to admit it was a little shocking to see so many players recently accused of serious crimes, including a pair that allegedly involved guns. Neither before nor since has there been such a rash of serious offenses within the Nebraska program to match that of the 1994-95 era teams. The players also brought much of the attention on themselves by committing their crimes when the program's profile was at its highest. Phillips' arrest came just hours after he was being hyped as the Heisman front-runner. And it all came at the dawn of the digital age and 24-hour news cycle, national cable sports outlets, sports talk radio shows and the nascent Internet spreading word of the Huskers' crimes around the country at lightning speed.

Years later, some within the Husker program were dismissive of all the negative attention, taking an "it happened everywhere" attitude. But others were quick to take ownership. The vast majority of the players on the team were hardworking kids who did things the right way and were great citizens, Ron Brown said. But there were also too many making serious off-field mistakes. "We had incidents with guns and women, guys in jail and all kinds of things, no doubt about it," he said. "I'm not going to point the finger and say we were poor victims. I'm pointing the thumb. . . . Bottom line, it was revealing something that was not right." Matt Vrzal years later agreed that the players had done their part to fuel the fire. "It was of our own making," he said. "We weren't bad people. We had some people who made some bad choices. We allowed people to take pot shots at our character and at us as human beings. We justly deserved some of it, and some of it not."

Pot shots aside, in the media siege Osborne would be confronted with some tough — and legitimate — questions. Why weren't the players' punishments more severe? For all his talk about the importance of character, what did these problems say about his players? Had he indeed lowered his recruiting standards to win a national title? Was this the price he had paid to win the big one? "Is it a coincidence," a Miami writer asked, "that Nebraska wasn't competitive with Florida State and Miami until it began fielding thuggish players capable of being in the end zone one minute and in handcuffs the next?"

Osborne also faced questions and criticism for his practice of conducting his own investigations into his players' criminal cases. When the woman had come forward with the rape allegations against Peter, Osborne had offered to arrange a meeting in his office with Peter and the woman so she could confirm for Osborne that he was her assailant — an offer seen by many as an effort to intimidate or influence the woman. Osborne said that since he knew the woman well, he didn't think she would find it to be an intimidating environment. Osborne also seemed quick to believe his players' version of events. Even when they admitted wrong, it would seem only natural they would try to minimize the seriousness of what took place. Based on such practices, Sports Illustrated came out with an article 10 days after Phillips' arrest questioning Osborne's methods. Titled "Coach and Jury," the story included an explosive new allegation from the chief Lancaster County prosecutor: that Osborne and assistant coach Kevin Steele had held and stowed away the gun Williams had fired at the car instead of immediately turning it in to police.

The university administration also faced legitimate questions about why it seemed to be deferring to its influential football coach on these matters. The school did investigate the Phillips episode through its regular code of student conduct procedures, as it would with any student so accused. In the end, the vice chancellor heading the review generally accepted all of the punishments and stipulations Osborne had imposed. But it raised the question: Is football the tail wagging the dog at the University of Nebraska?

Reporters who regularly covered Nebraska knew Osborne to be thin-skinned when it came to any criticism of his program. Such was his pride in what he and everyone at Nebraska had worked so hard to build. In the face of this onslaught, he didn't waver, defending everything that had been done. He wasn't proud of the criminal incidents but thought the entire team was being unjustly painted because of the actions of a few. The cases involved about a half-dozen players out of 150, and over a span of several years. Of course in a perfect world there wouldn't be any, he said, but that wasn't realistic when dealing with young men. He offered no apologies for standing up for accused players. The coach also defended his practice of interviewing players and witnesses, saying he needed to understand what happened to know how to discipline his players. To let the justice system take its course could take months. As for SI's charge about Williams' gun, Steele let the campus police know he'd secured the weapon. If Osborne had not used his influence to force Williams to produce the gun — the player retrieved it from the field in which he'd ditched it — did police think they ever would have seen it?

Osborne disputed that he was too close to the players to police and discipline them. A lot of the people now passing judgment on them knew nothing about them at all. For example, he felt "absolutely terrible" about the way Peter was being portrayed. Peter had indeed had numerous problems during his first years on campus, many of the incidents related to alcohol. Reined in by Osborne, Peter had had no more serious indiscretions in the past two years and become a great team leader.

Osborne denied his discipline system amounted to a slap on the wrist, maintaining it had proven effective over the years in changing players' behavior. He'd make them take responsibility for what they'd done and then set up a narrow, structured rehabilitation program. Always hanging over the player was the ultimate penalty of dismissal if the player did not stick with the program. Osborne didn't care if his second-chance philosophy was not in vogue in the get-tough-on-crime '90s. He wasn't willing to "send a message" if it meant throwing out someone he still thought could be redeemed. Outcomes, not appearances, were what concerned him. Osborne conceded he might be wrong in his thinking. But at least he was consistent. "I'm not going to sacrifice someone to make points," he said.

Interviewed in depth about the 1995 criminal controversies some 17 years later, Osborne said his views on the situation had changed little. He continued to defend his handling of the players, though clearly in Phillips' case, he conceded, it's easy to see in hindsight that his efforts to help the player failed. Osborne also acknowledged that much like parents who can't see the shortcomings in their children's behavior, it's possible he had a blind spot when it came to his players. At times that may have caused him to more readily believe they were telling him the truth or to not come down as hard as he should have. "You get to know them, you're invested in them, and you know where they came from," he said. "There's a fine line."

He particularly questioned in hindsight whether he had properly handled the incident in which Williams fired at the car. After his playing days at Nebraska were over, Williams would spend six months in jail in 1996 after his conviction in the gun crime. "That was serious, and probably in retrospect, maybe that should have resulted in a much longer suspension or a permanent dismissal," Osborne said. "He claimed he wasn't trying to hurt anyone. I don't know. There was a gun involved, and it was discharged." Osborne said the Williams case may have pointed out a flaw in the point system he and the Unity Council used. In the Williams case, he said he had adhered to the punishment the code called for when a player committed a criminal misdemeanor. But the code made no distinction whether that misdemeanor was public urination or, as in the Williams case, involved the firing of a gun. "I followed the code 100 percent," he said. "Maybe the code wasn't 100 percent correct."

Also in Williams' favor, Osborne said, was that he'd shown remorse, had no previous criminal offenses of any kind and cooperated with police. Another factor, Osborne acknowledged, was the affection he'd always felt for Williams. Williams had been a high school teammate of Tommie Frazier in Florida. While Frazier had come to Lincoln as a ballyhooed blue-chip recruit, the impoverished Williams scraped the money together to walk on, riding a bus to Lincoln. "I always thought he made quite a sacrifice to get here," Osborne said. Ironically, while the Williams case was the one in which Osborne most second-guessed his own actions, the result in the end was a good one. Williams had no more incidents in his two years in Lincoln and enjoyed a long and successful NFL career.

One issue neither Osborne nor his assistants would give an inch on years later was whether they had compromised standards in originally bringing any of the law-breakers to campus. Some critics would suggest the results spoke for themselves. Both Williams and Peter had come as part of the big Prop 48 classes in 1991 and 1992, players who likely would not have been in Lincoln were it not for the new push to get faster on defense. But Osborne and his coaches continued to insist they ignored no obvious red flags or character flaws with any prospects. Before coming to Lincoln, Williams, Peter, Washington and Phillips had no known history of serious problems with the law, gang affiliation, drug use or being disruptive in school — all things Osborne said would have been deal-breakers in recruiting. "We didn't cut any corners in recruiting, we didn't cut any corner academically, and we did the best we could to determine character," Osborne said. "It wasn't like we were the only school recruiting these guys."

Brown believed the issues were more a reflection of the risks all schools faced in recruiting. No matter whether a player grows up poor in the inner city or in a great home in the suburbs, you never truly know what you are getting. Even kids from great backgrounds can sometimes do crazy things when away from home for the first time. "I've walked into some of the toughest neighborhoods in this country in recruiting, and most of (those recruits) turned out to be great kids," Brown said. "It's easy to look back in retrospect and say this kid was a risk, or that one was a risk. In many ways, they're all risks."

Despite all the negative national publicity Phillips brought to Nebraska in 1995, his case caused few issues for Osborne in Nebraska. Of course, there was an element of the fan base that would support anything they felt would help the Huskers win. But most seemed to base their support on Osborne's track record for integrity, taking what he said at face value. They trusted him to do the right thing by his players. Knowing his makeup and commitment to his players, they weren't surprised by his choices. Some even gave him credit for trying to help his wayward players rather than just bleeding them for whatever he could and then discarding them by the side of the road when things got tough. Appropriately, these feelings were probably best summed up by the Rev. Val Peter, who at the time was carrying on Father Flanagan's legacy as the leader of Boys Town.

"You can quibble with what Tom Osborne did," he told a reporter that fall. "But I know one thing: His heart is big, and his intentions are good."

"If people want to rip me, that's OK.
That's what I get paid for.
But I hate to see players take
some of the stuff they have to take."

— TOM OSBORNE

Coming to Grips

I n the wake of the Lawrence Phillips attack and suspension, Tom Osborne gathered his players in South Stadium and dared them to be great. Adversity is going to come to every team, he said. We saw that last year when Tommie Frazier and Brook Berringer were hurt, and everyone pulled together to get through it. Great teams overcome these kinds of things. So Osborne gave this team a challenge: "Can you be that great team?"

It took all of 11 seconds the following Saturday for the Huskers to provide Osborne the answer. That's how much time had elapsed from the game clock by the time Clinton Childs, Phillips' replacement at I-back, took a handoff from Frazier and rumbled 65 yards for a touchdown against Arizona State. It was the fastest score in modern Husker football history. And it was only the beginning. The Huskers put up 63 points in the first half alone, a school record. That against a Pac-10 team Osborne had thought going in was capable of giving the Huskers a game into the fourth quarter.

The 77-28 trouncing showed that this team was little distracted by the events of the last week. Instead, the players had used them as a rallying point, taking out their frustrations on the team that had the misfortune of being the next one on the Huskers' schedule. The players had said nothing about the Phillips controversy during the week. It was the first time in at least 30 years the players had voted not to do any interviews. But their true feelings showed on this day. In the locker room before the game, Christian Peter gave another impassioned speech, but it was nothing like the WWF-inspired rant that had drawn blood the previous week. This one came from the heart, an emotional plea that the Huskers go out and give every ounce of effort they had for their coach.

During Osborne's entire tenure in Lincoln, there was perhaps no relationship with a player that was more unusual than the one with Christian Peter. The two were in many ways polar opposites. Osborne defined character. Peter was a character. A colorful cut-up with a booming Jersey voice, Peter was well-known for his comic antics and bombastic personality. And he regularly used foul words that Osborne would die before uttering. But Osborne enjoyed being around Peter, who constantly teased his coach. There was no player who could make him laugh out loud the way

Peter could. He once even got the staid Husker coach to go along with him and help toss a team trainer into a hotel pool. And Christian Peter absolutely adored Tom Osborne.

In the fall of 1990, running backs coach Frank Solich had come to Osborne asking him to watch some tape of a New Jersey high school intrasquad scrimmage. Solich had an eye for talent, and there was a defensive tackle he wanted Osborne to check out. Normally, the coaches would watch game film to evaluate a potential recruit. But this player had none. The night before he was to play the first game of his senior year, Christian Peter had been ruled ineligible. He had transferred too many times, having attended three different high schools due to struggles with a learning disability. Peter had actually only played one year of high school football, growing up a swimmer and soccer and hockey player. But based on that brief but impressive snippet of film, Osborne decided to award the raw Peter a scholarship. Peter was always grateful to Osborne for that chance, the foundation of their bond.

Peter arrived in the fall of 1991 and started practicing with the team, only to discover he was an academic casualty. The university did not accept one of the core courses he was counting on to meet Prop 48, forcing him to sit out that year. Even while sidelined, the 300-pound ball of muscle impressed coaches and teammates with how hard he worked in the weight room. You practically had to tear him out of the place. He would even sneak off to a local Gold's Gym late at night to get in more lifting. And from the moment he stepped onto the field, he stood out for his energy and drive. One time early in his career Peter had been ruled out because of a bad ankle. He begged the trainers to wrap it up anyway so he could practice, and they finally relented. Under Charlie McBride's tutelage, Peter over time would emerge as a great player, a force in the middle of the D-line on Saturdays that no one could consistently knock off the ball. The role of the D-tackles in McBride's system was often a thankless one. His job was to just tie up the blockers and keep them from getting to the linebackers, freeing them to make the play. Few did it better than Peter.

But Peter's strong and developed body belied an emotional immaturity. The big-city tough guy was excitable, and he may have set some kind of record for fights in practice. Osborne and McBride often had to settle him down. And he seemed to cause almost as much mayhem off the field as on it. That 1993 incident in which Peter was convicted of groping Miss Nebraska had been preceded by a litany of petty offenses — arrests or tickets for trespassing, disturbing the peace, failing to comply with a police officer, public urination, possession of alcohol by a minor and failure to appear in court. Peter came from a good family, his parents co-owning

New Jersey's finest French restaurant. But Osborne had to regularly lecture him on how to treat people and act responsibly.

Some teammates later said almost all the offenses had been fueled by Peter's abuse of alcohol. "Every parent who met Christian thought he was the nicest guy in the world," Phil Ellis later recalled. "Throw ten beers down Christian Peter and you don't recognize him." The groping incident had occurred in a bar. (After their NU playing days were over, Peter and several teammates would contend it wasn't Peter who groped the woman, Peter having taken the fall for another teammate they would not name.) There continued to be academic issues, too, as Peter didn't always get to class. With someone like Peter, Osborne wasn't one to expect an immediate transformation, Ron Brown recalled. The coach tended to meet players where they were, seeking to over time gradually change their ways. In one of the few interviews he gave after leaving the Husker program, Peter said Osborne constantly stuck his neck out for him as he sought to change and constrain him. "He continued to help me and help me," he said in the NETV documentary "Husker Century." "Without him, I don't know where I'd be."

But it appears the groping incident had been the last straw. Osborne required Peter to seek treatment for his alcohol problems and to stay out of bars, among other strictures. Peter completed the coach's program. If Osborne's mandates didn't make Peter a changed man, they were at the very least keeping him under control. There had been no arrests in the two-plus years since the groping incident. And while school was never easy for him, he was on track academically. It wasn't as if he'd been transformed into a beautiful butterfly. Peter remained more than a little rough around the edges. It was almost as if he couldn't help using foul language, apologizing to coaches on the spot whenever he was called out for it. And he remained a guy you didn't want to mess with. But in Osborne's eyes, he had come a long way, growing up a lot. Peter at the time expressed remorse for his past transgressions — at least the ones he admitted to. If he had really done all the things he'd been accused of, he said that fall, he'd be in jail. But Phillips' arrest conjured up Peter's past, causing him to be branded nationally as a rapist. He joined Phillips as a poster boy for Nebraska's new bad-boy image — a rap coaches and teammates later insisted was unfair. By that time, they said, Peter wasn't the same guy. Said McBride: "A lot of the stuff he went through was garbage."

In the process, Peter also emerged as a Husker team leader. Peter would lead by example, but he'd get in your face if he had to. If the scout team wasn't working hard enough to give the defense a good look, he'd let them know about it. No one

— not even a hardworking in-state walk-on — was more grateful to be wearing a Nebraska uniform than Peter. He was a guy that everyone knew would not only run through a wall for Tom Osborne, he could actually do it. His teammates that fall gave him the ultimate mark of respect by voting him one of five team captains. In fact, none received more votes than Peter. His teammates say that unless you were on the practice field or in the locker room, you could never appreciate what a unique leader Peter was. "That was the beauty of Christian," Matt Vrzal recalled. "Everyone thought he was this big dumb ogre, but he could motivate better than anyone has ever seen. He knew the buttons to push, and he knew how to push them."

Now as Peter got up to address the team before the Arizona State game, teammates could see this wasn't going to be another sideshow like the one in East Lansing. Eyes glistening with tears, he spoke to his teammates about his love for his coach. This man is like a father to me, he said. He's like a father to everyone on this team. And he's gone through one of the toughest weeks of his life. Osborne had stood up for a member of the team. Now the team needed to stand up for him. Let's win this game for him. Peter wasn't the only one in tears by the time he was done. And as everyone in Memorial Stadium would see, from the very first play, the Huskers went out and played with focus and passion. Afterward, in an emotional, private locker room scene that touched even the stoic coach, the players presented Osborne with the game ball. "We could see he was real hurt this week," Frazier told reporters. "We really wanted to win it for him."

Besides speaking to the emotional state of the team, the convincing win offered indications the Husker running game would be just fine without Phillips. Childs ran for 143 yards and two touchdowns on just 12 carries, and he did it for his friend. He and Phillips had been out together the night before the game, Childs feeling bad about the circumstances under which he was making his first start as a Husker. "Hey, you can't worry about that right now," Phillips told him. "It's your time."

When Childs was injured in the second quarter, true freshman Ahman Green took over and gave another early indication of why he would years later go down as one of Nebraska's all-time greats. He ran for 111 yards and two scores on 13 carries, his first of many 100-yard games as a Husker. He wasn't the punishing runner Phillips was. But with a low running angle, great balance and legs that never stopped churning, he was hard to knock off his feet. And there was no better athlete on the team, the Omaha Central High product having run up the highest scores in agility testing of any high school player who ever came through the Huskers' summer football camp. Osborne supposedly had been about as happy when the Parade All-American signed as he'd been when Nebraska won the national title. Now Green's confidence was growing daily. Osborne could see he was fast rounding into a big-time back.

Even though Phillips was nowhere to be found around Memorial Stadium that Saturday, the fallen star remained the story. A huge contingent of national media members showed up in Lincoln for the game, including four reporters alone from Sports Illustrated. While the Huskers were ready to move on, others clearly were not. "I don't expect it will be very nice," Osborne said of the forthcoming coverage. "But that's OK. We take it as it comes." Even Osborne, however, had a limit on how much of this he could take. He would hit his a week later, following the Huskers' next game against Pacific.

The Huskers for the second straight year drilled the overmatched Tigers. The 49-7 score would have been far worse had Osborne not had his quarterbacks throw the ball 36 times, most of them just little hitch routes a few yards down the field. Nebraska was the only team in the country that passed the ball when it was trying *not* to score. "This is a class program," Pacific Coach Chuck Shelton said afterward, "run by class people."

But the day after the game, Osborne arrived at work to stunning news. Craig Bohl was the team's linebackers coach, but he also served as a liaison and contact person for law enforcement — recently a busy position on this team. Bohl told Osborne he believed a player was going to be charged with rape. A woman had been at a party with some players and had been drinking heavily. She woke up Sunday morning crying, telling her roommates she believed she'd been raped the night before. Police were called.

Osborne couldn't believe it. Good Lord, he thought. After all the team had already been through, after all the warnings he had been giving them to stay out of trouble, how could this happen? He immediately spoke with the player. He acknowledged he'd been at the party and talked to the girl, but he denied even touching her. There were witnesses to prove it. Osborne found the player convincing. But he also didn't know what or whom to believe anymore. He advised the player to get an attorney.

Osborne would recall the next several days as the lowest point in his career. He was expecting any moment that the player would be arrested, setting off a media frenzy even more tumultuous than what his program had already endured. The Huskers were ranked second in the nation and undefeated, a team Osborne believed was his best. Yet it felt to him like they'd lost every game. "Man, I don't know if I can get

"I couldn't care less what people say.
The people I care about are
my teammates, coaches and family."

— CHRISTIAN PETER

through another of these deals," he thought as he sat in meetings that Sunday.

As he would write later, "this incident had literally and figuratively brought me to my knees." Over the next several days, he fell back hard on his faith. Osborne's Christianity was neither something he forced on people nor something he was reluctant to talk about. He was deeply grounded in it. And despite his position in a public university, Osborne was not afraid to incorporate spirituality into his program. He would generally talk to his players once a year about the importance of having a faith, whatever it was, and about acting in a way that honors God. "We shouldn't forget we are spiritual beings," he'd say in defense of it. Osborne and his assistant coaches also began each workday with a 10-minute voluntary devotional. Someone would read a verse of Scripture and they would talk about it, perhaps relating it to their lives. He thought it helped his staff focus on the broader view of the student-athletes and their welfare rather than personal goals.

Now in the wake of the rape allegation, Osborne prayed often, surrendering his predicament to God and leaving it in His hands. The coach accepted that whatever the outcome was, He would use it for His purposes. Osborne ultimately found peace in his meditations, not just with respect to the latest allegation, but with all of his program's recent turmoil. In the end, he continued to believe the culture within the program was basically sound and promoted the positive personal growth of his players. And he realized he had the fortitude to get through these trials. Osborne was grateful for the strength he found. He didn't know what the final outcome was going to be. He just resolved to put one foot in front of the other, make each decision with what he thought was his best judgment and live with the outcome.

While still in the midst of his internal and spiritual struggles, the embattled coach met with the team on Monday and informed them of the rape allegation. He didn't mention the player's name but said the story could break at any time, so they all should be prepared. Players could clearly hear the disappointment in Osborne's voice. It had a more powerful effect than if he had come in yelling and screaming. "He had a grandfatherly 'I'm disappointed in you' look that would just shrivel you to nothing," Vrzal recalled. The players also could see in his demeanor that he'd had about as much of the negativism as he could take. Some even read into Osborne's tone and beaten-down countenance that he was getting close to the point of cracking. Captains Peter and Ellis both met with Osborne individually the next day, concerned their beloved leader was about to step down.

Others also were seeing the strain on Osborne. In quarterback meetings with the coach every day, it seemed to Frazier that Osborne wasn't sleeping much, the pressure showing on his face. Brown recalled Osborne saying around that time, "I don't know if I can go on anymore. I don't know if I can keep doing this." But Brown didn't interpret it to mean Osborne actually was considering stepping down. It was more a reflection of the coach's frustration — that no matter what he told his players, they were just going to do whatever they wanted. It seemed to Brown that Osborne was losing faith in his team.

Osborne later recalled that he wasn't seriously considering retirement. But he said after his lifetime of work in Lincoln, it was painful for him to see what was happening to his program and its reputation. "I was really feeling very bad about the situation," he said. "We tried to build a program on character and representing the right things. We didn't cheat in recruiting, tried to hold players to a high standard, did well academically and had a reasonably good national image. Now all of a sudden we were the worst people on earth."

Osborne assured Peter and Ellis during his meetings with them that he was holding up OK. This is something we'll all have to get through, he told them. But the players decided to take the matter into their own hands. With fellow Husker captains Tony Veland, Mark Gilman and Aaron Graham, they called a players-only meeting before practice. There was a sense of urgency. "I didn't want to be part of the team that caused Coach Osborne to quit," Ellis, a Grand Island native, recalled thinking. "This is not going to happen on my watch."

The mood was tense as the players filed into the South Stadium auditorium. There was dissension within the team, some players upset that the irresponsible actions of a few were putting everyone in a bad light. There also was potential for racial rifts, too, as all the players who recently had gotten into trouble and the player facing the rape allegation were black. Osborne years later would recall that he had real concerns the off-field incidents could tear at the team internally, destroying their unity on the field.

Things did at times get ugly and contentious during the hourlong meeting. The player accused of rape stood up, assuring his teammates that nothing had happened. But regardless, Peter, Graham and the other captains were extremely animated, blunt and clear as they laid down the law for the rest of the team: Enough was enough. Recalled Jack Stark, the only non-player to witness it: "If you had been in that room, you would have been scared to death."

The captains no longer were going to tolerate off-field indiscretions. Not only did they reflect badly on the team, but they were putting a tremendous strain on Osborne. "Do you want Coach Osborne to quit?" Ellis recalled asking. The off-field issues also were becoming a huge distraction. Players were being asked about them every time they sat down for an interview. It was taking away from all that the team had been working so hard to accomplish. The team was on the cusp of greatness here. Why would they throw it all away over something stupid? "Let's stop sabotaging our season," Veland said.

The captains made it clear, and they repeated it several times: *There will be no more incidents.* For any player to even risk further damage now was outrageously selfish — putting himself above the team. As far as team leaders were concerned, it was now one strike and you're out. If you make a stupid mistake now, the reaction of Coach Osborne and the courts would be the least of your worries. "If anybody, and we mean anybody, gets in trouble, you're not going to have to face the media or the team," Graham said. "You'll face us."

It also was recognized that alcohol played a role in the off-field nonsense. The incidents landing players on police blotters almost always arose during Saturday nights on the town. Team leaders got the team to pledge to abstain from drinking for the rest of the season and to stay out of bars and parties. Nothing good happens in a bar after 10 o'clock. Every drunken knucklehead in town thinks he can show his manhood by challenging or taunting you. Don't even put yourself in that position. "It's about being smart in the people you surround yourself with and what you do," Frazier recalled saying.

Childs said the fact that the meeting was called at all spoke volumes to the type of leadership the 1995 Huskers had. He and other players say there's also no doubt the captains' message got through. "When your leaders tell you you're acting like a bunch of jackasses and to knock it off, you listen," Vrzal said. " 'We are giving people ammo to question us and cut us down. Don't put yourself in these positions. Use better judgment. And stop all the crap.' It was an eye-opener."

It's impossible to measure what had more impact — Osborne's pained disappointment or the captains' pointed threats. But it's notable that there would not be another off-field incident during 1995. In fact, other than a pair of players booted off the team the next year for alcohol-related arrests, there would be no notable black eyes for Nebraska during the rest of the Osborne era. "I think the players, to their credit, understood the painfulness of the whole thing," Osborne recalled.

"A lot of guys really pulled together to make things work and resolved it wasn't going to happen the next year or the next year."

And in the end, nothing would come of the rape allegation. Osborne said the player had witnesses that proved the woman left the party with others. It seems the woman also had some history of erratic claims related to football players. She'd concocted a fictitious romance with another player, even going so far as to buy herself an engagement ring and send out wedding announcements. Osborne said the player accused was nice and kind of naive. If even the allegation had ever been made public, it would have been hard for him to defend himself within the harsh climate the Huskers found themselves in.

Little was said about the players-only meeting until months later. Even then, accounts would place it right after Phillips' arrest, not after the unpublicized rape allegation that came two weeks later. Years later, Brown said he was glad the behind-the-scenes story of how the 1995 team persevered at a critical time could be told. Some teams crumble in the face of such strife. This one probably could have, too. "Through it all, that team never split apart, which was unbelievable when you think about it," Brown said. "I don't think to this day people really understand all that team went through, and all Coach Osborne and our staff went through, to keep that season together."

An internal crisis had been averted. This team was ready to move on. "It was painful," Osborne recalled of the 1995 team's trials. "But on the other hand, there were some good things that came out of it." Indeed, an amazing team chemistry was being forged. It was clear the players genuinely cared about each other and would stand up for each other — even those who had gotten in trouble. The Huskers became, Osborne said, "an unusually determined and focused football team."

The people in the media were going to continue to say what they'd say. But these Huskers were ready to get down to playing some serious football — some of the very best the college football world would ever see. As the Huskers gathered in the locker room just before kickoff of the next weekend's game against Washington State, Peter and the other captains spoke. And then they led the team in Nebraska's Unity Prayer. It was a ritual that had been performed before every game since the early 1990s, when former Husker safety Sedric Collins brought it to Lincoln from his high school in Louisiana. Stark and the Unity Council embraced it, and it became a treasured locker room tradition. Collins never played much before leaving the team in mid-season in 1994. But with the Unity Prayer, he left an enduring mark on Osborne's program. Even years later, players still could remember the words, and just thinking about it gave them goose bumps. Each game day, it became a powerful reminder of how they were going out there to play for each other. Given what they'd just been through, the words on this day meant more than ever. As always, the players huddled together, clasped their taped-up hands and bowed their heads, and recited the poignant words:

Dear Lord in the battles we go through in life

We ask for a chance that's fair.

A chance to equal all your stripes

A chance to do or dare.

If we shall win,

Let it be by the code

With our faith and honor held high.

If we shall lose,

Let us stand by the road

And cheer as the winners go by.

Day by day!

Getting better and better!

A TEAM THAT CAN'T BE BEAT!

WON'T BE BEAT!

"All week, Coach Osborne said
we could score on the first play.
And that's what we did."

— TOMMIE FRAZIER

A Relentless Team

For the second straight year, Colorado vs. Nebraska was a showdown of Top 10 teams, with all kinds of implications for the national championship race. The second-ranked Huskers came into Boulder facing the biggest crowd in CU history. The hostile student section was within spitting distance of the Husker bench, and there was cold Coors Light on tap at the concession stands. The students taunted the Huskers, calling them jailbirds and worse. A Samoan war drummer led the charged-up Buffaloes into the stadium, then led the pompom-waving crowd in chants of "Wartime!" Ralphie, CU's real-life buffalo mascot, charged so close by the Nebraska sideline that Tom Osborne feared he'd kill somebody. This figured to be Nebraska's stiffest test of the season.

But if the Huskers were in a slippery spot, they treated it like a day on a Colorado ski slope. Osborne told the Huskers just before kickoff that teams resort to gimmicks like the war drummer because they have doubt. And once again on the Huskers' first play from scrimmage, Lawrence Phillips' replacement ran untouched for a touchdown. This time it was Ahman Green taking a pitch from Tommie Frazier and rambling 57 yards down the sideline. Rick Neuheisel, CU's new boy-wonder coach, stood grim-faced as Green ran by him. By the game's final minute, Frazier and Nebraska's starters were in the same familiar spot they found themselves in throughout the 1995 season: watching as Brook Berringer and the rest of Nebraska's reserves mopped up.

It seemed no matter who Nebraska played during 1995, the story line remained unchanged: The Huskers kept taking hits off the field while delivering them on it.

The Huskers would play four Top 10 teams that season, ruthlessly outscoring them by an average of 49-19. The offense was piling up the kinds of yardage and points normally only seen by teams that threw the ball every play. With Phillips or not, the Huskers were averaging an astounding 7 yards each time someone carried the ball — setting an NCAA record by season's end — and were well on their way to another national rushing title. And much like a passing team, the Huskers could strike quickly. Half the scoring drives for the season covered five plays or less. Even in the biggest games, the third-teamers were seeing action. And the Huskers joked that punter Jesse Kosch, a meteorology major, had become relegated to providing weather updates on the sidelines. He'd often go entire halves without putting on his helmet. For the season, he would average two punts a game. "There were some royal butt-whuppings," Ron Brown recalled.

Everyone always knew that Osborne was a great coach. Now that he also had great players all over the field, it almost wasn't fair. From quarterback to place-kicker, where strong-legged freshman Kris Brown was hitting field goals at a school-record percentage, this team did not have a weakness. And the guys were brimming with confidence. Whenever the Huskers took the field, no matter who they were playing, Matt Vrzal was reminded of the line from the 1993 movie "Searching for Bobby Fischer": "You've lost. You just don't know it yet."

"I wouldn't say we were invincible," Vrzal recalled. "I'd call it a realistic expectation of perfection." Game days on Saturday seemed no tougher than playing the scout team, everything moving in slow motion. "It was crazy," Phil Ellis recalled. "That was just the confidence that we had. No one was going to stop us."

Along with the confidence, the Huskers were more motivated than ever. If there had ever been the potential for this team to become complacent during the long season, it was gone now. The team developed a classic us-against-the-world mentality. The 1994 team had a little bit of that going, in the face of the people who didn't believe they could win a national championship. But in the end, the rest of college football had been rooting for those Huskers. Ironically, this 1995 bunch was pretty much the same team, with most of the same players and the same coaches. But the view nationally could not have been more different. These Huskers wore black hats. This time, the world truly was against the Huskers.

In response, the team hunkered down, refusing to be beaten down. The Huskers convinced themselves that what others thought, wrote and said about them had no impact. "We just sort of built up these walls," Jason Peter recalled. If anything, the Huskers used all the jibes as ammunition. There became a direct correlation between the boos and taunts of opposing fans and the number of bruises their players received on the field. It was the only place where the Huskers could punch back at their critics. This became one punishing football team. Usually by the third quarter, opponents were looking for a corner of the stadium to curl up in. It particularly angered the Huskers that everyone on the team was being branded thugs and gangsters because of the actions of a few. "We knew who we were. We knew what type of people we had in that locker room," Frazier recalled.

"To see how we were being portrayed really fueled us."

And the Huskers were downright furious about what was being said and written about Osborne. The players saw strong character as Osborne's very essence. "The worst thing is to have people talk about Coach Osborne in the wrong light," Aaron Graham told a Sports Illustrated reporter that fall. "I don't care who you are or what kind of media you come from. You do not know Coach Osborne, and you do not know this program." It now provided huge motivation to have the outside world questioning Osborne's integrity. "We knew what kind of person he was," Grant Wistrom recalled. "It was like someone attacking your father or grandfather."

The Huskers worked hard to keep their indignation within South Stadium, rarely vocalizing it to the media or anyone outside the program. It would have been misconstrued as just another sign that Nebraska condoned what Phillips had done. Brown would later recall it was good that Facebook and Twitter didn't exist back then. The feelings would have been hard to contain. But they quietly served as a powerful driver. Another great motivator, players later admitted: not giving their critics the satisfaction of seeing them lose. "If we thought what people were saying was bad, if we had lost a game it would have been a million times worse," Vrzal said. "We never would have heard the end of it."

The closest the 1995 Huskers would actually come to losing a game would be against Washington State, Nebraska's first game after the rape report. Strangely, while never to be confused with a football power, Washington State had made three previous trips to Lincoln, and three times left with wins. This Cougar team seemed intent on making it four. Salty Cougar defenders were tagging Husker running backs and receivers. And after WSU's running back broke off an 87-yard TD run against the Blackshirts near the end of the first quarter, the Huskers found themselves trailing for the first time all season. "OK," Tony Veland thought when he got back to the sideline. "These guys aren't scared of us." It was strange to look up at the scoreboard and be behind.

Not for long, though. Green came off the bench to get the Husker offense going, running for 176 yards on just 13 carries. He increasingly had fans asking, Lawrence who? Green revved up both the crowd and NU sideline with his tenacity. On one play, he was gang tackled by eight Cougars but refused to go down, still driving the pile. "He was intense!" Christian Peter raved. And Nebraska was more than happy to match the Cougars' physicality. Frazier set the tone by throwing a crack-back block on a reverse, taking out a 6-6, 260-pound defensive end by targeting him

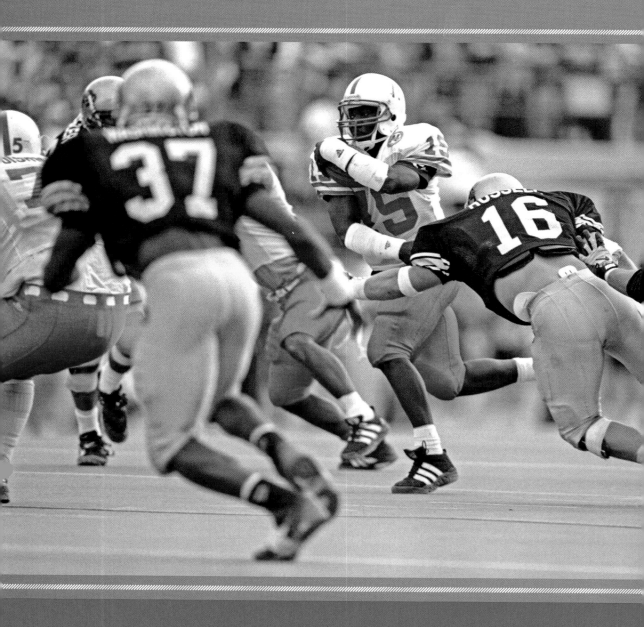

"(Tommie Frazier) played as great
a game as he can play. From here."

— ASSISTANT COACH TONY SAMUEL, POINTING TO HIS HEART

right between the numbers. Frazier was unusually animated during the 35-21 win, pumping his fist and talking a little trash in the face of a Cougar after one score. He was agitated by the attitude the Cougars brought to Lincoln. "When you come to our place, you don't intimidate us," he said. "We try to intimidate you."

The next week the Huskers mauled Missouri's Tigers 57-0. Mizzou over the years had tried some strange tactics against Nebraska, but none more curious than what they brought to Lincoln that week. The Tigers pulled out the option, against a defense that practiced every week against the best option offense on the planet. "I don't know what they were thinking," Jared Tomich said afterward. The Husker offense for the first time all season picked up less than 500 yards, but only because they took over on so many short fields. Goal lines were the only thing stopping Frazier and Co. in that game.

Then Kansas State came to Lincoln with its highest-ever national rank, at No. 8, and boasting the nation's No. 1 defense. The Wildcats once again had designs on ending its generation-long losing streak to the Huskers. "Ain't gonna happen today, baby!" Peter roared during warm-ups, words the KSU players surely heard a few times once the game kicked off. Scoring on offense, defense and special teams, the Huskers led 42-6 late in the third quarter, when all the starters went to the bench. Only several scores against the reserves made the 49-25 final score halfway respectable. Mike Rucker provided one of the signature plays of the year during a punt return, hitting a Wildcat with a block so savage his helmet flew off. "We wanted to make sure they knew they played Nebraska," Tomich said.

The next week, the Huskers went into Boulder and pillaged the place. Osborne never expressed such thoughts, but some players suspected he always wanted it a little more against Colorado. (When his program was failing to meet the state's lofty expectations in the late 1970s, Osborne at one point had actually interviewed for the Colorado job. Many have pondered what would have become of the program had Osborne taken that job). Osborne again put in several new offensive plays against the seventh-ranked Buffs, including the one that produced Green's opening-play touchdown. Osborne had been telling the Huskers in the days leading up to the game they'd have a great chance to score on the first play. The Huskers put an extra blocker in the backfield and used two wideouts, a formation they'd never shown before. Having a pretty good idea what formation the Buffs would come out in, Osborne figured the Huskers would simply outnumber Colorado on the short side of the field. Not only did the Huskers put a helmet on every Buff over there, fullback Jeff Makovicka took out two with a single block. Green, now the Huskers'

"We matched them in intensity,
we matched them with speed. We were just
unable to match them with execution."

— COLORADO COACH RICK NEUHEISEL
AFTER NEBRASKA PLAYED WITHOUT A PENALTY OR TURNOVER

starter at I-back, simply outran everyone else. Neuheisel was being billed as a young chalkboard whiz, but he was no match for the old master.

In his final chance to stick it to Colorado, Frazier may have had his greatest game. On one of his most memorable plays as a Husker, Frazier dropped back to pass and while looking downfield took a full-speed, chest-high shot from a blitzing linebacker. Almost any quarterback would have gone down. But Frazier somehow absorbed the blow, recocked his arm and then zipped a pass in the flat to Green, who breezed 35 yards down the field. "Once in a while," Osborne recalled, "Tommie would make a play you knew nobody else could make." Frazier threw for two first-half touchdowns, including another deflating one-play scoring drive on a long play-action pass to Clester Johnson. His touch and accuracy were never better as he completed 14 passes for a career-high 241 yards. Personally responsible for 14 first downs, the option maestro was at his play-making best.

Overall, the Huskers played a near-perfect game, putting up perhaps the best all-around performance of Osborne's tenure. Nebraska for the second straight week never trailed against a Top 10 team. It was assessed no penalties, committed no turnovers, gave up no sacks and nearly perfectly balanced its offense between passing and running. "I guess they can just go and buy their suntan oil now," ABC play-by-play legend Keith Jackson said when the Huskers took a 31-14 lead just before halftime. Indeed, it didn't appear there was anything that was going to stop this team from getting to the national championship game in Tempe. With 15 national writers on hand, this was the performance that finally convinced the pollsters to jump Nebraska over Florida State into the No. 1 spot. This team by all appearances was on a collision course with history. Osborne refused afterward to be drawn into comparisons of these Huskers with the 1994 national champs. About the time you do that, he said, is when somebody comes in and pins your ears back. But Osborne verbally embraced his team, words that were particularly notable given what they had put him through this year. "I like the chemistry of this team. I enjoy being around them and I like their approach to the game."

Not that the rest of the country was ready to throw their arms around this Nebraska team. The off-field controversy was about to heat up again. That's because five days before the Colorado game, Lawrence Phillips returned to the Huskers' practice field.

A Controversial Return

In mid-October, the Lawrence Phillips ordeal was once again fodder for discussion on an Omaha call-in radio show. The host was a little surprised to learn the name of the next caller on hold: Lawrence Phillips. And in an 11-minute interview — the only one Phillips would give during his suspension — he vowed that he would do right by Tom Osborne, the Huskers, the university and himself. "I'm going to look this right in the eye," he said. "I'm not going to be afraid or I'm not going to be embarrassed or nothing. I did wrong. Everybody does wrong. I'm just going to take care of it."

Osborne and Phillips' friends would later say his words that day accurately reflected his determination to deal with his personal demons. He could have just left Nebraska and headed back to California to get ready for the NFL draft. He had agents telling him they'd give him $100,000 to live on until then. But Phillips ultimately decided he wanted to get back on the field with the Huskers. Osborne and Phillips' friends say he was remorseful for what he had done, felt badly for how his actions had affected the team and wanted to take responsibility. "He'd faced adversity his whole life," Clinton Childs recalled. "He wanted to take this head on."

The first step in his return came 10 days after his arrest, when he pleaded no contest to two misdemeanors in the attack on Kate McEwen. The prosecutor recommended — and the judge later accepted — that he should receive a year of probation for his offenses. No one thought time in jail would do anything to solve Phillips' anger problems. Phillips also for the first time apologized to McEwen, releasing a statement expressing his regret for what had happened that night.

The legal hurdle now cleared, he was off to Topeka and the Menninger Clinic for

"I was hoping they wouldn't boo him.
If they want to boo me,
I'm the guy who put him out there."

— TOM OSBORNE AFTER LAWRENCE PHILLIPS' RETURN

several days of intensive evaluation and counseling. A big and strong member of the Husker strength staff accompanied Phillips to provide 24-hour supervision of the running back while he was there. Ordinarily, even the fact that someone was admitted to Menninger would remain confidential. But with Phillips' permission, Osborne would later release the results of the Menninger evaluation, excerpting key passages in his 1996 book. The report gave Phillips a relatively good bill of health. Menninger doctors determined Phillips was not psychotic, had no abnormal personality, nor was he in general a threat to others. He had an "adjustment disorder," one of the most minimal diagnoses in the spectrum of psychiatric disorders. It simply meant that Phillips had trouble coping with the stresses of his life. In this case, the termination of his romantic relationship with McEwen was said to be the stressor that set it off. Not surprisingly, the disorder was traced to the voids during Phillips' youth.

"(H)is experience of childhood was that he was never quite good enough to keep the people he needed around him," the report said. "His father left him and was absent from the time Mr. Phillips was quite young and his mother, while available for a number of years, when Mr. Phillips was age 12, was involved with another man. The patient developed a sense that something was 'messed up' and, as a result, other people would not be there for him. The incident with his girlfriend led unfortunately to yet another loss of a significant person in his life."

The clinic said Phillips needed intense psychotherapy, but as further evidence of how mild it considered his disorder, did not recommend that he be put on medication. Significantly, the report also considered the role football could play in Phillips' rehabilitation. It called football a mixed bag for Phillips in that it was both quite stressful and rewarding. But to not play, the doctor wrote, would be psychologically difficult for Phillips given football's importance to his identity and self-esteem: "I think that what will be most important psychologically for this man is not to prevent him from doing those things which he is able to do well and from which he can gain a considerable amount of self-esteem and positive responses from others, but to add to that some additional activities such as psychotherapy. . . ."

If Osborne was looking for medical backing for his contention that Phillips needed football, he had it — and from one of the best brand names in the world of psychiatry. It was just what the doctor ordered. It was also, Jack Stark would later conclude, quite likely wrong. Stark is a psychologist, not a psychiatrist. But based on the continued incidents of Phillips lashing out at women after he left Nebraska, Stark said it's not a stretch to say he more than likely had a significant personality disorder. Stark said he wasn't blaming or criticizing Menninger. Such evaluations are fraught with potential to not reach the full depth of the problem, especially if the subject does not tell evaluators everything.

The positive evaluation that Phillips received from Menninger didn't mean he had to play again during the 1995 season. However, to those around the program, it was pretty clear that that was the course Osborne and Phillips were on. Phillips, or course, wanted to get back on the field right away, even early on unrealistically believing he could still get back into the running for the Heisman. There seemed to be a lot of sentiment from Husker fans he should get back soon, too. In fact, it was a little unsettling when his court case was resolved how quickly fan focus turned to a timetable for when the star back could return to the field. With big upcoming games against top 10 teams in Kansas State and Colorado, there was much speculation that Phillips would not be out much longer.

Osborne, though, said Phillips had to show through his weekly counseling and psychiatric sessions that he was making progress in controlling his feelings. On October 17, four days before the KSU game, Osborne squelched any talk of an early return, saying Phillips would not be back on the field until some time after the Colorado game. Osborne years later acknowledged he made the decision in part because putting Phillips back on the field then would have played right into the common belief that Phillips' return was all about winning games. Phillips was disappointed and discouraged that he would be sidelined so long. But Osborne said Phillips continued to keep up with school and stuck with his rehabilitation program. His general demeanor seemed better. It also was around that time that Phillips called into the radio show. Sounding at times both nervous and excited, he talked of the situation he'd put himself in and how he refused to run from it. "I did it," he said. "I'm facing up to it." He said it bothered him that people were talking about him like they knew him. For the first time since the story broke, Phillips looked and sounded like a real person, not just a name and mug shot in the paper.

 Clearance of the final hurdle for Phillips came on October 23, the Monday before the Colorado game. The university announced it had resolved its case against Phillips for violating the student code of conduct, deciding his offenses, while bad, did not merit expulsion from school. As Vice Chancellor Jim Griesen would later recall, Phillips' assault "was not the bloody brutal attack it was made out to be" in the press. That decision left Phillips' fate solely in Osborne's hands, and he almost immediately allowed Phillips to rejoin the team. He would not make the trip to Boulder but would see his first game action the following week against Iowa State, ending what in the end became a six-game suspension. Defending his decision, Osborne said it was unrealistic to say Phillips had been transformed or would never get angry again. But he now had better tools to cope. Ever stubborn, Osborne said he didn't care if there was a public outcry. His voice quivered and almost cracked when he talked to reporters about how he was trying to do the right thing for Phillips.

Also accompanying Osborne's announcement was a statement from McEwen, her first of any kind in the six weeks since the assault. She said she was glad the situation was coming to an end but offered no words either opposing or blessing Phillips' return. However, Griesen would recall that McEwen and her father were quite upset that Phillips wasn't expelled, demanding a meeting with the chancellor. McEwen's biggest statement on the matter would come later with her civil suit against Phillips, for which she would eventually receive a substantial settlement out of his first NFL contract. She would go on to lead a happy and productive life in Kansas as an attorney, wife and mother. (The author inquired through McEwen's attorney to see if she wanted to address the Phillips matter. She did not respond.) Angela Beck, who coached McEwen on the Husker women's basketball team, followed the university line at the time, but she made it clear in an unusual press conference that she was biting her tongue.

Phillips was all smiles as he rejoined the Huskers in the locker room after their practice that Monday. They laughed and joked together just like before. Even Green and Childs, the two backs who had gotten most of the carries in Phillips' absence, were smiling. They wanted him to again feel he was part of the team. Fullback Joel Makovicka said years later it would be disingenuous to suggest players' happiness to have Phillips back had nothing to do with what he could do on the football field. He was the Huskers' best back. But more than that, Makovicka said, on this close-knit team, Phillips was "family."

"If you're family and a brother makes a mistake, you're not going to kick him out in the cold and say, 'That's it, we're done with you.' Everybody wanted him back and felt this was the best place for him." Grant Wistrom agreed. If there was one thing that set the Nebraska teams of that era apart, he said, it was the way the guys all cared for each other. And the tone for that, Wistrom said, was set by Tom Osborne.

Phillips wouldn't go right back to the top of the depth chart. He actually got his first work in practice the next day as a member of the scout team and would have to work his way back into a role. During that week, injuries were beginning to pile up at running back. Green already had a bum ankle from the KSU game, and then

Damon Benning suffered a hamstring injury. When James Sims bruised his hip during a freak collision in practice, Childs was suddenly the only completely healthy running back going into the battle in Boulder. For the second time in two years, team captains approached Osborne with a question about Phillips' playing status: Would the coach change his mind and allow Phillips to make the trip and play if needed? Despite his own concern about the injuries, Osborne refused. As it turned out, Green proved plenty healthy come game day.

Going into the Iowa State game in Lincoln, Phillips could barely control his excitement. "I'm going to run for 500 yards in that game," he told a friend back in California. Phillips would be the first back off the bench in relief of Green. Everyone wondered and anticipated what kind of reaction he would get from the crowd. The answer came five minutes in when Phillips trotted out to join the huddle. He was greeted with warm applause, a roar beginning in the student section and rolling in a wave across the stadium. Certainly not every fan was happy at the sight of No. 1, but those fans showed their disapproval with silence, not boos. Phillips picked up 2 yards on his first carry, and the words "Ball carried by Phillips" echoed through Memorial Stadium for the first time all season. From his first carry, Phillips looked sluggish and out of sync. He had hit the weights hard while sidelined, packing eight more pounds of muscle on his frame. But he wasn't carrying it well, by the end huffing and puffing his way to 68 yards and a touchdown on 12 carries. Osborne could see he wasn't the same player. "He looked like a guy who hasn't played for six weeks," Osborne said afterward.

Phillips wasn't even the best runner on his team during the Huskers' 73-14 rout. Carrying the ball the same number of times as Phillips, Green ran for 176 yards to bring his season total close to 1,000 yards. A week later he would become the first freshman in Nebraska history to top that milestone. After the game, Phillips talked to reporters for the first time since his arrest, expressing regret for his actions and gratitude for his second chance. The next week against Kansas, Phillips again was not sharp, running for only 47 yards in the Huskers' 41-3 win. He was still not even close to the back who ran roughshod over everyone those first two games.

Of course, with Phillips' return also came the uncomfortable glare of the media spotlight. It started as soon as Osborne announced Phillips was back and continued each time he took the field. Since Osborne said Phillips' six-game suspension had been double what the team's code of conduct would normally have called for when a player committed such misdemeanors, a Philadelphia columnist suggested Phillips now had one free woman-beating in reserve for future use. A New York Daily News

story likened giving Phillips anger management counseling to sending a T. Rex to charm school. Numerous national and local publications quoted women's groups decrying Osborne's decision, one quoting the director of the university women's center saying Phillips was being brought back because the Huskers wanted him for their coming bowl game. Osborne said he was prepared to take the heat. But even Osborne couldn't have anticipated the ambush awaiting him at his weekly press conference just before the Iowa State game.

CBS sent reporter Bernard Goldberg to Lincoln to do a piece on Phillips. He came with two cameras — one trained on Osborne, the other on himself. He asked a provocative question, one seemingly intended to get a reaction out of Osborne, and it did. It appears the question had been borrowed from a letter to the editor in the Omaha paper that morning in which someone questioned how Osborne would have handled the Phillips matter if his own daughter had been attacked. "Coach, I understand this may not be the most popular subject to bring up in Lincoln, but let me try anyway. If one of your players had roughed up a member of your family and then dragged her down a flight of steps . . . "

Osborne, who had two daughters of his own, cut him off, and then asked Goldberg to identify himself. "I'm not going to talk about that, OK? And I kind of resent that question, to be very honest with you." Osborne told Goldberg he would answer his question, but this was not the time or the place. They later met in the hall, and a red-faced Osborne gave Goldberg his answer. "The answer is yes, OK. The answer is yes." Osborne didn't think of it at the time, but he later wished he'd asked Goldberg a question of his own: If Phillips had been your son, what would you have wanted me to do?

Goldberg's piece aired on Dan Rather's CBS evening newscast the night before the Iowa State game, and it was as much a hit job as journalism. The Huskers were "leading the league in making bail," Goldberg said, and of course it included video of his press conference exchange with Osborne. There were several obvious

"Hard work pays off. I came into two-a-days
not thinking of where I would be during the season."

— AHMAN GREEN

"No other team loves each other
the way we do, baby! Nobody!"

— CHRISTIAN PETER PSYCH-UP VIDEO

inaccuracies, including identifying the oft-arrested victim in the Riley Washington case as a convenience store clerk. Goldberg's stated, and off-base, premise: Osborne was bringing Phillips back because it was all about the money. If you could get down to the true nub of why anyone associated with the Huskers wanted Phillips back, you'd probably find a myriad of motivations, including the belief they needed him to win another championship. But money surely wasn't among them. Regardless, it was another big national black eye for Osborne and Nebraska. CBS wasn't done yet. The CBS news magazine "48 Hours" later that month aired a piece on the Huskers. It generally portrayed Nebraska as a place in some parallel universe where woman-beaters are idolized, rapists are voted team captain, and fans paint their faces red and blindly cheer through it all.

Osborne was extremely upset with the treatment the Huskers got from CBS. In fact, the whole team was weary of the media blitz and the hits they were taking. "Nobody wants to talk about how Nebraska is trying to win another national championship," Jared Tomich said after the ISU game. "It's that we're a bunch of trouble-makers." The Huskers were at another boiling point, one that would best be defined by Christian Peter in a video message to his teammates just before the next week's game against Kansas.

One little spoken-of tradition within Nebraska football during the 1990s was the psych-up tape. Produced by team psychologist Stark in conjunction with the video crews from HuskerVision, it was a compilation of Husker football highlights set to music. The tape would be played to the Huskers on Saturdays just before they boarded the bus for games, intended to help get them into the right frame of mind. Even years later, some Huskers said they still got chills thinking about the psych-up tape the team watched just before taking the field in the Orange Bowl against Miami, set to Phil Collins' "In the Air Tonight." To paraphrase the lyrics, they had been waiting for that moment for all their lives. Emotionally, it hit all the right notes for a Husker team that went out and played inspired football. There was indeed something in the Miami air that night.

Psych-up videos during the 1995 season often also included specially taped inspirational messages from team captains. As it happened, the Kansas psych-up video was the first put together after Goldberg's piece had aired. Stark still had a copy of it years later, and another version somehow found its way on to the Internet video website YouTube. The Stark version bleeps out the considerable rough language Peter used in his message. The Internet version does not. There's some question which one the Huskers actually were shown that Saturday. One player called the

Stark copy "the Tom Osborne edition," recalling that the team watched the un-bleeped one (Osborne usually was doing other things to prepare for games and typically wouldn't watch the tapes with his players). Stark was almost positive he showed the bleeped-out version, though he acknowledged over time he allowed some profanity in the tapes, the players arguing the censorship robbed the messages of much of their emotion. Either way, nothing better sums up the team's internalized anger over how the Huskers were being portrayed — or how they used it to their advantage — than Peter's message to teammates before they took the field against the 10th-ranked Jayhawks.

It opened with Peter looking like he had just come off the practice field, wearing a gray Nebraska football T-shirt with the sleeves cut off over a long-sleeved top. HuskerVision crew members later would recall how he had paced in the hallway before the shoot, working up the emotion he needed to say what he wanted to say. He was at times breathless, at times raging, but always animated as he spoke into the camera about the Huskers' showdown in Lawrence.

"You know, [takes deep breath and starts calmly] a lot of people are trying to take us down. When you're up here [raises arm over head], everybody tries to take the cheap shots at you, always knocking you down. Saying things about your players. [Voice rising] Saying things about your head coach, the guy who would cut off his arm for any one of us! They're saying things about him! Fellas, that ain't right. We gotta go out there and show everybody what we can do. Because we are the best team in America! Everyone else is down here! Dogs sit at our feet!

"I tell you what, we're going down to play in their house. They think they got a f------ edge on us. [Voice again rising] We've been to places! We've played in the f------ Orange Bowl! We've played against Miami. We've gone into Colorado's house. We've been called f------ rapists. We've been called women beaters and everything else in the book. They think this place will be a bitch to play in. Nah. Nah. It ain't going to be nothing like that. We're going to go into this place! We're going to be called every f------ name in the book! But I tell you what, I tell you what. We are going to shut their mother f------ crowd up, and we're going to do it fast!"

Then Peter did something not seen in any of the other psych-up videos from that era. He called on all the players and coaches in the room to join hands. That would have included Lawrence Phillips, the man at the center of all the public outcry. Stark would recall it as one of the season's most powerful and unifying moments. No one could break the unity of this team. It was also, Stark said, another example of why no player in that era was a better motivator than Christian Peter.

"Fellas, [takes deep breath] what we got in this room is something special," Peter continued. "Why doesn't everybody grab each other's hands, coaches, players. . . . Feel the strength, baby. Feel the love running through. Feel the electricity, baby. We got something in this room [voice rising] that nobody can take from us! No other team plays like we do! No other team loves each other the way we do, baby! Nobody! And this has carried on throughout the season. From day one, we've stuck together. We've made it this far. We're on our 10th game, fellas, we've stuck through it all. People have tried taking f------ shots at us that aren't right, that aren't right! But through the love, for everybody caring for each other, we've stuck through and we've risen. We've risen to the top!"

There's little wonder why a charged-up Husker team went out two hours later and pummeled the Jayhawks. Kansas had its best team in decades, but it still was no match for this Nebraska team on a bitterly cold day. Frazier wowed the 20,000 Nebraska fans who took over much of KU's stadium with an option run that years later still showed up in highlight reels. Making instinctive cuts and stop-and-go moves, he faked three Jayhawks right out of their jock straps before being hauled down at the 1. He had no explanation afterward for how he did it. "I was just doing my best not to get tackled."

And then the Huskers came back to Lincoln and blasted Oklahoma, 37-0. Not only did the Blackshirts shut out the Sooners — the first time Nebraska had done so since World War II — they scored two touchdowns of their own on interception and fumble returns. In their last three games, the Blackshirts had now surrendered a total of 17 points. And Phillips for the first time offered glimpses of his early-season form. Against a stout front seven geared toward stopping the run, he led Nebraska rushers with a hard-earned 73 yards on 15 carries.

The OU win wrapped up Nebraska's fifth consecutive Big Eight championship. But most importantly, the top-ranked Huskers had punched their ticket to Tempe. The opponent in the national title game wouldn't be determined for another week, but pity to whoever it would be. At this point, it seemed the only team able to give Nebraska a fight was the Huskers themselves. In fact, that proved true during a practice right around that time — when a drill provoked a knockdown, drag-out brawl between the first-team offense and first-team defense.

Once a week, Osborne would pit the top units against each other in a goal-line drill,

"(A national championship) is all I think about. Well, maybe not all I think about. Just 90 percent."

— HUSKER FAN AFTER WIN OVER OKLAHOMA

going at it for about eight plays inside the 5. It was mano a mano, and there would be lots of pride on the line. If the offense could get into the end zone a couple of times, that was huge. If the defense could hold them out, there were big bragging rights there. "They were the enemy, and we would do whatever we could to make sure they didn't get in, and they took the same approach," Jason Peter recalled of the drill. "It was full-go, pure chaos."

But on this day, it got ugly. And not surprisingly, Christian Peter was at the center of it. Peter never had much use for offensive linemen anyway, usually referring to them as "slobs." But on one goal-line play, reserve offensive lineman Steve Volin cut-block Peter — going low to hit him on the thigh and take him down. It was a perfectly legal block, but it sometimes wasn't considered good form to cut a team-mate in practice, because you're hitting dangerously close to the knee. "Damn it, don't cut me!" Peter screamed. But Milt Tenopir insisted his guys not back off. We're going at game speed here. If the only way you can reach the guy is to cut him, cut him. So on the next play, Volin cut Peter again.

Then it was on. Peter went after Volin. Center Aaron Graham came to the defense of his linemate, jumping on Peter. If Jason Peter saw someone go after his brother, he wasn't going to stand around. And if the Peter brothers were involved, Wistrom and Tomich weren't going to be far behind. While the Nebraska coaches officially discouraged fighting, the D linemen had long figured out that McBride actually liked it when they scuffled. It showed they had fire in their bellies. Soon all the linemen on both sides of the ball were getting after it. At one point, legend has it, Christian Peter lifted Graham up off the ground and literally tossed him. "All I'll say is the captain of the offensive line got into it with the captain of the defensive line, and somebody went flying," Tony Veland recalled. The linebackers and running backs also squared off, and even some reserves not on the field got involved. "Dadgummit, knock it off!" Osborne called out, but he was pretty much powerless to stop this melee. This was an outlet the team had needed for some time. It ran its course and the guys finally got separated, Osborne sending Christian Peter and Volin up the stadium stairs.

But afterward in the locker room, it was as if nothing had happened. Guys laughed it off. If there's such a thing as a healthy fight within a team, this was it. The Huskers even turned it into another bonding experience, on both sides of the ball. This team had been hunkered down and fighting side by side for each other for nearly three months. Now more than ever, there was a feeling that whenever you went into battle, your teammates had your back.

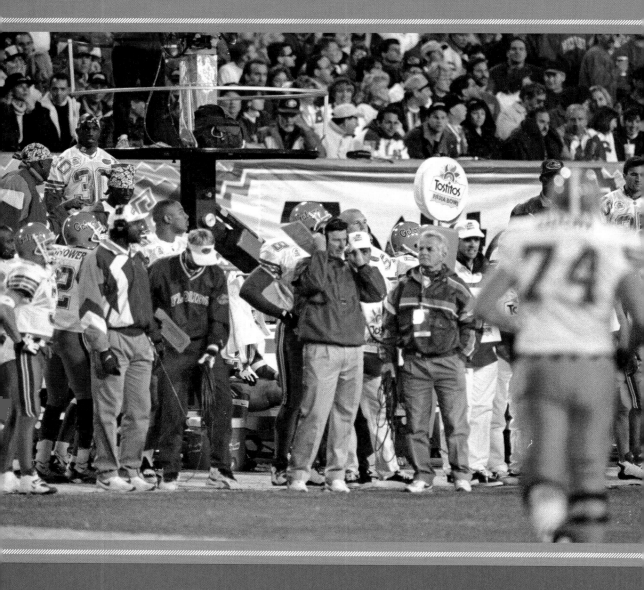

"He's a guy who is very confident and has
no fear of failure in anything he does."

— FLORIDA ASSISTANT ATHLETIC DIRECTOR NORM CARLSON
ON STEVE SPURRIER

Gator Bait?

A t a team function during the week of the Fiesta Bowl, Steve Spurrier was holding court, the Florida coach talking and yucking it up, a big smile on his face. Charlie McBride was just walking by when he was stunned to overhear the Florida coach jokingly say, "Where's this McBride guy?" The Nebraska defensive coordinator went right up and introduced himself to Spurrier, who seemed a little taken aback. Spurrier wasn't being rude, McBride later recalled. It was just Spurrier being Spurrier, the coach notorious for his bravado and supreme confidence in himself. But after McBride walked away and disappeared into the woodwork, his brief conversation with the Florida coach had left a big impression. For the rest of bowl preparations, McBride couldn't help thinking, "I want to see if we can't pour the coals to this guy."

In what was being billed as "The Duel in the Desert," the Huskers and the University of Florida Gators would be facing off January 2, 1996, for all the nachos in the Tostitos Fiesta Bowl. Part of the new Bowl Alliance, it was the first bowl game specifically set up to match the nation's No. 1 and No. 2 teams. Few college football games to that time had been subject to more pregame hype and hoopla. Much of the talk before the showdown centered on the two teams' contrasting offensive styles: the high-torque threshing machine from the Corn Belt against the high-tech, high-flying passing attack from the Sun Belt. But much like McBride in his encounter with Spurrier, the Huskers couldn't help but feel they weren't getting much respect.

Nebraska was coming in with the top ranking, a 24-game winning streak, three straight title game appearances and as defending national champion. But they also came in as an underdog in the eyes of many. ESPN's talking heads, Sports Illustrated and other national pundits were favoring the Gators. The media was completely enamored with Spurrier's "Fun 'N Gun" passing attack, though Nebraska's 52 points-a-game offense had led the nation in scoring. And in spite of Tom Osborne's reputation for innovation, Spurrier was the coach who was being labeled an offensive genius. One reporter termed the battle of the two offenses to be the Space Age vs. the Stone Age. Recalled Osborne: "The assumption was we were still back in the 1800s as far as football, and they were the guys who had it figured out."

Of course, no one had a higher opinion of the Florida attack than Spurrier himself.

"Field goals," the coach once boasted, "we don't kick many of those." Florida's quick-strike attack featured a fleet of receivers that Spurrier would send zipping all over the field. If defenders played off them, they'd find an open spot and get the ball. If defenders played them tight, they'd run right by them. And they had a quarterback who could get them the ball. Danny Wuerffel, a future Heisman winner, was known for pinpoint accuracy, having thrown for 35 touchdowns in the season. The Gators used their passing game to set up the run, a pair of good backs helping them average 174 yards on the ground. The Gator attack put up video-game offensive numbers, and many thought that wouldn't change in the Fiesta Bowl. "Spurrier, you give him a month and he'll dissect any defense," said Lee Corso, the ESPN personality and former college coach.

The Gators also were fast — too fast for Nebraska, it was said. Even after Nebraska's bowl performances against Florida State and Miami, a common story line bowl week became whether the Blackshirts had the speed to keep up with Florida. Most of the experts questioning Nebraska's speed also were noting that the game was being played on grass, the surface Florida had played nearly all its games on. Conversely, Nebraska had played every game on artificial turf. Corso said grass would slow down the Nebraska pass rush, keep Nebraska defenders from hanging with Florida receivers and make it harder for Tommie Frazier to get around the corner on the option. "I think grass will be very, very important," Corso said. "I think it's the determining factor in who wins the game." For his part, Osborne thought it was all a little ridiculous. He assured reporters that Nebraskans knew what grass was and had run on it some. To read about it all, it was as if everyone still thought this was Nebraska circa 1990. "Lord have mercy," guard Aaron Taylor muttered to an Omaha reporter as he stood to the side during one Fiesta Bowl media session. "You would think we'd get some respect sooner or later."

Such talk aside, there was a more complex and critical X's and O's battle going on behind the scenes. And it pitted the Blackshirts vs. the Fun 'n Gun, McBride vs. Spurrier. While Florida typically operated out of a one-back set, Spurrier frequently would empty the backfield, sending five receivers out on routes. One of the big questions going into the game was how Nebraska would defend this no-back set. Some teams would rush only three players and drop back eight into coverage to try to stay with all those receivers. But five-receiver sets also left a team vulnerable to blitzes, with no running back in to help protect the quarterback. Osborne recalled that one of Nebraska's coaches previously had heard someone ask Spurrier about the blitz threat against the no-back formation during a coaching clinic. The Florida coach wasn't concerned. They're not coming, he said. And if they do, a receiver will be open, and we'll get him the ball.

But the gambling McBride did plan to bring the heat. The blitz was part of the Blackshirts' identity. And while McBride and his staff would change some tendencies and throw in some new wrinkles, the game plan wasn't going to change. Whether Florida went one-back, no-backs or whatever, McBride's plan was to bring two or even three of the Blackshirt linebackers right up to the line of scrimmage. He often still would be rushing only four guys, but he'd keep Wuerffel and the Florida coaches guessing as to how many, and which, would be coming. Even if the Huskers didn't get great coverage, McBride figured he had guys who could get to Wuerffel awfully quickly.

McBride was pretty open about his primary strategy for stopping the Fun 'n Gun: shutting down the Florida running game. He said as much during a bowl week press conference, a comment that drew derisive laughter from reporters. Hadn't he heard? The Gators liked to throw the ball. But McBride was serious. If Nebraska shut down the Gators' running game and made them one-dimensional, the blitzing Blackshirts would really be able to target Wuerffel.

During bowl week, the Husker coaches sensed Florida's coaches were concerned about what McBride was going to do against the no-back set. Tenopir's offensive line counterpart from Florida actually brought it up as they sat together at a bowl luncheon. "I wouldn't empty the backfield," Milt Tenopir warned the Florida coach. Was Tenopir trying to stir the pot, knowing the Gator coaches were stressing over the issue? Tenopir later said no. It was just two coaching colleagues sitting down for a chat. The veteran Husker coach also was confident the Blackshirts would have a good plan, no matter what Spurrier did. Just weeks after the bowl game, Tenopir again talked to the Florida coach at a coaching convention. The coach said he had told Spurrier what Tenopir had said, but Spurrier wasn't overly concerned. They won't get to us, Spurrier had assured him.

However, Florida coaches weren't the only ones losing sleep over the coming battle. McBride always felt a special burden in these championship games. He couldn't help feeling that shortcomings on defense had cost Nebraska titles in the past. The 1983 Huskers had that world-beating offense but a defense that allowed a school-record 368 yards a game. They couldn't hold up their end of the deal in that heartbreaking 1984 Orange Bowl loss. And even after the 1994 title, McBride would not let such thoughts go. "It bothers me more than anything I've ever done in coaching,"

McBride still was saying years later. For that reason, McBride refused to put on his 1994 championship ring. He figured it should have come at least a decade earlier.

Now stopping the Fun 'n Gun was Charlie McBride's War. McBride and the Black-shirts were spending hours in meeting rooms, breaking down tape of Florida and drilling on the game plan. It was so exhausting that during one drawn-out session, backup defensive end Mike Rucker fell asleep. He must have had some kind of nightmare, because he woke up with a start, screaming out. Normally, a player fall-ing asleep during tape study would be doing some extra running after practice. But McBride took this as a sign the Blackshirts had had enough. He turned off the tape. We're done, he said. Let's go play some football. "Looking back," George Darlington said, "we were foolish to be as concerned as we were." Indeed, the Blackshirts' battle with the Fun 'n Gun aside, Nebraska and its coaches knew they had lots of advan-tages going for them heading into this game. And many of the Nebraska strengths were getting scant attention amid the media love affair with Spurrier's offense.

Nebraska had Frazier, who already had proven himself an unflappable, big-game quarterback in two previous championship games. This would be his fourth straight major bowl game against a top-three team, surely a first for any college quarterback. And now he was coming off a snub in the race for the Heisman. The trophy for college football's best player had been awarded to Ohio State's Eddie George. History would show the voters blew it. Frazier would go down as one of the greatest college quarterbacks ever. Lawrence Phillips indirectly may have cost Frazier the award, so many sportswriters being down on Nebraska. Frazier was gracious about his runner-up finish. A second national championship was what he was after, he said. But Osborne sensed that No. 15 was burning inside. In the last game of Frazier's illustrious career, Osborne figured Florida would pay for what had happened. For his own part during bowl week, Frazier had been smiling a lot and saying little. It was a good sign for Nebraska.

The Huskers were again confident in their trademark ability to physically beat down their opponent. The Gators had yet to face a team that would just come right at them on both sides of the ball. Though Osborne figured the Gators would score some, he still didn't think they were capable of getting a big lead against the Black-shirts. Then it would just be a matter of wearing them down. He figured Nebraska would win by a couple of scores in the end. As in bowls past, the Huskers had stayed physically sharp. They took little time off after the regular season and arrived in Tempe more than a week before the bowl. As always, they trucked half their weight room down from Lincoln, lifting throughout. And they ran some hard-hitting practices and scrimmages. "They worked us like Hebrew slaves," cornerback Michael Booker recalled. Conversely, Florida was counting on its ability to finesse, scheme and outrun the Huskers. Nebraska coaches later would hear from a Colorado coach who had visited a Florida practice that if you closed your eyes you wouldn't have known the Gators were practicing at all. There were hardly any pads popping. Nebraska is going to crush those guys, the coach thought. Against Nebraska, fancy schemes weren't going to cut it. Grant Wistrom may have put it best in the week leading up to the game: "They're a good team and everything. But you've still got to line up and play football."

The Huskers continued to play their us-against-the-world card. They were amazed at the disrespect. Wingback Clester Johnson at one point pulled aside Corso and challenged his prediction. "Have you looked at our offense?" he asked. When Aaron Graham was told by a Sports Illustrated reporter the magazine was picking the Gators, he begged for five minutes to convince him otherwise. "Never before have I felt so much confidence in this team," he said. "It's something I can't even describe." They were tired of being portrayed as the villains. Every time they faced the media, there were the questions about Phillips and the off-field problems. Most Fiesta stories mentioned Phillips and his assault. Almost never mentioned was that two of the starting Gator defenders who would be trying to tackle Phillips had been arrested in the previous year for assaults on women. Each had received a one-game suspension. Osborne was also none too happy the game was being televised by CBS, the same network whose news division had skewered his program. Most galling to the Huskers were the cheap shots and piling on related to Phillips. Sports Illustrated, for example, said that playing in national title games was becoming as "routine for the Huskers as fingerprinting and mug shots." The Huskers said all the right things during the week, not betraying just how infuriating it all was. But that kickoff just couldn't come fast enough for the Huskers. "They can call us heathens, America's Most Wanted or whatever they want. It doesn't bother us," Wistrom said during the week. "Those people aren't going to play the game or affect the outcome."

And the most overlooked Husker advantage: the old Lawrence Phillips was back. Osborne and the Huskers first saw that December 18 during a scrimmage inside Cook Pavilion, Nebraska's indoor practice facility. Working against the Blackshirts, Phillips took a swing pass for a touchdown. And then on a draw, he showed the acceleration of old, zooming up the middle through the entire defense for a score. The Huskers had seen this guy before. And even though it invited another round of negative publicity, Osborne the day after Christmas named Phillips the starter for

"If they give us a few seconds,
we'll have a good rush on them."

— JARED TOMICH

the championship game. To many, it was further proof that Phillips had come back to help Nebraska win the title. Osborne said Phillips had simply graded out above Green and the other backs and deserved to start. Going into the game, few were talking about Phillips other than to mention him as a black mark on the Husker program. But Osborne believed the old Lawrence Phillips would be the best player on the field on January 2.

During an otherwise yawner of a Fiesta Bowl media day that had some writers longing for the trash-talking Hurricanes, Phillips' past problems made him the center of attention. But in his first major interview session since he was suspended, Phillips acquitted himself well. Seeing a never-ending stream of reporters over a full 60 minutes, sweat ringing his mouth by the end, Phillips dodged only one query. "Next question," he said in a clear voice when asked to explain what had happened September 10. But he said he'd learned a lot about himself in the past months and was trying to control his anger. When asked what causes his anger, he said he didn't know. "I'm working on finding that out right now," he said. "I'm not used to talking to people. I'm used to keeping to myself. I'm working on being a better person and making up for my mistake. Now I think I deserve a chance to play."

Phillips was grateful for the chance. Jack Stark and the Husker captains put together one final psych-up tape for the team, played just before the Huskers headed to Sun Devil Stadium for the game. Tony Veland talked of how sick he was of hearing about the Fun 'N Gun, reeling off all the formidable weapons Nebraska was bringing to the table. Mark Gilman spoke of putting an end to all the Husker bashing. Phil Ellis told the team he'd give his "right nut" for any of them. Graham reminded the Huskers they'd played in these big games before. Christian Peter was his usual bombastic self. He said Nebraska's smash-mouth style was going to leave the Gators on their knees in the fourth quarter, just like "them pussies" from Miami. And for the first time all season, a non-captain delivered a video message to the team.

"I really appreciate you guys standing by me and supporting me and accepting me on the team," Lawrence Phillips said. "Really not making it a big issue with me coming back. Just being there. I love all you guys. And I hope we get it done." Just the fact Phillips was allowed to address the team in this forum was another testament to the way the Huskers were embracing their fallen teammate. Now at the end of a long and trying season, these guys were ready to go out one last time and play their guts out for each other.

A Fiesta in Fiesta

The way Sun Devil Stadium is laid out, it makes for an unusually long walk from the locker room to the playing field. But after Tom Osborne led his Huskers from the dim tunnel into the glare of the stadium lights, they could hardly believe their eyes. On a cool, starry night in Tempe, Nebraska's fans had painted the buff desert landscape red. Nearly two-thirds of the seats in the 77,000-seat stadium were filled by Husker fans with their cornheads, red sweatshirts, foam No. 1 fingers and "Go Big Red" chants. Take away all the Tostitos logos that were prominently displayed all over the field and stadium — about 70 in all — and the Tostitos Fiesta Bowl looked a little like game day in Lincoln.

Nebraska fans would seemingly go to any length to see their team, even willing to buy a season ticket in an opposing team's stadium to make sure they had a seat. They weren't about to miss the chance to see their Huskers try to become the first consensus back-to-back national champs in four decades. After all those years of playing Florida schools in Florida — seven times in its previous eight bowl games — in this one, Nebraska would finally have the home crowd advantage. "This thing is over," Phil Ellis thought as he took in the scene. Indeed, it would be one long, joyous and unforgettable night in Arizona for Ellis and up to 50,000 others dressed in red. The Huskers were about to crush Florida like a corn chip under foot.

Before the game, Osborne calmly chomped his gum as he walked around under the stadium lights giving his players words of encouragement. He felt oddly relaxed. He knew he had a confident team that was ready to play. In fact, just before the team had left the hotel, he had recited to the Huskers a Bible verse someone had just sent him, one that Osborne felt typified the character of this team.

> "I had a great career at Nebraska,
> and there's no better way to end it."
>
> — TOMMIE FRAZIER

"For God has not given us a spirit of timidity, but of power and love and self-discipline," read the verse from 2nd Timothy.

The coach wasn't out looking for converts, he'd say later. And he always thought it was ridiculous for anyone to believe God cares who wins a football game. But to Osborne, those particular words of Scripture well described these Huskers. They obviously were not afraid of any team. They were powerful. They cared about each other, their bonds only strengthening as adversity rose. And to him, they had great self-discipline. Those kinds of virtues often are rewarded, he told his team. "Go out and play with that in mind," Osborne told them. "You have certainly done everything you had to do to get here."

During warm-ups as a HuskerVision camera moved among the Huskers stretching on the field, you could see the confidence in their eyes. Said a fiery Mark Gilman: "We will not be denied."

"We're going to make some people real mad today," Tony Veland said.

"Let the Fun 'n Gun die," Grant Wistrom said. "Big Red is rolling tonight."

They were anxious and ready to show the Gators what Nebraska football was all about. But if the camera had made it over to the offensive line station, Milt Tenopir wasn't so sure about his own guys. The Pipeline had only warmed up a minute or two, and they all were sweating profusely. It seemed Chris Dishman had an aunt living in the Phoenix area who had taken in all the linemen and fed them homemade Mexican food all week. Tenopir figured they'd gained 10 pounds each. He shut warm-ups down early, deciding to wait until it was time to run a few snaps with the whole offense. Osborne, of course, noticed and asked Tenopir what was going on. Are you sure they're ready? "Coach, just look at them. They're all lathered up," Tenopir replied. He didn't tell Osborne, but he worried whether they'd even make it out of the first quarter. He would laugh about his concerns years later. "They came out like biting sows," he said. "They were something."

That described the entire Husker team. After the Gators took the opening kickoff back nearly 40 yards to set up a field goal, Nebraska answered. Lawrence Phillips ran 23 yards through a gaping hole to get the Huskers into Gator territory. Frazier kept the drive alive on a third-down play by bulling through three Gator defenders for four yards. Then on first down, Osborne turned to a new play he'd installed just for this game.

The I-back counter sweep was a bread-and-butter play for the Huskers, and they also often ran one of their most effective pass plays off of the look, Frazier faking the handoff, rolling out and hitting a tight end downfield. Osborne knew the Gators would be well-schooled in both of those plays. But this time Osborne created a new variation. The play had worked great in practice leading up to the bowl, and Osborne sent it in now: Fake 42 Counter Sweep Screen Left. Frazier took the snap, faked the handoff to Phillips on a run to the left and rolled right as if to pass downfield to the crossing tight end. Instead he suddenly turned around and zinged a pass all the way back across the field to Phillips, who had continued toward the left sideline after the fake. Osborne couldn't have drawn it up better. The entire Gator defense had been sucked over to Frazier's side of the field, the only bodies anywhere near Phillips being the two offensive linemen who had pulled with him on the fake counter. Phillips hardly needed his two huge escorts as he powered into the end zone, tumbling over the goal line to complete the 16-yard score. The Gators didn't know what had hit them. It wasn't hard to read Steve Spurrier's lips after he watched the play unfold from the sideline: What was that? After a blocked extra point, the Huskers led 6-3.

Later in the first quarter, Danny Wuerffel again took the Gators down the field, capping a scoring drive with a one-yard sneak. The Florida quarterback was dropping back just three steps and hitting quick slants down the field to beat the Husker rush. It appeared to back up those who questioned whether McBride and the Black-shirts could keep up with the Fun 'n Gun. "Nebraska better not get too far behind," CBS announcer Jim Nantz said after the Wuerffel TD put the Gators up 10-6. These early leads by Florida were only the second and third times all season Nebraska had trailed.

Again, Nebraska would not be behind for long. The Huskers scored in just five plays, running the ball right at the Gators. The drive was capped by Phillips, who ripped off one of the most dynamic runs of his Husker career. Taking the ball on a simple dive play up the middle, he found no hole and broke the run to the outside, eluding a tackler. He darted to the inside and broke two more tackles, and then simply outran everyone else 42 yards to the end zone. For most Husker fans, a run Frazier would break off later in the game through a tired and dispirited Gator defense would be the most memorable of the game. But to Husker players, no run surpassed Phillips' — one of the best any of them had ever seen. Among those marveling was Frazier. As the Husker quarterback watched Phillips gallop like a thoroughbred down the field, he knew this would be the junior's last game as a Husker. Even with

"They got tired of getting blocked,
and we wore them down."

— LAWRENCE PHILLIPS

the running back's baggage, anyone could see Phillips was a sure-fire first-round NFL draft pick.

With the Huskers now up 13-10, this was looking like the wide-open offensive shootout it had been billed to be. But the Phillips score, coming on the second play of the second quarter, actually had kicked off what would build into one of the most dominant periods in more than a century of Nebraska football. The next points in the Nebraska scoring barrage would be delivered by McBride's Blackshirts — and by a player who was running the wrong assignment.

A pair of penalties backed the Gators back up to their own 8. Even up against his own end zone, the brash Spurrier still wasn't afraid to throw the ball. Still more brazenly, he went with his no-back set. McBride decided to go after Wuerffel, sending weak-side linebacker Terrell Farley on a blitz. Farley walked up to the line before the snap and smiled right at Wuerffel, and then was on the Florida quarterback before he could even think. Wuerffel fought to reach the ball just over the goal-line before going down to the turf. The Blackshirts thought they had the safety. Farley and fellow linebacker Jamel Williams were upset, both unsuccessfully pleading the case.

As the Gators huddled up again, McBride made his next move, this time calling for the Huskers to rush four and drop seven back into zone coverage. But just before the snap, there was suddenly confusion within the Husker formation. Even down inside the 1, the cocky Spurrier again emptied his backfield, sending the running back in motion. Seeing that, middle linebacker Doug Colman, quarterbacking the defense, got excited and checked into another defense, one calling for him and Jamel Williams to go in on an all-out blitz. But the problem was the defense McBride had called was one the Blackshirts were never supposed to check out of. As a result, guys didn't know what to do. Some went with the check. Others recognized the mistake and stuck with the original call. It left the Husker secondary trying to cover five Gator receivers with a confused mix of zone and man-to-man coverage. Veland, the safety responsible for setting the Husker pass coverages, could see the Blackshirts weren't on the same page. He frantically tried to get Williams' attention, wanting him to stick with the original call and drop into coverage. But there was no stopping Williams. As soon as Colman made the check, the linebacker's eyes lit up. He already had Wuerffel locked in his sights. As Williams recalled years later: "I was going regardless. Once (Colman) said that, it was over."

With Williams and Colman blitzing, unintentional as it was, Nebraska had six guys charging in and only five linemen to block them. "It was like Christmas all over again," McBride recalled years later. On the snap, Colman surged up the middle. And Williams came flying around the edge like the 10.5-second 100-meter man that he was. Even if Spurrier had anticipated the Huskers might all-out blitz his no-back set, he surely didn't realize they'd be coming as fast as they did. Because few linebackers in college football could run like Williams.

Williams had led the state of Indiana in rushing in high school. He didn't know anything about Nebraska when the Huskers started recruiting him out of that basketball hotbed, but a friend was a huge Husker fan and sent in the initial paperwork for him. Williams had once hoped to play I-back for the Huskers, but a knee injury in a high school all-star game put an end to that. The NU coaches, who always wanted him on defense, convinced him the knee would take less of a pounding on that side of the ball. The junior ultimately found a home at strongside linebacker. Now he was about to deliver the biggest play of his Husker career.

The guard locked up with Colman and Williams ran right by them, untouched. He got a little lucky that Wuerffel turned his back to his side, never seeing the Husker blazer coming. Williams hit Wuerffel like a bolt of lightning and drove him into the back of the end zone. There was no doubt about this safety call. For the second straight year, the Nebraska defense had scored a momentum-grabbing safety in the national championship game. Looking back, if there was one signature play to define the speed transformation of the Huskers in this era, this was it.

After Wuerffel went down, the Blackshirts were jumping all over Williams and each other. "You know you weren't supposed to go," Veland told Williams when they reached the sidelines. Oh, well. They just laughed. It was a lucky play all the Blackshirts could laugh about years later. "I don't think we had everyone covered," Darlington recalled. "But because of Jamel Williams' exceptional speed at a position you don't expect a blitzer to run that fast, a partial screw-up resulted in a safety."

Now it was all Nebraska. Taking Florida's free kick, the Huskers scored again, this time in only seven plays. Frazier provided the key play on a third-and-seven. Running a quarterback draw, he bumped into the back of his own lineman, bounced off two tacklers and then squirted 32 yards to the Florida 16. Ahman Green pounded it in a minute later from the 1. The Huskers minutes later added a field goal to make it 25-10.

The Blackshirts by now had the Gators flummoxed. Per their plan, the Huskers had shut down Florida's running game. The Gators would gain only 12 rushing yards on

"A lot of people were talking about their offense. They aren't saying anything now."

— JAMEL WILLIAMS

21 carries, a figure that turned to minus-28 when you threw in 40 yards of losses on quarterback sacks. And the Florida coaches by now had made a rude discovery. Going in, they'd see Farley or Williams covering a wide receiver and likely believe they had a great matchup. It didn't work out that way at all. Despite all the talk going into the game about Florida's speed, it became obvious to Nebraska's coaches that their outside linebackers actually were faster than the Gator receivers.

And McBride kept bringing the pressure. On some plays, McBride was running zone blitzes, with one or two of the defensive linemen dropping off into pass coverage to free linebackers or safeties to come after the quarterback. The zone blitz had been popularized by the Pittsburgh Steelers, and the Huskers had used the defense as part of its mix in recent years. Nebraska had athletic defensive linemen who could make such a scheme work. But against Kansas earlier in the season, the Huskers' six zone blitzes had resulted in six Jayhawk pass completions. "I'm sure Florida's coaches figured we wouldn't be stupid enough to run that coverage," Darlington recalled. But the Nebraska coaches were that stupid. And on the Gators' next possession, it paid off.

After the Gators got their only first down of the quarter on a Blackshirt offside penalty, Wuerffel again dropped back to pass. This time he had a running back to help block, but Nebraska ran a zone blitz that jumbled the Gator pass protection. Jared Tomich and reserve defensive tackle Scott Saltsman dropped back into coverage so Williams and Farley both could come hard around the corner. As the pocket was collapsing, Farley pushed a big lineman into Wuerffel's face, and the quarterback floated an ill-advised pass downfield.

Going into the game, everyone knew the Gators would be trying to pick on Michael Booker, the junior who had stepped into Barron Miles' old cornerback spot. Even Booker knew it, telling everyone back home in Oceanside, California, the Gators would be coming after him. But he also told them he was going to pick one off and bring it back. On this play, Booker did just that, slipping in front of Ike Hilliard at the Florida 42, gathering the ball in and taking it all the way back for six. If Spurrier had been wearing his trademark visor during this night game, he surely would have thrown it down in disgust about now. Instead he just grimaced and shook his head, staring vacantly into the distance. The Fun 'n Gun was done. Checkmate Charlie McBride.

The Gators were out of answers on both sides of the ball. This would be the longest night of Spurrier's coaching career. Before the quarter was over, the Blackshirts would sack Wuerffel twice more, both again coming on zone-blitz plays where tackle Jason Peter dropped back into pass coverage. Then Kris Brown tacked on another field goal to make it 35-10. The second-quarter numbers: Nebraska outscored the Gators 29-0, tallying the most points any team had ever put up in one quarter in bowl history. "We have no answers, no answers," a humbled Spurrier would say later. "They were just too good for us."

The game was essentially over. But Osborne still was exhorting his players to stay after the Gators, telling them in the locker room at halftime he didn't care what the score was. They needed to hit them even harder, to play "very, very physical." His players said later the coach seemed fired up, at least by Osborne standards. "One last thing, fellas. You've got a chance to make a statement. Not an ugly statement, but a chance to make a statement to show who the best football team in the United States is. And, by golly, this half, let's let it all fly."

His words suggested that this one meant something to Osborne. Was this a chance to stick it to his critics? Asked about it years later, he dismissed it as a typical halftime speech for a blowout. Teams can recharge and refocus at halftime and turn things around. If that truly was the case, Osborne may have been the only person in the stadium who thought that was even possible on this night. By this point, it didn't even look as if the Gators wanted to be on the same field as Nebraska.

Either way, the Huskers didn't let up, continuing to pile up the punishing hits and the points. The second half became the joyride that, absent off-field drama, the whole season should have been. Late in the second half, Phillips stiff-armed a Gator during a nice run along the sidelines, ironically looking much like the iconic stiff-arm trophy that at one time could have been his. He would pick up one more touchdown in the fourth quarter on a 15-yard run, finishing his final game as a Husker with 165 yards on 25 carries and three scores. "How do I look now?" he was overheard screaming on the sidelines at one point. "How do I look now?" Like a guy ready to skip his senior season. Frazier was right. Phillips and Osborne were indeed now both ready for him to move on, the running back taking his mixed legacy into a future filled with both promise and peril.

But it was Frazier who would leave the biggest mark in the game's second half, firmly cementing his place in Nebraska football history. Early on, he scored the touchdown that iced the game beyond any reasonable doubt. On a third-and-long play, Frazier ran a quarterback draw play right into the teeth of a blitz and ripped 35 yards up the middle for a score. As he strutted into the end zone, he held up an index finger to the crowd. If the sportswriters didn't wish they could have their Heisman votes back after that run, they surely did after Nebraska's next possession. That's when Frazier capped his Husker career with a run for the ages.

Rolling right on a sprint option, Frazier showed his strength by fighting off a tackler just past the line of scrimmage, and then was wrapped up by two Gators, one trying to strip the ball. Three other Gators converged. Frazier kept his legs churning and escaped them all, and then fought through one more defender who ran up and tried to corral him as he broke from the pack. Suddenly Frazier was sprinting all alone down the sideline. He reached the end zone and looked back, shaking his head in disbelief. The Gators couldn't believe it, either. At least seven of them had a shot at him. Afterward, the Gators admitted they'd been surprised by the Nebraska quarterback's toughness. "We had heard he was kind of a crybaby when things didn't go his way," Florida's Ben Hanks said. "But he showed our team he's a guy with a lot of character."

Frazier for the game rushed for 199 yards and a pair of touchdowns. For the third straight year, Frazier was the MVP of the national championship game. One other thing also was now as crystal clear as Nebraska's pair of national championship trophies: Tommie Frazier was the best player Nebraska ever had behind center. You could look at all kinds of numbers to try to back that up, but you really needed just a couple: 33-3. That was Frazier's record in four years as Nebraska's starter. It was a sterling 28-1 over the last three. The final touchdown of Touchdown Tommie's career wasn't his best, but it's one that would visually define his Husker legacy. It was also this Nebraska season in microcosm: Taking hit after hit after hit, but refusing to go down, refusing to be stopped.

The unforgettable Christian Peter also would have one final great moment as a Husker in the second half, and true to form it was a comic one. After the Gators returned a kickoff for a touchdown, Osborne put the starters back in to defend the two-point conversion attempt. The play broke down, the ball ended up on the field, Peter scooped it up and started rumbling the other way. He broke out of his lumbering gait to prance the final 10 yards into the end zone and then was hauled down by Colman from behind. Peter just lay there, exhausted, but it had all been for naught. The refs had blown the ball dead 90 yards earlier. "For crying out loud," he wailed afterward. "I about had a heart attack at the 10." It was an appropriate capper to a laugher of a game.

"We felt if we could play our style
of football — which is physical —
we could beat these guys up."

— CHRISTIAN PETER

"It wasn't ho-hum, certainly.
But it was more matter of fact."

— TOM OSBORNE, COMPARING HIS SECOND NATIONAL TITLE TO HIS FIRST

Osborne mercifully had Matt Turman take a knee at the Gator 1 on the last play. As the final gun sounded, McBride looked up at the scoreboard reading 62-24 Huskers and winked to a reporter. "Now you know why Lee Corso doesn't coach anymore." McBride's men in black had sacked Wuerffel seven times — four coming off of blitzes — and intercepted him three more. They held the high-powered Gators to 269 yards, half their average. McBride should have felt free to wear this championship ring. Despite that loss in the 1983 championship game. And despite all the awful things Husker fans had said about him over the years. This was the night that cast McBride's Nebraska legacy as that of a defensive whiz. Over time, no member of Osborne's staff would be more fondly remembered by fans.

The Cornhuskers had completed their imperfectly perfect 12-0 season, repeating as national champions in convincing fashion. The old saying is that the second championship always comes harder than the first. But somebody forget to tell that to this Nebraska team. And if that first title had been for Nebraska's long-suffering fans, this one had been for the history books. After this ridiculously easy victory, you no longer could just talk about these untouchable Huskers as the best team in the country. You had to begin to consider whether this was the best team ever to strap on helmets in a college football game.

Their 62 points were the second-highest ever in a bowl. No bowl team had ever topped the 524 yards the Huskers ran up on the ground. For the year, Nebraska outscored its opponents by an average of 53-15, the victory margin against Florida actually equaling the Huskers' 38-point average for the season. They demolished the teams that ended up second (Florida), fifth (Colorado), seventh (Kansas State) and ninth (Kansas) in the final AP Top 10. During 720 minutes of football, they had trailed for less than 14. No team was closer than 11 points of them at halftime. No team got closer than 10 after the half. Their biggest deficit of the season: 7-0.

If this team had any peers, they certainly weren't playing college football in 1995. You'd more likely have to go back to legendary Notre Dame teams, Oklahoma of the 1950s or this team's own kin, the 1971 Cornhuskers. Terry Donahue, the former UCLA coach and color commentator for CBS, was among those who immediately recognized the historic nature of what everyone had just witnessed: "We may have seen the greatest team in the history of college football."

The team's legacy would only grow with time. Tom Osborne's 1995 Cornhuskers would consistently compete at the top with the 1971 Huskers when pundits in subsequent years ranked the greatest college teams of all time. The Sagarin computer ratings, looking since 1956 at each team's strength of schedule and how each performed against it, put the 1995 Huskers a clear No. 1, just ahead of 1971 Nebraska. One ESPN exercise ranked the Huskers as the No. 4 all-time great team out of any sport — right up there with the 1985 Chicago Bears and 1927 Yankees. Outside of the NFL, this was arguably the most fearsome collection of football players ever put together.

As he left the sideline, Osborne got the traditional Gatorade bath from Frazier and others. But the celebration did not compare to the pandemonium seen on the Orange Bowl field the previous year. It certainly wasn't a ho-hum deal, as Osborne would put it. But it was like this one had been expected, almost routine. Players said it still was satisfying and sweet. "We wanted to show people that we're not a bunch of bad guys," Graham said. "We're a bunch of college students who love to play football." Said Frazier: "When you go through everything we did and still defend your title, it makes it even more special."

It was notable that both Huskers had invoked the off-field problems in assessing the season. Even in celebration, the Phillips controversy — and its sting — was never far from the surface. At the very moment the Huskers were being recognized for winning, the on-field reporter from those buzz-killers at CBS alluded to the cloud. How does it feel, she asked Osborne, to win a championship after all the team has been through? "We'll take it," Osborne responded curtly, feeling the time and place for the question had been inappropriate. He repeated his belief that he believed his team had great character. But the win did nothing to change the nation's sour opinion of this team. In the eyes of many, there always would be tarnish on this trophy and an asterisk next to the team's accomplishments in the record book. Unlike the 1994 champions, who were feted by President Clinton for their "character, tenacity and spirit," there would be no White House invitation for these Huskers. Justified or not, this title wouldn't be celebrated by anyone outside of Nebraska and its fans.

Osborne barely cracked a smile during all the post-game proceedings. Still, there was no doubt he was fond of this team, even after all it had put him through. It was the way they had responded to the adversity that he so admired. They were talented at every position, but they also were unselfish, disciplined, focused and driven, never self-centered, and they never took anything for granted. And their togetherness would stick with him forever. In the locker room, Osborne told the Huskers how proud he was of what they'd accomplished. "A lot of it was because you simply cared about each other and worked hard," he said. Then his eyes glistened.

"You'll remember this, and I'll remember you. We appreciate everything you guys have done."

Now that the season was over, Osborne could finally say it. This was his best team, he told reporters, his most complete team. But his 23rd team also had admittedly been a trying one to coach. By the end, it seemed to those watching Osborne in his post-game press conference that the weight of the past four months had left its imprint on his face. "Why don't you go on to basketball," he told reporters at one point. He was joking, but there was truth in it, too. It had been both a great and terrible year, he said, a season that at times had him running on empty. He was happy about the championship. But he was even happier at the moment that this season was over.

It would become the legacy of the 1995 Cornhuskers, a team that produced some of the program's greatest days on the field and worst days off of it. But as the Huskers celebrated their back-to-back titles in the desert that night, they didn't realize that their very worst day was yet to come.

"God allowed Brook to throw one more pass today. The question is simply this: Will we receive it?"

— RON BROWN AT BROOK BERRINGER'S FUNERAL

One Final Blow

I t had not at all been the senior year Brook Berringer was hoping for. He had been absolutely critical to the Huskers winning the national title in 1994, leading the offense during seven do-or-die wins. But other than when he took over for an injured Tommie Frazier in the Michigan State game, he had seen nothing but mop-up duty for the 1995 champions. Given the previous year's success, everyone knew it had to be tough. Teammates felt for him. But what could you do? He was behind Frazier, who had a shoulda-been Heisman season.

True to his character, though, Berringer's disappointment rarely showed. He quietly walked out of the team meeting where Frazier was named the starter. He continued to work hard in practice to get better every day. He remained confident in his abilities. And when called on to play, he did his job with dignity, even though it usually meant simply handing off to reserve running backs with the game in hand. He could have been a huge distraction on this team but did nothing to shake the chemistry that was its great strength. While traveling on a bus during Fiesta Bowl week, Berringer told Jack Stark of his frustrations. "I'm competitive. I want to play," he said. "This has been tough on me." But he said he understood it and wasn't making an issue of it. It was what was best for the team.

Berringer epitomized what it meant to be a team player. The Huskers respected him as much for that as for what he'd accomplished on the field the previous year. Berringer also continued to be one of the team's best goodwill ambassadors, regularly visiting with children in schools and hospitals. And he remained extremely popular among Husker fans. Once when he was out hunting, several pickup trucks pulled up with six or seven people toting posters and other memorabilia for him to sign. He signed them all. Berringer was leaving Lincoln with a legacy, a young man who whenever called upon always delivered. Despite the nation's preoccupation with Lawrence Phillips, it arguably was Berringer who best defined the essence of the Nebraska program.

Tom Osborne, in particular, had a special appreciation for Berringer. He was close to all his quarterbacks, spending an hour and a half in meetings with them almost every day. But he'd grown particularly fond of this quarterback over the past two years. With their shared love of the outdoors and strong Christian faith, Osborne considered him a friend. And Osborne admired and respected the way Berringer dealt with standing on the sidelines his senior season. Osborne believed the Huskers would have gone undefeated with either Berringer or Frazier at the helm. The coach had agonized over how to play Berringer, knowing he deserved the chance but not wanting to mess with the delicate timing of the option. The quarterback's attitude had eased the coach's burden. It pleased Osborne that in the final quarter of the Fiesta Bowl, he'd been able to call a quarterback sneak down by the goal line, enabling Berringer to score one last touchdown as a Husker.

Now as Berringer was leaving the program, it appeared all his hard work and dedication was about to be rewarded. He was projected to be a mid-round pick in the coming NFL draft. Berringer actually was a better NFL quarterback prospect than Frazier. He had the prototypical NFL body type and a decent pro-quality arm. If the NFL didn't work out, he had his business degree in hand and thoughts of possibly following his uncle into a career as a commercial pilot. He had a wonderful girlfriend, too, a medical student. Berringer was truly ready to take flight, leaving nothing but fond memories of his days in Lincoln. Weeks earlier during filming of a HuskerVision documentary on the '95 season, Berringer wore his Nebraska letterman's jacket and spoke with pride of his college career. "Ten or 20 years from now," he said, "I'll still be telling people what it was like to play for Nebraska and the experience of being a Husker."

If only he would have had that chance. On Thursday, April 18, Berringer was staring at one of the biggest weekends of his life. That night, he was to speak at a state Fellowship of Christian Athletes banquet. The next night — on the eve of the Huskers' annual spring game — there'd be a formal dinner with all the other departing senior football players. That would be followed by a huge Memorial Stadium ceremony in which Berringer and the rest of the Huskers would receive their national championship rings. On Saturday, Berringer would be back in Goodland, Kansas, watching with his family as his name was called in the NFL draft. His mom had even installed a satellite dish just so they could pull in ESPN2, which was carrying the draft live.

With all of this in front of him that afternoon, it seemed to Berringer a good time to get away and go flying. Berringer had developed a relationship with a Lincoln man who owned a Piper Cub and allowed him to borrow it. Berringer's girlfriend was in town for the championship celebration. Her brother, 32-year-old Tobey Lake, joined Berringer on the trip out to the small rural airstrip just outside Lincoln.

"Denial is the first thing that set in.
You're thinking, 'No way, I just saw this guy.'"

— DAMON BENNING

As much as Berringer loved flying, he knew it wasn't fun and games. He had a healthy respect for its dangers. It was a cloudless, warm and windy day, with gusts of up to 28 mph. But Berringer had some experience in such conditions when he and Lake climbed into the World War II-era single-engine plane. Berringer fired up the engine and around 2:30 p.m. lifted off from the grassy runway. He ascended over a house and a windbreak into a beautiful clear blue sky. Moments like this were why he flew.

A pair of farmers witnessed what happened next. They said the plane was about 250 feet into its climb when its engine sputtered and coughed. Federal investigators would later determine Berringer had failed to ensure that the plane's fuel selector was fully in the "on" position before takeoff. That caused the plane to be starved of fuel during its climb. The plane then shuddered, lost airspeed and stalled. The left wing dropped, sending the plane plummeting to earth like a stone. Berringer had no hope of pulling out of the sheer nose-first dive. The plane exploded on impact in an alfalfa field and burst into flames.

Osborne had just finished a workout that afternoon when his secretary tracked him down, her face ashen. Shocked and dismayed, Osborne, Ron Brown, Turner Gill and Frank Solich climbed into a van and drove to the crash site. They were carrying Berringer's dental records and the mold for his mouthpiece — requested by sheriff's investigators trying to identify the two bodies. The coaches passed through a checkpoint filled with media and were escorted down a narrow road to the crash site. The plane was just in the distance, surrounded by emergency vehicles and still smoldering. There was almost nothing left of it or its occupants. Years later, Osborne still vividly remembered the sight and the awful smell.

Osborne called Jan Berringer, Brook's mom. There's been an accident, he told her. She was in some denial, asking Osborne whether Brook had thrown out an elbow. No, I'm out here in the country, Osborne replied. She then asked whether he'd had a hunting accident.

"No, there was an airplane involved," he said. Jan Berringer's heart sank right down to her feet. On the other end of the line, Osborne was almost as devastated. He would shed a lot of tears over the next several days. Some 17 years later, his eyes still welled up in recalling the time. "It came about as close as it could to losing one of my own children," he said.

Osborne attended the FCA banquet that night. He hoped against all hope that Berringer would show up to give his testimonial. He had been the night's first scheduled speaker. Osborne later got a call during the event confirming that the dental records had identified Berringer's body. Many tearful remembrances were offered at the banquet. It was a powerful night.

The championship celebration for the next night was canceled. Saturday's spring game turned into a wake. Some fans wore black shirts with Berringer's No. 18 jersey number. The game was preceded by a stirring video tribute to the fallen Husker on the Memorial Stadium video screens. It left few dry eyes in the old gray house. There were football highlights and images of Berringer reading "Green Eggs and Ham" to first-graders. At another point in the video, Berringer talked about his late father, who he said watched his games as a Husker from "the best seat in the house." One of the few comforts anyone took in all this was that Berringer was now with his dad.

Berringer's death was a huge shock to his teammates, and almost all of them years later remembered where they were when they first heard of it. When you're that young and strong, you just have a feeling you're going to live forever. They already had learned so many lessons together: Dealing with adversity. Hanging together. Accepting responsibility for your actions. Standing up for your convictions. Now Brook had taught them the most painful lesson of all — Live every day to the absolute fullest.

Dozens of Husker players, staffers and coaches traveled by bus to Goodland for Berringer's funeral. Standing near Berringer's casket, the quarterback's Husker helmet on top, Osborne told those gathered he was a better person for having known Berringer. "I've coached more than 2,000 players," he said, "and there is no one I coached who had better character than Brook Berringer." It wasn't just those Berringer knew who were touched by him. His mom would receive 10,000 letters of condolence, most from people she had never met. And as the funeral procession moved down the highway, people stood along the side holding Husker flags, a sight that again moved Osborne to tears. It spoke to the kind of legacy Berringer had left behind.

The death of Brook Berringer was one final, devastating blow for a team that had been through so much already. And its timing sucked still more joy out of what should have been the most satisfying of seasons. As Tom Osborne and the Huskers moved on from the spring game, they were ready to put 1995 completely behind them, from its great highs to tremendous lows. They certainly didn't ever want to go through another year like this one.

Osborne probably said it best 17 years later when he bluntly summed up the 1995 season: "It was a great year from the standpoint of our football team. But it was my worst year of coaching."

The Final Journey

"I think one of the big things we're
all going to try to do is to instill
that confidence we had two years ago."

— JASON PETER BEFORE THE 1997 SEASON

A Frosty Reception

I
n the Huskers' first fall scrimmage of the 1996 season, new quarterback Scott Frost broke loose down the field on a bootleg. The native of Wood River, Nebraska, had his eyes locked on the cornerback along the left sideline, putting a stiff arm on the Blackshirt and turning toward the middle of the field. He never saw Eric Stokes coming. The senior safety lowered his head and shoulder and blasted Frost almost head-on. The vicious hit sent Frost flipping backwards and literally de-cleated him, both of his shoes flying off.

After transferring from Stanford and being forced to sit out the 1995 season, Frost had been looking forward to taking the first hits of this new season. This hit from Stokes — one Frost later recalled as the hardest he ever took on a football field — had been a little more than he'd been hoping for. But the sturdy, 6-foot-3, 215-pounder rolled with it. While dazed, he instinctively popped up, retrieved his shoes and returned to the huddle, later giving his teammate credit. "He got a good piece of me," he said.

With the pads again clashing in Memorial Stadium, excitement was once more rising within the Husker Nation. The Huskers were on an incredible roll, winning 25 straight en route to those two national titles. And now Frost and his teammates were chasing history. They openly talked about a three-peat, something no major college school had ever pulled off in the six decades since the poll system had been established. There was no reason to think they couldn't get it done. They likely would be favored to win every game on their schedule. And for the first time in their recent run, the Huskers were starting the year atop the polls.

To hear the Huskers speak, they were as hungry as ever. "I still haven't forgotten about the Florida State game," said senior rush end Jared Tomich. Yes, he was talking about the 1994 Orange Bowl, some two and a half years earlier. That was the

"There are going to be some doubts
anytime a guy is new in the offense."

— SCOTT FROST BEFORE THE 1996 SEASON

only game he and other Husker seniors had ever lost, the group entering its final year with an unheard-of 36-1 mark. Tom Osborne wasn't feeling any pressure to win another title. Pressure, he knew from experience, is when you go 22 years without winning one. And that was perhaps the most amazing thing about this team's roll. Just two years earlier, the college football world had wondered whether Tom Osborne would ever win a national championship. Now you had to wonder when he would ever lose one.

Clearly the biggest question heading into the season was Frost. After somehow turning the simple 105-mile trip between Wood River and Memorial Stadium into a circuitous one by way of northern California, the 21-year-old had won the battle to be Nebraska's No. 1 quarterback. But could he fill the oversized Adidas shoes left by Tommie Frazier? Could he take Nebraska to the finish again? About the only thing his teammates knew for sure at this point was that he could take a hit.

To succeed as Nebraska's quarterback, Frost would indeed need to be able to take hits — and not just on the field. And he would need to be tough, not just physically. He initially faced hazing, cold shoulders and hard shots from his new teammates, many of whom harbored unspoken resentments. He would face boos, belittlement and doubts from his team's own fans. In fact, much of Frost's career at Nebraska would come to be defined by his struggle to gain acceptance, from fans and teammates alike. And it was all rooted in the fact Frost had done something considered next to heresy for a high school football star growing up in Nebraska: When Tom Osborne came offering a scholarship, Frost had said no.

Scott Frost had been the biggest thing to come to Wood River since the old Lincoln Highway. In the fall of 1992, the towheaded quarterback had the central Nebraska farm community of 1,100 buzzing, ranking as one of the nation's best prep players. The four-year starter had run and passed for more than 11,000 yards in his career, almost double the Nebraska state record and the third-most in national history. He was a Parade All-American, but that was only the beginning of the hype. He had been featured in a full-page ad in Sports Illustrated as the Old Spice Athlete of the Month. ESPN brought its cameras to town, showing images of Frost spearheading Wood River's veer running attack on a gridiron flanked by cornfields. Frost was such a tremendous all-around athlete, he was a state champion in both the shot put and the 110-meter high hurdles. He also grew up in a football family, his dad the head coach at Wood River, his mom the receivers coach. A coach is often accused of favoritism if he plays his own son at quarterback. But you didn't hear talk like that around Wood River.

While just about every school in the country wanted him, it seemed only natural Frost would end up down in Lincoln. Home-state kid. Grew up worshiping Turner Gill and rooting for the Huskers. Tools that seemed perfectly honed for the deadly Nebraska run-and-pass option attack. His dad had even been a Husker, the last starting wingback at Nebraska before a guy named Johnny Rodgers came along. Dad Larry wasn't even the best athlete in the family. Scott's mom, Carol, had been a 1968 Olympian in the shot put and had once coached the women's track team at Nebraska. It was actually Osborne, then a young assistant on Bob Devaney's staff, who had first recruited Larry Frost to Lincoln in the early 1960s. Devaney had sent Osborne to watch the kid from tiny Malcolm, Nebraska, play, Osborne reporting back the next day that Frost had carried the ball eight times and scored eight touchdowns. Nobody tackled him. Osborne had worked even harder to land Larry's son, one day calling Scott seven times. With Scott's athleticism, durability, speed and strong arm, Osborne thought he could be a tremendous quarterback in the Nebraska system. The Nebraska coach rarely whiffed when trying to recruit in-state standouts. He would later recall that in all his years as a coach, he never put more effort into recruiting a player than he did with Scott Frost.

Nebraskans didn't just hope Frost would end up in Lincoln. It was the expectation. But for Frost, it wasn't that simple. He had become infatuated with the thought of one day playing quarterback in the NFL. He could be the next Joe Montana, he'd been told. And it seemed there was no one who could better get him there than Montana's old coach, Bill Walsh. Walsh was an NFL legend, having led the San Francisco 49ers to three Super Bowl championships. And as the inventor of the West Coast offense, he was considered the guru of the NFL passing game. In 1992, he was the head coach at Stanford, and he, too, recruited Frost hard. When Frost made his official visit to Palo Alto in December 1992, he had dinner at Walsh's house. And who should happen to show up but Joe Montana himself. It was made to look like Montana was just dropping by, but considering Frost and a top running back recruit were both in Walsh's home that night, it was surely no coincidence. Stanford would later get a wrist slap from the NCAA when the facts of the night came out. But Frost, Montana and Walsh spent 45 minutes talking about the heyday of the 49ers.

Walsh compared Frost not to Montana but to another great 49ers quarterback, the mobile gunslinger Steve Young. Come to Stanford, Walsh told him, and we'll get you to the next level. You'll learn the very same offense more than a half-dozen NFL teams are using. In four years, you'll be a millionaire. It was just what every 17- or 18-year-old football star wanted to hear. How could Frost resist that?

Frost became quite open in the Nebraska press about his desire to one day be a pro and his belief that Walsh was the coach who could best mentor him. "I think he'll help me be the best quarterback I can become," the still-uncommitted Frost said after his trip west. Of course, no pro teams ran the Nebraska option. But that, in Frost's mind, wasn't even the biggest strike against Nebraska. The rub actually had to do with NU's treatment of Frost's older brother, Steve.

Even more than Scott, Steve had grown up worshiping the Cornhuskers. And when he came out of Wood River two years before Scott, the offensive lineman wanted a scholarship offer from Nebraska more than anything in the world. Steve wasn't quite good enough for a four-year offer in Osborne's eyes, but the coach did decide Steve Frost merited being a recruited walk-on. If Steve came to Nebraska, the coach would guarantee he'd have a scholarship by the beginning of his junior year. Many of the most prominent players to walk on at Nebraska during this era received such pledges, which Osborne would put down in writing. It allowed Nebraska to stretch its available scholarships and was a huge competitive advantage, especially at a time the NCAA was ratcheting down scholarship numbers in the name of parity.

For Steve Frost, that would have been enough to bring him to Lincoln. But for whatever reason, Nebraska's recruiting office never communicated that offer to Steve. Seeing nothing from Nebraska on the table, Steve committed to Colorado State. It wasn't until Nebraska was recruiting Scott that Steve learned that the potential to play at Nebraska had ever been there. When Steve found he could have been a Husker, he was crushed. He literally cried about it. At the time, he was very unhappy at Colorado State, so much so he would eventually join his brother at Stanford. But seeing Steve's emotional reaction to the previous scholarship mix-up kind of put Nebraska behind the 8-ball with Scott. He thought Steve had been mistreated.

Between that, Scott's NFL aspirations and the general compulsion many kids feel to go off somewhere more adventurous for college, Scott Frost didn't even want to take an official recruiting visit to Nebraska. He was sure he wasn't going there. His father, who personally hoped Scott would pick Nebraska, insisted he take the trip. You don't want to burn any bridges, he told him. If things don't work out at Stanford, you might want to come back.

While Scott enjoyed his visit to Lincoln in mid-January 1993, it wasn't enough. Frost would later come to love and respect Osborne so much he'd simply call him "the best man that I know." But he didn't fully appreciate the coach at the time. He told Osborne he was going to Stanford. He then made the choice official during a press conference in Wood River on January 28. He almost apologetically announced it, saying the Stanford offer was just too good to pass up. To many Nebraskans, he was a traitor.

The two years in Palo Alto turned out to be among the most miserable of Scott Frost's life. Stanford was just not a good fit. He was used to being in a place where football meant something. Stanford students cared little for the sport, as few as 15,000 fans showing up for games in the school's 85,000-seat stadium. And culturally, Frost could see from day one he didn't fit in. The conservative, God-fearing kid from small-town Nebraska landed with a thud on one of the nation's most liberal and elite campuses. Palo Alto is not Berkeley, but you can see it from there. During student orientation, Frost was a little taken aback when part of the entertainment included a flamenco dance between a cross-dressing man and a cross-dressing woman. It was the strangest thing the Nebraska boy had ever seen. Other times he'd see kids going around campus carrying "We shall overcome" signs. Frost couldn't figure out exactly what they were overcoming, considering their parents were paying for their expensive Stanford educations. "Where am I?" he thought.

And things weren't going a whole lot better for him on the football field. He sat behind four-year starter Steve Stenstrom during the 1993 and 1994 seasons. And while Walsh always assured him he was the quarterback of Stanford's future, at the start of his sophomore year Walsh asked whether Frost would consider playing some safety. Frost was willing, as long as he remained the team's No. 2 quarterback. So during the odd season that followed, Frost started five games at safety and two others at quarterback after Stenstrom got hurt. Frost's first college interception was one he caught, not threw. The quarterback guru who compared Frost to Steve Young now publicly compared him to Ronnie Lott, the 49ers' Hall-of-Fame safety. In a pair of games, Frost saw snaps at both quarterback and safety. Frost finished the year 33 of 77 throwing the ball for 464 yards and two touchdowns while running for four other scores.

To make matters worse, in their efforts to turn Frost into the next great NFL quarterback, the Stanford coaches had tinkered with his throwing motion. Frost's original mechanics certainly weren't classic. But he had a very natural release — fluid, quick and compact. He winged the ball around so effectively in high school all the nation's top passing schools wanted him, including Miami, Florida State and BYU. But the Stanford coaches felt he needed to raise his relatively low release point to better get the ball over those big defensive linemen he'd face in college and the

NFL. They had him watch film of Joe Montana. The awkward result was a throwing motion that harkened back to Frost's high school shot-put days. His smooth high school delivery had been replaced by a robotic one in which he hitched the ball up high and then seemed to push it. His new over-the-top motion would frequently result in balls diving to the turf short of his receivers. When Frost missed, he usually missed low.

Frost years later didn't blame Stanford coaches for fouling up his mechanics. It had been the unfortunate result of their efforts to improve his motion and his body's failed effort to process it. But once the new motion was ingrained in his muscle memory, it became almost impossible for him to shake it. It wasn't until he was playing safety for the NFL's New York Jets years later that he regained his old high school form. Just screwing around on the sideline one day, he suddenly was zipping the ball. A Jets executive standing nearby told him the team would have drafted him as a quarterback if he'd thrown like that at Nebraska. "I throw the ball a hundred times better today than I did in college," Frost would say almost two decades later. But in the interim, Nebraska fans would become all too familiar with Frost's shot-put throwing style. It would frequently drive them crazy.

To top it all off, the worst thing about Stanford football to Frost was the losing. Walsh's brief attempt to return to the college game fell far short of most people's expectations. The Cardinal went 4-7 in Frost's freshman year and followed that up by going 3-7-1 in 1994. Frost wasn't just unhappy with football. He was unhappy with life, fighting borderline depression. He originally tried to hide it. He didn't want to admit things weren't working out. When The World-Herald sent a reporter to Palo Alto in September 1994, Steve at one point started to suggest in an interview that his brother was frustrated. "Wait a minute," Scott interjected, cutting his brother off. "I don't want to see an article that says Scott Frost is unhappy at Stanford. I'm not."

But he was. And by the end of that season, he didn't care who knew it. Frost was back in Wood River by Thanksgiving, talking to his parents about transferring. When Walsh resigned in early December, there was no question Frost was leaving. He received a release from his scholarship and started shopping around for a new school. Larry, the one who had warned him about burning bridges, made the first overtures to Osborne. The coach was very receptive, holding no grudge over the snub two years earlier. Frost visited with Osborne and Gill during Nebraska's Orange Bowl preparations that December and liked what he heard but still wasn't sure. He was now being re-recruited by Stanford, too, new Cardinal coach

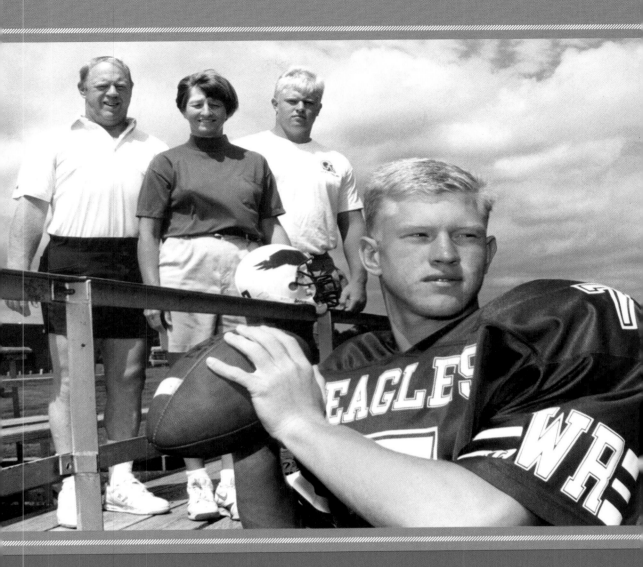

"Scott had reached a point at Stanford
where we were seeing his self-confidence
and attitude get down."

— LARRY FROST

Ty Willingham encouraging him to reconsider.

Frost found himself back in Palo Alto the first week of January 1995. The semester was about to start, but he was still torn. He called back to Lincoln and talked with Osborne. Hearing the young man's emotional struggles, Osborne actually encouraged him to stay another semester at Stanford, just to be sure he was making the right choice. Go through spring ball and see if it works out, Osborne told him. If it doesn't, you can join us in the fall. But Osborne's words had the opposite effect. Frost could see the coach wasn't just interested in whether he could help Nebraska win football games. Osborne wanted what was best for him as a person — a quality of the man Frost had not appreciated enough during the recruiting process two years earlier. "No," Frost replied at that moment, "I don't want to be here." He jumped on a plane for Lincoln the next day.

Surprisingly, Frost expressed no regrets years later about his initial decision to go to Stanford. It was all part of growing up, he said. He'd learned some things about himself and what was important to him. And while Stanford didn't work out for Scott, Steve thrived there. He got two Stanford degrees, met his wife, started a Silicon Valley career and even became the public address announcer at Stanford football and basketball games. Steve belonged in Palo Alto. Scott said he would go through it all again just for his brother. But there's no question there had been sacrifices. Osborne years later used the words "almost tragic" to describe Frost's decision to go west. Frost could have spent 1993 and 1994 in Lincoln getting valuable experience in the Nebraska system, likely taking a redshirt in there. If that had happened, who knows how the course of the college football history to come could have been altered?

When the prodigal son returned, the Lincoln campus still was basking in Osborne's first national championship, secured just days earlier with the win over Miami. Frost was scrambling. The new semester had already started. Dennis LeBlanc of the Huskers' academic support staff got Frost enrolled and then rushed him off to class, LeBlanc's car sliding on the ice along the way and nearly crashing into a pile of bricks. There was another unfortunate incident that first day, too. Frost had not yet had time to go out and buy a winter coat. The only warm thing he had to wear was his Stanford letterman's jacket. Frost's return was big news, and the campus Daily Nebraskan newspaper got the scoop and an exclusive photograph that morning. The first look most teammates got of Frost was the newspaper shot of the golden-haired boy arriving on campus wearing Stanford's cardinal and white. Not a great first impression.

The boyish-faced quarterback joined his new teammates for winter conditioning, beginning with physical testing in mid-January. In a shell, Frost decided to go last, settling against a wall inside Cook Pavilion and just taking it in. What he saw left him in complete awe. The players lined up to run the 40, and Mike Minter went 4.3. So did Tyrone Williams. Damon Benning and Clinton Childs clocked in at 4.5. Terrell Farley went 4.4. Then the 300-pound Christian Peter ran a 4.9. And so it went, an endless stream of incredible athletes, all faster than anyone back at Stanford. This was big-time football.

Athletically, at least, Frost fit right in with this group. He was one of only 20 players to hit position goals in each of the obscure feats of athleticism tested that day. Even before setting foot in that incredible weight room, he rated as the strongest quarterback ever at Nebraska. But that didn't stop teammates from giving him the brush-off — and worse. The attitude of some Huskers: Hey, we weren't good enough for you. And now you want to come back and be one of us?

Frost hadn't even been in Lincoln a month before he arrived at his locker one day to find someone had sealed it shut with white trainer's tape, topping off their handiwork with a sign that read, "You are evicted." Frost never told anyone about it. "I knew what was going on," he later recalled. "I'm not a stupid person." Osborne said he never heard of any hazing of Frost and said it wouldn't have been tolerated. But he said he wouldn't have been surprised if players, particularly those from in-state, would have made things tougher on a player who had spurned the Huskers previously. Joel Makovicka, a fullback and Nebraska native, years later didn't deny there were some hard feelings for the newcomer. "If we're being honest, the guys were pissed," he said. "He had a lot to prove to a lot of the guys. 'Hey, you didn't want to play with us. Now you have to earn it.' "

Some players were more welcoming to Frost. He was befriended by fellow quarter-backs Brook Berringer and Matt Turman, who didn't seem to bear any ill will. Frost was grateful for their support. And when spring ball rolled around, Frost was able to step right in and compete, even though he wouldn't be eligible for a year. He even had a good spring game, throwing for three touchdowns against the lower units to help the White team to victory.

But come fall, it was a different story. With the Huskers now going into the regular season, a redshirting player like Frost would be relegated to scout team duty. For a big-time player, it could be a humbling experience. And as athletic as Frost was, he would most often be put up against the first-teamers. Some coaches may

have treated such a blue-chip player differently, figuring he'd be the quarterback of the future and having him instead run with the 1's and 2's. But that wasn't Osborne's way. And as Osborne put it later, "If I had given him special status, it would have made it even harder for him to gain acceptance. That he went out there and took his licks was important."

And take his licks he did. Throughout the next four months, Frost would imitate the likes of Tony Banks and Danny Wuerffel while the Blackshirts beat the tar out of him.

The Peter brothers were particularly physical. Any scout team quarterback was always going to be a target, Jason Peter later said. But given Frost's history, "we were going to make him really earn his way back into Nebraska." If he had the ball, they were going to hit him. And even if he got rid of it, they were still going to hit him. One time the Blackshirts knocked off Frost's helmet, and then to pour salt in the wound someone chucked it halfway down the field. "Let's go. Get your helmet back on," they told him.

But Frost was raised by his parents not to back down from a challenge. That led to more than a few practice conflicts and skirmishes. One day Frost got mad at the Peters and altered his snap count to draw the linemen offsides. The volatile Christian in turn got so upset about it that when he rushed the quarterback during a non-tackling drill, instead of tagging off on Frost, he punched him. Undeterred, Frost again changed his cadence, and then the big, physical quarterback who could run like a fullback escalated the tensions even more by flattening a Blackshirt during a long run. Soon a fight broke out. Defensive end Jared Tomich, who later would become a good friend of Frost, grabbed the quarterback by the facemask and tossed him like a discus. That was pretty much how it went much of that fall. Frost's parents later recalled that Scott once gave this assessment of going up against the Peter brothers in practice every day: Jason hits harder, but Christian punches harder.

"As long as I think I'm playing well and my coaches and teammates are happy with my play, then I'll feel fine."

— SCOTT FROST

As tough as things got on the practice field, the hardest part for Frost was watching the games. Sitting with the other redshirts, most of them two years his junior, Frost usually left before the final gun. He also tried to keep a low profile, both within the team and publicly. But that became pretty tough when he found himself caught up in the middle of the Lawrence Phillips affair. When Phillips cornered his former girlfriend in Frost's apartment, Frost had to fight his new teammate to free her. Frost avoided the reporters who flooded him with calls after the incident. It was a bad deal for everyone, including himself, and yet another wedge between him and his new team. When that wearying 1995 season was over, Frost was almost as happy about it as Osborne.

The coming of spring in 1996 brought renewed life for Frost, as he joined Turman and others in a five-man battle to succeed Tommie Frazier. Itching to get into the mix, Frost soon won the job, setting himself up as Frazier's heir apparent. Along the way, he earned a grudging respect from his teammates, some of whom privately marveled at his resiliency. Among those publicly offering praise was, significantly, Jason Peter. In the mind of the Blackshirts leader, Frost over the previous year had earned his place on the team. He was a Husker. Peter said fans should stop sweating over Nebraska's future quarterback. "He'll do fine this fall," Peter said. "Just his athletic ability alone makes him a great quarterback." Frost's face lit up when a reporter relayed Peter's words. Given his behind-the-scenes struggles to earn acceptance in the Husker locker room, the words meant more to Frost than most anyone realized. During the summer months to follow, Frost asserted his own leadership role with the team, organizing seven-on-seven passing drills for players on both sides of the ball.

That fall, perhaps no Nebraska player ever attempted to step into bigger shoes. Osborne said he didn't believe the play at quarterback would drop off as much as people expected. Frost said he knew there would be doubters, but he said he didn't care what people thought. His teammates and Osborne were the ones who mattered. Frost publicly offered no sense of the largely no-win situation he was stepping into: following a legend, taking over a team that had won 25 straight, with fans expecting nothing short of more perfection. In fact, showing the brashness typical of quarterbacks, Frost embraced the challenge of taking Nebraska to a three-peat. "I want to do the same thing Tommie did, and that's win a national championship," Frost said in an interview. "He got his in '95. It's my turn in '96."

On September 7, the season for both Frost and the Huskers got off to a great start against Michigan State's Spartans. Frost thought he was on top of the world the first time he led the offense out on the field. It was exciting to be quarterbacking the nation's top team. Frost certainly didn't make anyone forget Frazier, but he kept the car on the road. He ran for 58 yards and his first Husker TD while completing 5 of 11 passes for 75 yards and a score. With six brand new starters on offense and some shuffling on the offensive line, it was going to take a while to get things really rolling. And with the way the Blackshirts were playing, they'd have that time. With seven returning starters, a pair of All-American rush ends and playmakers all over the field, Charlie McBride's guys were smothering. They forced four turnovers, ran back two interceptions for TDs, ran a punt back for another score, and held Michigan State to 83 yards on 49 rushes. This was arguably the best defense of the entire championship era.

Even Osborne, who had spent 24 seasons preaching to his players to not look past the next game, talked to his team in the locker room before kickoff about the chance the Huskers had to make history. "Not many teams have ever had the opportunity that you have this season," Osborne said. "So let's go get it." Days later, Sports Illustrated put out a warning to the rest of college football. The magazine's cover featured a photo of Ahman Green taking a handoff from Frost and the headline "Red Alert."

But in actuality, it was Frost, the Huskers and their winning streak that were in peril. Within just over a week, that story on Nebraska's bid for three titles would be seen as yet another case of the notorious Sports Illustrated cover jinx.

Debacle in the Desert

Nebraskans were ready for another big night in the Arizona desert. Just 251 days after the Fiesta Bowl flogging of No. 2 Florida, more than 25,000 Nebraska fans returned to the site of that triumph and again helped fill Sun Devil Stadium to capacity. Riding high on their 26-game win streak, the Huskers were about to face an Arizona State team they had hung 63 on in just the first half the previous year. This was going to be a blast.

But Nebraska coach George Darlington already had a sense this night was going to be different. During warm-ups out on the grass turf, a friend and Husker booster who was standing by the rail of the stands asked Darlington how he thought the team would play. Darlington just glumly gave him a thumbs down. Confused, the booster repeated the question. Darlington repeated the gesture, with more emphasis. The friend was in disbelief. By the end of this one, he certainly wouldn't be the only one.

After all the winning over more than three seasons, it appeared for the first time a dangerous complacency had crept into the Nebraska locker room. Certainly not everyone was of that mind-set. But there were too many players on this field who had the idea they could just toss their helmets out there and win this game. Tom Osborne and all his coaches could see it in practice. The Huskers had a bye week between the Michigan State game and this one. It was always tough to get the players motivated in a bye week anyway, with little to play for at the end of the week. But this bye, combined with an upcoming game against a team the Huskers had absolutely manhandled the previous year, helped produce what Darlington

"I think in football there's a tendency when things don't go well to cast too much blame on the quarterback."

— TOM OSBORNE

would recall as the worst two weeks of practice he saw in more than two decades in Lincoln. As much as the Husker coaches harped on the players about their efforts, they couldn't get through. They were losing the battle with human nature. The letdown was coming at a critical time, too, when a new quarterback was still trying to develop a rhythm in the option game with his offensive line and backs. Recalled Darlington years later: "We got just what we deserved."

Nebraska's motivational problems aside, even the Husker coaches weren't prepared for what was waiting for them in Tempe. Despite the previous year's result, the Sun Devils were a talented team, led by a pair of future NFL standouts in quarterback Jake Plummer and safety Pat Tillman, along with eight other defenders who would be chosen in the NFL draft over the next two years. ASU at the end of the year would finish one play away from an undefeated season and possible national championship. And the Sun Devils had been laying for Nebraska for a whole year. It wasn't just that the Huskers had annihilated them the previous season. It was the way they had done it.

Particularly sticking in the craw of Coach Bruce Snyder and his team was a late touchdown the Huskers had scored near the end of the previous year's 77-28 blowout in Lincoln. With third-stringer Matt Turman in at quarterback and less than a minute to play, the Huskers were facing a third down. Osborne had spent the entire second half trying to hold down the score. But he wanted to pick up the first down to give Turman and the other reserves a few more snaps. They deserved that chance. So Osborne called a pass play, with fourth-string wingback Lance Brown assigned to run a 12-yard hook route just beyond the chains. But Brown and Turman were also trained in practice that if the safety jumps the route, you run by him and go deep. And that's exactly what happened. Brown streaked toward the end zone, and Turman hit him with a perfect pass for a 39-yard touchdown. Osborne was embarrassed by the final-minute score, one made worse when the acrobatic Brown celebrated his first collegiate touchdown by turning a back flip on the Nebraska sideline.

Snyder was livid afterward, refusing to shake the hand of the apologetic Husker coach. "That was not right," Snyder curtly told him, "and I didn't appreciate it." He didn't seem to buy Osborne's explanation. Husker coaches years later would say there's no question Osborne wasn't trying to run up the score. If he had, the Huskers probably would have hung a hundred on the Sun Devils that day. But teams don't forget plays like that. Joel Makovicka later played in the NFL with both Plummer and Tillman. They told him that during the entire off-season, the rematch in Tempe was the only game the Sun Devils thought about. The game would be played at night, an atmosphere sure to put a big charge into the Sun Devil crowd. Nebraska players and coaches were even being taunted by ASU fans the night before the game during their walk-through. Put it all together, and the Huskers were walking into a desert rattlesnake pit.

The 17th-ranked Sun Devils set the tone for this ambush right away. They won the toss, and rather than deferring to the second half like most teams, they wanted the ball. Plummer proceeded to drive it right down the Blackshirts' throats. The touchdown came on a pass in which the Husker coverage was completely busted, three guys playing man-to-man while the other was in zone. The Husker defense woke up after that, holding the Sun Devils to just a pair of field goals the rest of the game. But it didn't matter by that point. Because the Nebraska offense on this night would prove shockingly inept.

The 60 minutes of offensive chaos began with a holding penalty that backed the Huskers against their end zone. Even though a third of the fans in the stands wore red, this was where the Huskers would discover just how loud the stadium would be this night — the loudest any of them would face in their careers. Standing in his end zone, Frost attempted to audible, but only about half the team heard it. The option play broke down, and Frost was forced into a rushed pitch that hit Ahman Green's hands and bounced off. The back tried to regain possession and bobbled the ball out of the end zone. Safety. Just five minutes in, the Huskers trailed 9-0.

On the next NU possession, Frost drove the Huskers from their 21 all the way down to the ASU 5. But on a third-down play, Frost tried to get a pitch to Green while being tackled. A lineman got a hand on the ball, and ASU recovered. The offense and a slumped-shouldered Frost left the field, knowing a touchdown there could have completely changed the face of this game.

ASU was playing with an edge, while the flat Huskers continued to shoot themselves in the foot with penalties and mistakes. Football is a game of emotion and momentum, and once they're going against you, it's hard to turn things around. It's why most upsets happen. And crowd noise would continue to be a big factor, disrupting Husker play-calling. Osborne ultimately told Frost to stop calling audibles. Sometimes, though, the Huskers even had trouble hearing in their own huddle. At one point, Frost called for a counter sweep reverse. But in the din, one player didn't hear the word "reverse" — the offensive lineman who was supposed to pull and lead the ball carrier down the field. That was kind of like taking the word

"People expect us to do well.
We tried to do our best tonight,
and it wasn't meant to be."

— AHMAN GREEN

"not" out of the Ten Commandments. On film, Huskers could later see that missing block could have been the difference between the short gain Nebraska got and the play breaking wide open. It was just that kind of night.

Then just before the end of the horrendous half, the Huskers were backed up against their own goal line yet again. To beat the noise, Frost was now lifting his foot to signal for the snap. Aaron Taylor, an all-conference guard who had moved to center this season, mistook a more subtle Frost foot shift for the snap signal and fired the ball before Frost was ready. It sailed past his ear into the end zone. Frost got on it, but the result was another safety.

This was about the time Husker fans in the stadium that night started letting their feelings be known about the play of their quarterback. "Get the bum off the field!" one fan screamed within earshot of Frost's parents. Many others had harsh words, the verbal abuse so blatant and bad that fans sitting directly around the Frosts started getting uncomfortable. Nearly all Husker fans looked on in stunned disbelief as their team went into halftime down 17-0. Even Osborne had to admit to himself, "We're in a world of trouble here."

Osborne tried to get his team to regroup at halftime, but the Huskers' slapstick act on offense continued. Second-half drives were killed by a sack, a running back's fumble and a pass dropped by a tight end as he streaked open down the field. And then to top it off, another holding call again put Nebraska's back to the end zone. Two ASU defenders beat their guys and sacked Frost in the end zone for the third safety of the game. Three! Osborne couldn't remember the last time the Huskers had surrendered even one. In 106 years of football, no Husker team had suffered as many in a game. While Frost laid on his back in the end zone, he showed his own frustration by firing the ball against the goal post. It was a fitting capper to a 19-0 meltdown that would go down in Husker history as the Disaster in the Desert.

There were tears in the locker room, and the team was still in shock as it arrived back in Lincoln in the early morning hours Sunday. But Husker fans weren't just shocked. Many were irate. As Osborne later put it, "We came back here, and it was like we'd never won a game. We were a terrible team with a bad coach and a bad quarterback." A passionate fan base that didn't tolerate losing was one of the reasons Nebraska football was a cut above other schools around the country. Mediocrity was not an option in Lincoln. But these Huskers were about to be exposed to the ugly underbelly of that passion. And most of the angry howls would be directed at Scott Frost.

Frost returned to Lincoln to find death threats on his answering machine. He became the scapegoat, flogged around bar stools, in the newspaper and on talk radio. "Although one player can't make a game by himself, Scott Frost proved one player can break one," a fan wrote. Many fans were predisposed to not like Frost anyway, given the Stanford episode. And his confident comments at the start of the season were now rubbing some the wrong way, too. "Must we now have a quarterback with more arrogance than skill and more talk than action?" another fan asked. The criticisms would become common refrains for the next 12 months: Frost can't throw the ball. He doesn't make good decisions. He's not the leader Tommie was. Is he really the best we have? "He's tentative, he's scared, and he made bad decisions," one fan said. "There's a reason he was playing defense at Stanford."

Fans immediately started calling for Osborne to turn to his two backup quarterbacks, Turman and Frankie London. The World-Herald's Tom Shatel offered some of the sharpest assessments, calling Nebraska's option game nonexistent with Frost at the helm. If Tommie Frazier had been out there, he wrote, there wouldn't have been the mistakes and ineptness. It was the start of a frosty relationship. For the rest of his Husker career, Frost would give the columnist the cold shoulder.

Quarterbacks always face criticism when things go badly, and Frost had indeed played poorly — the worst game of his life. Snyder's plan going in had been to take away Nebraska's other weapons and put the game in Frost's hands. The strategy clearly exposed Frost's inexperience, as he went six for 20 passing for 66 yards. But there was plenty of blame to go around. The Pipeline had sprung some major leaks, the line playing a horrible game. Frost was getting hit almost every time he dropped back to pass. While the line returned four starters from the previous year, two of them were playing at new positions, the whole unit seeming out of sync. One Husker lineman lined up against a quick Sun Devil defensive end who pretty much stole his lunch money all night. The backs and receivers also had their share of fumbles and bobbles. The dad of one offensive lineman came up to Larry and Carol Frost in the Denver airport the next day. "I know Scott is going to take a lot of the blame for this," he said. "But I was watching my son, and he didn't touch anybody all night."

It took the ASU loss for Frost to grasp how much pressure he faced trying to repeat as champion and follow Frazier. He felt ashamed to even go to class the next week. He stopped at a dorm to visit a girl he was dating, and another female student across the room screamed a vulgarity at him. One of Frost's most vivid memories in the days that followed was walking into a huge auditorium for a business class and finding the floor and chairs littered with copies of the campus paper discarded by students. Prominently featured was a photo of one of Frost's lower moments in the ASU game, along with a story that said the only thing he and Frazier had in common was the first two letters of their last names. Everywhere he looked around that room, Frost saw reminders of his failure.

Husker coaches were concerned about what the loss would do to the confidence of their quarterback and team. Unity was also an issue, as there was some finger-pointing in the locker room. Due to the offensive struggles, the Blackshirts had been forced to play 85 snaps in the brutal desert heat, and they weren't very happy about it. Grant Wistrom felt the horrible play of certain Huskers had reflected their lack of off-season dedication. And it raised his ire even more that he didn't see any remorse for it. Years later he wasn't naming names, but he was clearly still perturbed by what he saw as a preventable loss — one of only two he'd see during his four years in Lincoln. Wingback Jon Vedral acknowledged to a reporter after the game that there were likely some players in the locker room who doubted Frost's ability. The whole season could have unraveled at that point. But it was times like these when the Huskers fell back on the emotional rock that was Tom Osborne.

Osborne gathered the team in the South Stadium meeting room on Monday and calmly set the course for the rest of the season. "This was probably the best thing that could have happened to us," he told his players. The team had gotten fat and happy, believing it would never lose another game. Arizona State had exposed some real weaknesses. He quickly turned the players' focus from the past to the things they would now work on to get better. It was always Osborne's way to turn a negative into a positive. And he told the team all of their goals — including a national championship — were still attainable. There's still a lot of football to be played. Crazy things can happen.

The next day, Osborne came strongly to the defense of Scott Frost. Facing a barrage of questions about the quarterback during his regular meeting with the press, Osborne at one point leaned forward in his chair, his voice rising. "People can come down on his head all they want. But what else are you going to do? You might as well support the guy. He's the best we've got. Believe me, I know that. I may not know much, but I know that."

Most comforting and calming to Frost was that win or lose, Osborne was the same. He quickly got his quarterback focused on the things he needed to work on. He also told Frost to avoid reading the papers or listening to all the talk, the press and fans always inflating the good and overblowing the bad. Just try to stay on an even keel, he said. Teammates were also supportive, Frost particularly appreciating how safety Mike Minter reached out to him right after the ASU game. Frost's parents were always there, too, talking to him several times a week, not bringing up football unless Scott did.

But what best helped him cope, he said later, was a friendship he developed with Art Lindsay, a Lincoln insurance salesman. Lindsay, who long had been active in the Fellowship of Christian Athletes, a year earlier had become a spiritual adviser to Brook Berringer, helping the quarterback deal with the disappointment of his senior season on the bench. Five days after the Arizona State loss, Frost also turned to Lindsay, and the Lincoln man again ministered to the spiritual needs of a Nebraska quarterback. They began meeting weekly for Bible study, Frost becoming rededicated to his faith. It helped him to see there was more to life beyond football. Frost's parents noted a new calm in their son. Through his work with Lindsay, Frost came to appreciate what the Bible means when it says God causes all things to work together for good. That's how he began to see the Arizona State loss and his trials. Frost had thought Osborne was crazy when he said the loss was the best thing that could happen to the team. He now could see Osborne had been right.

And to the great credit of Frost and the Huskers, over the next two months they did quickly turn things around. Nebraska reeled off nine straight wins, most of them just the kind of demolitions Husker fans had grown accustomed to. The average margin was 49-9. The Blackshirts had firmly established themselves as the nation's No. 1 defense. Nebraska got its running game going, despite huge injury problems at I-back that plagued the team throughout the season. Green, who had rushed for 1,086 yards as a freshman while being only a part-time starter, fell off to 917 in 1996, missing two games and parts of three others due to toe and foot injuries. Damon Benning and James Sims had bum ankles that also forced them to miss time. Still, the Husker run game rolled on.

Frost's play improved. Osborne could see he'd grown markedly in his ability to tailor the play to what the defense was showing. That only came with experience. And Osborne wasn't sure he'd ever had a quarterback who'd run with such toughness. One thing Osborne had challenged Frost to do was completely shed any thought of hook sliding or running out of bounds, lingering habits from his days at Stanford that would still occasionally pop up. Osborne wanted his big-framed quarterback to run over people. Now it was clear: Frost wasn't afraid to stick his nose anywhere.

By the end of the season, Frost's statistics would closely mirror those of Tommie Frazier's sophomore year — the Husker legend's first full year as a starter. In fact, the similarities were striking: Frost had 1,878 total yards compared to 1,863 for Frazier; 22 touchdowns compared to Frazier's 21. By any reasonable standard, Frost had a solid year.

Not that the young quarterback seemed to get any credit for that. The critics continued to throw their barbs throughout the season. It got so bad his parents abandoned their usual seats in Memorial Stadium, instead moving to a corner of the east stands where the state high school coaches' association had a block of seats. These coaches knew them. And they also understood the game well enough to know that when things went badly, it wasn't just Scott's fault.

As it turned out, Osborne had also been right when he said that loss to Arizona State might not derail the Huskers' title hopes. After outslugging No. 5 Colorado 17-12 in the regular-season finale, the third-ranked Huskers appeared on track for a date in a possible national championship game against top-ranked Florida State. If Nebraska beat the Seminoles and ASU lost in the Rose Bowl — which it subsequently did — the Huskers would in all likelihood be champs again. Husker seniors in particular relished the chance to play Florida State, the only team besides Arizona State to hand them a loss during their careers. Only one thing stood in the way of that matchup: a game against an underachieving, 7-4 Texas team in the first-ever Big 12 Conference championship game.

"We're not making excuses.
We've got to give Texas credit."

— SCOTT FROST

Getting Hooked

Over time, Nebraska football fans would develop a healthy hatred for all things Texas. And it all had its roots in 1996, Nebraska's first season in the new Big 12 Conference.

The Big 12 had been sold originally as just an expansion of the old Big Eight, with Nebraska and its longtime conference brethren taking on four Texas schools left homeless by the collapse of the scandal-plagued Southwest Conference. It was all about adding eyeballs and TV sets to make the league more attractive to the TV networks that now pretty much ran college football. But when the league presidents got together for the first time, it almost appeared one of the first orders of business was to knock Nebraska down a peg or two. The Big Eight had allowed schools to take Prop 48s, and Nebraska at the time was taking two a year. But all Nebraska's old Big Eight friends joined with the new schools in an 11-1 vote to bar them. While the schools had their reasons for doing so, Nebraska Athletic Director Bill Byrne couldn't help feeling there was some kind of anti-Nebraska backlash going on. Especially when he was hearing comments during side conversations like, "It would be nice if you could lose a few games now and then." The academically sacrosanct Big Ten, along with the Pac-10 and the SEC, would all take Prop 48s, but the Big 12 would not.

Much to Tom Osborne's disgust, the new conference also threw out the Big Eight record book. All those great accomplishments by the likes of Mike Rozier, Turner Gill and so many others didn't count for much considering Texas, Texas A&M, Baylor and Texas Tech weren't in the league back then. Nebraska was on the wrong end of another 11-1 vote when it came to whether the conference would hold a championship game. The other schools liked the money such a game would raise. But Nebraska wasn't looking for money. Nebraska was about winning national championships. All that game would do in Osborne's eyes was put one more hurdle in the way. The results of the first game in St. Louis would prove him right.

Nebraska went in a 21-point favorite. But in the end, a key personnel loss on defense, plus an inexplicable oversight by a coach who seemingly was prepared for everything, would help lead to the Huskers' downfall.

To start the 1996 season, Terrell Farley's face had been on magazine covers. The all-world linebacker who hunted down ball carriers like a puma looking for lunch was being touted as a potential All-American. The Husker coaches often just allowed Farley to freelance, the linebacker usually following his instincts right to the ball. But just days before the season opener, the Georgia native was arrested on suspicion of driving drunk. The timing was unfortunate, allowing the national press to run another round of out-of-control Husker stories just as the team was trying to turn that page. Other players had previously expressed concern to Osborne about Farley and drinking. Osborne suspended the linebacker for the Michigan State and ASU games, required him to go into counseling and started randomly testing him for alcohol several times a week. Farley seemed committed to sobriety — for the short term, at least. He somewhat oddly told reporters he couldn't see himself swearing off alcohol forever because he was too young.

But with alcoholism, relapses are also common. And on a fateful November night, Farley allowed a friend to talk him into going out. He was later clocked by Lincoln police going over 61 mph in a 35 mph zone. When officers gave chase, the Husker drove his car over a curb and through a muddy field before crashing into two parked cars. Farley got out and took off. There was a reason to run: Osborne had told him he'd be off the team if he drank again. Though almost no one on the football field could keep up with Farley, in his impaired state the police ran him down. The self-destruction of Terrell Farley was complete. Osborne booted him from the team.

Teammates were upset at Farley's selfishness. After all the Huskers had done to fight their way back into the national championship picture, Farley had let down the whole team. Farley's dismissal created a huge void in the middle of the defense, and at a critical time. Nebraska was days away from the showdown with Colorado that would decide the champion of the Big 12's North Division. To replace Farley's critical speed at linebacker, Husker coaches shifted safety Mike Minter into Farley's spot and shuffled other players around in the secondary. The Husker D passed that test, holding up against a strong Colorado passing attack. But Farley's absence would be keenly felt in the championship game against Texas. A Longhorn coach later told Husker coaches that from what they'd seen on film, they would have had no way to stop the Husker lightning bolt.

Compounding Farley's loss, during the week before the Big 12 title game, the flu ran through the Husker locker room. Under Osborne, the Huskers were always looking for something to give them an edge. They couldn't move Lincoln closer to all the great prep players in Dallas and Miami. They couldn't change the weather.

But whether it was football or the supporting academic, nutrition, training or strength departments, Osborne always made sure the Huskers had the most up-to-date equipment, the best staff and the latest, most innovative practices. No detail was ever too small. But during this season, the Huskers hadn't gotten their flu shots. Osborne recalled that trainer George Sullivan had approached him about it earlier in the fall. But since a few players would inevitably get laid up for a time as a reaction to the vaccination, Osborne had put it off.

It was a decision that would come back to haunt Osborne and the Huskers. In the wake of the Colorado game, played in the cold, rain and sleet of Lincoln on the day after Thanksgiving, the bug insidiously struck. Dozens of players missed practice time before the Huskers headed to St. Louis, with the defense particularly hard-hit. And it was a virulent strain. Safety Eric Stokes lost 14 pounds in the week. He ended up playing with a 103-degree temperature and dehydrated, afterward barely remembering being out there. Linebacker Jamel Williams, who didn't practice during the week, spent the game shuffling in and out of the lineup. Lots of guys were a couple of steps slow.

Despite its ho-hum season, Texas had the offensive horses to expose the sudden gaps in the Husker defense. The Blackshirts made athletic quarterback James Brown look like a comic-book hero. He threw for 353 yards. And future NFL standout running back Priest Holmes repeatedly gashed the Huskers on a simple running play, one that magnified the loss of Farley. On the play, a guard would pull and take on Minter, who as a safety wasn't used to having to fend off big linemen. Holmes in the end ran for three scores against a Blackshirt unit that had not surrendered a single rushing touchdown all season. Then late in the game, Minter's replacement at safety got hurt, and the Oklahoma native was forced to return to his old position. Just minutes later, the safety who hadn't covered a deep pass in two weeks was burned by Brown for a 66-yard touchdown. Minter appeared to mistime his leap, barely missing the deflection.

Nebraska also struggled some on offense, with the season-long injuries at I-back forcing the Huskers to start DeAngelo Evans. Even the true freshman was gutting out the game with a painful pelvic injury that would require surgery by the end of the year. Evans played courageously, scoring three times. But the pain essentially transformed the player who could run a 4.5 40, into a 5.0 man. Reviewing the game tape later, Osborne would lament numerous plays that would have normally gone for eight to 10 yards that were netting just a few.

Even after all that, the Huskers still had a chance to win the Texas shootout. Trailing 30-27 with just over two minutes left, the Huskers were looking to get the ball back one last time. The Blackshirts forced Texas into a 4th and 1 from its own 30, what would normally be a punting situation. Based on his offense's second-half momentum, Osborne was confident that if the Huskers could get the ball back here, they could drive to tie or take the lead. Leery of just such a scenario, Longhorn Coach John Mackovic decided to roll the dice.

When the Texas offense came back out on the field, Osborne thought it was surely a bluff, expecting that Brown would just try to draw the Huskers offsides. A stop here and the Huskers would already be in position for a game-tying field goal. But Brown had barely settled in behind center when the ball was suddenly snapped, putting Mackovic's risky gamble into motion. With three running backs stacked behind Brown, the Blackshirts were sure Texas was looking to power it right up the middle. The 10 Husker defenders who had been crowding the line of scrimmage all crashed forward. That included Ralph Brown, the Huskers' freshman corner. When no receiver lined up on his side of the field, he abandoned his post, moving up as another inside backer and then blitzing. James Brown faked a handoff to Holmes. Wistrom tackled the back, thinking he'd saved the game. But then he saw James Brown rolling out with the ball. Uh-oh. Longhorn tight end Derek Lewis, uncovered by Ralph Brown, slipped off the line and was running 10 yards behind any Husker defender. Lewis hauled in James Brown's pass, finally dragged down 60 yards later by Jamel Williams. The game was essentially over, the Huskers having no way to stop the Longhorns from running out the clock. Holmes then ran through a dispirited Blackshirt unit for another touchdown on the next play, capping Texas' 37-27 win.

No one knew it at the time, but it was Tom Osborne's last loss. Years later, he would call it the one he agonized about the most — even more than the 1984 Orange Bowl heartbreaker. And the flu shots became one of his biggest regrets. As he saw it, the oversight had cost the Huskers a shot at four straight national titles. "That game hurt," he said. And if that's the way the even-keeled coach felt, one can imagine how his players were taking it. Instead of going to the Sugar Bowl to play for a third straight national title, the Huskers landed back in the Orange Bowl for a largely meaningless game against No. 10 Virginia Tech. They felt they'd let a golden opportunity slip away. There was still no question in their minds they were the best team in the country. Playing in the Huskers' place, a Florida team that was pretty much the same one the Huskers had crushed the year before ended up beating Florida State for the championship.

There were huge questions as to whether the Huskers would even be motivated to play their bowl. An 11-2 season and Orange Bowl win at most places would be considered reason for a campus-wide parade. But in the warped world in which Nebraska now resided, it was like ending with a trip to the Poulan Weed-Eater Bowl.

Scott Frost by that point was mentally and emotionally exhausted. He weathered more kicks after the Texas loss, despite having a pretty good game. As the Huskers' plane landed in Miami, he was listening to Bob Marley, losing his troubles in the feel-good reggae beat. It was the first time he had felt so relaxed in four months. "Nebraska was the worst place for me in the country at that point," he later recalled. In fact, it was good for all the Huskers to get away from the football fishbowl in Lincoln. For a week, they could just practice and hang out together.

Mustering their pride, the Huskers played well before a half-empty stadium. A big motivation was sending out the team's seniors the right way. With a win, they'd finish with a four-year record of 47-3, the best in NCAA history. Jason Peter had a key play early, scooping up a fumble and returning it for a touchdown. And against the defensively minded Hokies, Frost had what Osborne considered his best game of the year. Running with authority, he picked up 62 yards and a pair of touchdowns on the ground to complement an MVP performance by oft-injured senior running back Damon Benning. Nebraska won 41-21 and finished No. 6 in the country.

For Frost and the Huskers coming back in 1997, the bowl win provided a nice boost of momentum going into the offseason. Frost in particular had grown a lot during the year. At the start of the season, he had just been trying to avoid mistakes. Now he was taking charge. Teammates could see his confidence growing week by week, and their confidence in him grew, too. Many fans had yet to warm up to him. But among the Huskers, there was now no question: Scott Frost was their quarterback. Among those who sought out Frost after the game was Milt Tenopir. From the day Frost had transferred to Lincoln, the Husker offensive line coach had been very supportive, making him feel welcome and giving him encouragement. The quarterback now considered him to be almost an uncle. Tenopir told Frost he'd had a great game and a great season. And then the line coach made a prediction.

"Next year, Scott," Tenopir said, "you'll take us to it all."

A Dynamic Duo

Tom Osborne was walking across the floor of Memorial Stadium as players in shorts, T-shirts and sweat clothes went through the rigors of summer conditioning, building the sweat equity that would carry them through another grinding season. Out of the corner of his eye, Osborne suddenly saw a big guy streak across the field and tackle another player from behind. It was Jason Peter.

"What are you doing?" Osborne asked his standout defensive tackle.

"The guy's loafin'," Peter responded.

And that was something neither Peter nor his roommate, Grant Wistrom, would tolerate from this 1997 Nebraska team. If anyone was late for these supposedly optional workouts. If anyone wasn't running those stadium stairs until their lungs burned. If anyone didn't squeeze out one more rep on the bench press. They were going to hear it from Wistrom and Peter. There was only one acceptable outcome for their senior seasons. This team was going to win another national championship, their third ring in four years in the program. And no one, least of all a lackadaisical teammate, was going to screw that up. The entire Husker team came into the season motivated by the pair of losses the previous year. But arguably no Huskers were more invested in the coming year than Peter and Wistrom. They would become the heart and soul of the 1997 Huskers.

In the days after the Orange Bowl win over Virginia Tech, both players had come into Osborne's office. The coach suspected this might be goodbye. Peter and Wistrom had worn Blackshirts for two years, and Wistrom was a first-team All-American. Based on NFL executives Osborne had talked to, both players were projected to be possible late first-round picks if they decided to forgo their final college seasons.

> ## "When Jason makes a play, I'm just as excited as when I make one."
>
> — GRANT WISTROM ON ROOMMATE JASON PETER

"We could have a great defense this year,
but it all depends on how they play together."

— CHARLIE MCBRIDE

But instead of telling Osborne they were hanging up their Husker gear, the coach and players later recalled the conversation going something like this:

"Coach, we lost two games this last year. We don't think that was very good." Osborne agreed it was a little disappointing. "We're coming back. We want to finish this thing up right." The players later recalled the coach's reaction as typical Osborne. "Well, that's fine. We'll see you in the weight room."

Did anyone expect Tom Osborne to dance on a table? But while the 1997 season was still months away, Osborne knew well this was a huge win for the Huskers. (The players' decision also would change his thinking on another weighty matter, a subject for a later chapter.) Graduations had produced a changing of the guard in Lincoln. By 1997, Wistrom and Peter were among just a half-dozen or so Huskers who had played major roles on those previous title teams. Osborne considered Wistrom and Peter the best players at their positions in the nation. If they had left the program, Nebraska would have returned only one starter on defense. Even though there were other experienced players and up-and-coming talent, it's hard to imagine a team that green on one side of the ball being able to compete for a title.

And then there was the tremendous leadership the two defensive co-captains would be bringing back to the Huskers. In many ways, Wistrom and Peter were the epitome of the peer leadership that drove all the Husker teams of this era. Sure, speed on defense and offensive playmakers were important. But one little-appreciated ingredient of all the Osborne championship teams was great leadership in the locker room. Osborne, Charlie McBride and sports psychologist Jack Stark would all agree years later: There may never have been a better pair of leaders at Nebraska than Grant Wistrom and Jason Peter. Neither was going to put up with any nonsense this year as they sought to lead Nebraska back to the top — in their eyes, the natural order of things. As starting middle linebacker Jay Foreman later put it, "They didn't come back to mess around with some knucklehead college kids."

Wistrom and Peter. Peter and Wistrom. Almost from the time freshman Wistrom joined redshirt freshman Peter in the program in the fall of 1994, the two were inseparable. Back then, Jason would sit with the upper-class D-linemen at lunch, having an in with that group because of older brother Christian. But the big-city boy from New Jersey early on noticed the tall and skinny Parade All-American from rural Missouri on the practice field. He thought Wistrom was a guy he could get along with. One day, Jason Peter invited Wistrom to sit with him and the older guys at lunch. From that point on, the two were like brothers.

When Christian left the program in 1995, Wistrom and Jason became roommates. To be around them, you might think they loathed each other. They'd wrestle for the remote control. They incessantly ribbed each other. Peter called Wistrom a Missouri hick. Wistrom made fun of Peter's leather jackets and imitated his Jersey accent. They constantly questioned each other's manhood. When Wistrom showed up at a press conference after the 1997 spring game with a broken pinky finger, Peter couldn't resist taking a shot. "She'll be alright," he told reporters. Wistrom gave it back when Jason got hurt months later. "Is Pumpkin OK?" he asked McBride. But in a game or practice, when one made a big play, the other would be just as excited. And each knew the other would always be there, on and off the field. They were teammates at Nebraska by chance, they liked to say later, but became friends by choice.

Jason Peter, of course, had followed his brother to Lincoln. The day in 1993 that the defensive tackle committed to the Huskers, he said he dreamed of lining up in a national championship game, looking next to him and seeing his brother. In 1995, that dream became reality. They were the first pair of brothers to start at Nebraska since Jimmy and Toby Williams in 1981. Even with Christian now off to the pros, Jason Peter was still known by many around the program as the little brother. But in the past two years, he'd established himself as a great player in his own right. At 6-foot-5, 285 pounds, he wasn't as heavy as Christian, but he was taller, quicker and faster. And like his brother, he was an emotional leader. He was quick to grab your face mask and get in your face if you were falling short of expectations. And as a three-year starter with previous family ties to the Blackshirts, nobody better understood what it meant to wear that black practice jersey. When you earned one, you weren't just playing for yourself or your team. You were playing for everyone who ever wore one before you. After a big play, no Husker was quicker than Peter to "throw the bones" — crossing his forearms below his head to mimic the Blackshirts' skull-and-crossbones symbol.

> "We're going for the national title.
> There's no ifs, ands or buts about it.
> This team is for real."
>
> — JASON PETER

"I wanted to be one of the people
who really mattered to the team
and one of the leaders for the team."

— GRANT WISTROM AFTER BEING ELECTED CO-CAPTAIN

But with the Peter name also came a lot of baggage. Jason was often linked to the indiscretions that had dogged Christian, even though Jason kept a clean off-field slate in Lincoln. It didn't help that months after leaving the Nebraska program, Christian had been convicted of disturbing the peace after grabbing a woman by the throat in a Kearney, Nebraska, bar. Christian Peter acknowledged after his first run-in with the law in nearly three years that he had a drinking problem. The incident didn't keep Peter from being drafted by the NFL's New England Patriots in April, but the team dropped him days later when the team owner's wife objected to having him on the roster. While playing the 1996 game against Arizona State months later, Jason couldn't help noticing the sign a Sun Devil fan had held up: "Jason, Don't Be a Christian." But Jason loved his brother and thought much of the grief he'd taken was unfair. After Christian moved on, Jason paid tribute to his brother by changing his jersey number from 95 to Christian's 55. For the rest of his Husker career, he'd always be playing for his brother.

As the 1997 season began, there was still another Peter brother in the Husker program. Damian Peter had been the best of all the football-playing Peter brothers, the offensive lineman recruited by almost everyone out of high school. He eventually chose Notre Dame. But the summer before he was to head to South Bend, Damian broke his neck in a diving accident. Doctors said he might never walk again. Damian, Christian and Jason all shared a lot of tears that summer. It particularly bugged Jason Peter that Tom Osborne seemed to show more concern for Damian than Notre Dame Coach Lou Holtz. Osborne had called several times to check on his condition. Jason and Christian helped see to the needs of their halo-wearing brother, massaging his feet and helping him bathe and shave. Damian did eventually recover, though his football days were over. That didn't stop Osborne from offering Damian an undergraduate assistant job with the Huskers, allowing him to keep a hand in football. It was another example of why Jason Peter, like brother Christian before him, loved Tom Osborne with a passion.

While Wistrom was a terrific football player, he was above all else a winner. He had won two state championships in high school before coming to Nebraska, and he'd been an integral part of the back-to-back title teams. At one point, he'd won more than 50 football games in a row. It wasn't a coincidence. Jason Peter years later would say that in college or the pros, he had never seen a more fierce competitor. And Wistrom had a motor that would not quit. Combine that with his quickness and speed, and the 6-5, 255-pounder was a terrifying sight for any quarterback as he came around the edge.

Recruited by top schools all over the country, Wistrom chose Nebraska so his dad would never have to miss a game. He could also see how his skills fit well into Nebraska's attacking defense. Though coming in as a high school All-American, Wistrom arrived in Lincoln humble and hard-working. While most freshmen ultimately redshirt, Wistrom decided he was going to make it hard for Husker coaches to sit him out, laying it on the line every day. Not only did he get on the field right away, he even recorded 1½ sacks in his first college game, the Kickoff Classic to open the 1994 season. He was almost immediately compared to Husker All-American Trev Alberts, who helped define the new rush end position in Nebraska's 4-3. In the national championship game against Miami, Wistrom as a backup was on the field making plays. From there, Wistrom moved up the ladder. He was a starter and all-conference player as a sophomore. He was first-team All-American and Big 12 defensive player of the year as a junior. By the time his career would end, he'd be the Husker career leader in tackles for losses and second only to Alberts in sacks. Quite simply, he was one of the greatest Blackshirts ever.

His physical attributes aside, few players possessed Wistrom's on-field smarts. That despite the fact that film study wasn't necessarily his thing. Teammates loved to tease Wistrom about how he frequently fell asleep when McBride turned on the tape player. "As soon as the lights went out, Grant was out," Foreman recalled. McBride started making Wistrom stand up during the sessions. But Wistrom always insisted he heard everything after dozing off, once proving it by reeling off not only his assignment on the play but everyone else's, too. He was no slouch in the classroom, either, twice earning academic All-America honors while majoring in pharmacy.

As Wistrom went into the final 1996 home game against Colorado, he knew it might be the last time he'd play in Memorial Stadium. So he decided to just drink in the whole spectacle. He listened to the band. He watched the balloons take to the sky after the first score. He felt the roar of the crowd. Lincoln was a special place on game day. It became one of his most memorable games at Nebraska. He and Peter did seriously consider the NFL at season's end. With the potential to improve their draft stock and move up in the first round the next year, both ultimately decided it could be to their financial advantage to stick around. But for all games they had played in and won at Nebraska, the two that stuck out the most were the two they'd lost. And that, as much as anything, was why they wanted to come back.

Few players were respected in the locker room more than Wistrom. He had a sensitive side, the player a teammate could talk to about a breakup. But he could be tough with you, too, especially if you weren't taking care of your business off the field. By this time, a system of internal enforcement had firmly taken hold among the Huskers. Osborne didn't have to worry whether players were going to the bars, not getting to class or finding trouble. Team leaders would take care of it, often without the coaches even knowing about it. Report of a freshman drinking at a party Friday night? I'll handle that, Wistrom would tell Stark. And in his kind but firm way, he would. "Hey, Little Brother, that's not going to happen anymore, is it?"

Like Peter, Wistrom was now riding his Husker teammates to make sure they earned that third title in four years, something no team had accomplished since Notre Dame in the 1940s. Stark would later recall watching Wistrom that summer double over on the field from his own exertions and then berate the offensive linemen. "You're lazy, you're out of shape and you're fat!" McBride also recalled Wistrom's intensity that summer, at one point seeing him order defensive lineman Jason Wiltz to get his butt up the stadium stairs. Wistrom, Peter and other Husker captains liked the attitude they were seeing during drills that summer. They thought the team was paying attention to some things they'd gotten away from the previous year. But as Wistrom told reporters at the beginning of fall camp, "Now we have to take it to the field."

If the preseason No. 6 Huskers were going to win another title, the schedule ahead was a daunting one. Already looming was a September 20 trip to Seattle to take on Washington, a Top 5 team with its own national championship aspirations. Everyone in the country knew that one was going to be huge.

Scott Frost was another major story line entering the season. He was once again ready to show he had what it took to lead Nebraska to a national championship. But with the lessons of the previous year, he was facing the challenge with more perspective, humility, inner strength and resolve.

The season also figured to be special for Osborne, who was marking his 25th year leading the Cornhuskers. "I think it will be a very interesting season of Nebraska football," Osborne said on his opening TV show that fall.

He wasn't ready to reveal it yet, but Osborne knew another reason that statement would prove true.

Coming Up Big

They were a vocal minority in Memorial Stadium that day, many sitting in the southeast corner student section. But when Scott Frost ran out on the field to huddle with his Husker teammates, they made themselves heard. "Booooooooooooo!" It was unmistakable, a sound heard not only in Memorial Stadium but also reverberating across the state. For one of the rare times in the history of Cornhusker football, NU fans booed one of their own.

What would become a defining moment of the 1997 season came during Nebraska's second game, a 38-24 win over Central Florida. The Knights came in as 42-point underdogs, so nobody paid a lot of attention when Tom Osborne talked them up before the game, as he did most every weakling on the Huskers' schedule. People should have listened this time. UCF was quarterbacked by the talented Daunte Culpepper, a future NFL Pro Bowler who would give the inexperienced Blackshirts fits.

After UCF kicked a field goal to take a 10-7 lead in the second quarter, Osborne inserted backup quarterback Frankie London into the game. Osborne's intention was to give him some experience in a meaningful situation. He had told reporters two days before the game he'd be doing it. London proceeded to take the Huskers down the field to score, giving them their first lead of the game. The sophomore flashed some of his raw athleticism while doing it, completing a 30-yard pass and running the final 8 yards for the score. So when Frost subsequently re-entered the game on Nebraska's next possession, his many detractors decided to let him know how they felt. As the boos rained down, Frost's parents sat in the stands not believing their ears. *They're booing our son.* Even 15 years later, his mom got emotional talking about it. The student section followed the boos with chants of "Fran-kie! Fran-kie!" No matter how Frost played, it seemed to many Husker fans

"It shouldn't have happened. I was surprised that the fans would do something like that."

— FRANKIE LONDON AFTER FANS BOOED SCOTT FROST'S RETURN TO THE GAME he would always be Benedict Arnold.

Nebraska trailed at the half 17-14 before wearing the Knights down in the second, Frost leading three third-quarter scoring drives to put NU in control. That this game was close had more to do with the Blackshirts, who were scorched for 318 yards by Culpepper. Overall, Frost had a strong game, completing 9 of 15 passes for 120 yards and a score while running for 52 yards and another TD. While his throwing mechanics still weren't pretty, he was accurate and threw a very catchable ball. Most importantly, he had made no big mistakes. In NU's two games against Akron and Central Florida, Frost had yet to throw an interception or lose a fumble, and in each game Nebraska had generated more than 500 yards in offense. The most ironic thing about the booing: Under Osborne's grading system, which looked at not only execution but whether the quarterback was getting the Huskers into the right play in the first place, Frost had scored 1.97 that day on a 2.0 scale. Osborne could never recall a quarterback scoring higher.

The booing was ringing in everyone's ears after the game. The whole NU team had been booed at home once during the early 1980s. No one could recall an individual Husker player getting such treatment in Lincoln. Osborne was visibly irritated, scolding the fans. "I don't think that has any place in this stadium," he said. Osborne also slammed the door on the idea Nebraska had some kind of quarterback controversy. While fans had seen Frost and London play a little bit, he had watched them both make thousands of plays in practice. There was no question Frost was Nebraska's best quarterback. Indeed, despite what the so-called experts in the stands and press box were saying, London would never start a game at quarterback for the Huskers. By the next season, even with Frost gone, he'd be playing wingback. "I didn't see anything he did wrong today," Osborne said of Frost. "There might have been one or two passes he might have completed. But for heaven's sake, Joe Montana didn't complete every pass." Osborne praised the way his quarterback had handled his many detractors. "Scott Frost has kept his head up, with a tremendous amount of criticism that I don't understand."

Frost said little to reporters about the booing afterward, saying he didn't pay much attention to it. But inside, he quietly seethed — not just at the fans, but at his coach. It would be the only time during his three years in Lincoln he would get mad at Tom Osborne. He loved Osborne. It was almost impossible to play for him and not feel that way. But Frost felt his coach had opened him up to the criticism by taking him out when the Huskers were behind, making it look as if he'd been yanked. It raised questions in fans' eyes as to whether Scott was the guy for the Huskers.

After the fresh start of the new season, the move had helped create yet another negative situation with the fans. Frost was very emotional about it as he spoke to his parents after the game. He later talked it out with his coach. Osborne explained that he felt the need to keep his pre-game commitment to London, despite the fact that NU trailed at the time. But he did see how it had made Frost's situation more difficult. He felt bad that it happened. The quarterback quickly got over his feelings toward Osborne — but not his feelings for the fans.

Now Nebraska would be going into its biggest game of the year with questions about the confidence of its quarterback. The seventh-ranked Huskers' game against No. 2 Washington figured to be an early-season playoff game in the race for the national championship. Most everything the Huskers had worked for in the past year could be lost. Washington boasted the nation's stingiest run defense, holding its first two opponents to a combined -5 yards. The Huskies' 16 returning starters included quarterback Brock Huard, the nation's top-rated passer, and big-play receiver Jerome Pathon. Huard may have been the best pure passer Nebraska faced in this era. And Husky Stadium was considered one of the toughest places to play in all of college football. The stands went up steeply from field level, so it seemed the fans were right on top of you, stomping on the metal bleachers. Plus, there was a huge cantilever roof that held in the sound and caused it to bounce back all over the field. The Huskers had lost in Seattle five years before, and it was the loudest environment Osborne had encountered in his career. The sound that night had been measured at 135 decibels, approaching the roar of a jet engine. To get ready for this game, Osborne had cranked up the noise in practice so much during the week he'd drawn complaints from faculty for disrupting nearby classes.

During preparations, Osborne continued to be disturbed by fans' treatment of Frost and concerned about its potential impact on the team. His words after the Central Florida game had failed to quell talk of a quarterback controversy. Osborne didn't understand how a boy who was as Nebraskan as beef steak could be so badly maligned in his home state. Contrary to what some might say, he didn't believe this stuff should "go with the territory" when you played quarterback at Nebraska. Frost was not a pro. He was a 22-year-old kid, playing for a scholarship worth less than $10,000. Osborne privately feared that a loss to Washington would give Frost a place of permanent scorn within the annals of Nebraska football.

For his own part, Frost tried hard to tune out the negativity, becoming increasingly isolated. While most Huskers would say they were playing for the fans and the state, the circle of people Frost was playing for at that point was not much larger than his teammates, parents and coaches. Those were the people he drew strength from. He tried to view the fans and outside critics as absolutely irrelevant to his life and to this team's success. While he forced a smile in the Huskers' weekly press conference and joked about the booing, he hinted at the true depth of his feelings in a telling ESPN interview days before the game. "I'll remember my team fondly," he said, "but I might not have such special memories of the university." Anyone offended by his words just didn't know what it was like to be in his shoes, he said years later. "Honestly," he said in a 2012 interview, "you could not have given me two cents at that point for most of the people sitting in the stands."

But the criticism also gave him huge motivation. He went to Seattle absolutely determined to stick it to his detractors. In the locker room before the game, Frost put on his wrist bands. He wasn't one to wear his religion on his sleeve, but inside the wrist bands he had written "Exodus 14:14." It was a Bible verse Art Lindsay had given him that week. "The Lord will fight for you. You only need to be still." It reflected the peace he felt inside. He knew he had a great team around him, buddies who believed in him and supported him. They would be with him every step of the way. While others may have been wondering about Frost's confidence, he had complete faith in what he was about to do.

Frost wasn't the only one ready to play that day. As the underdog Huskers went out for warm-ups on a gorgeous fall afternoon beside Lake Washington, Grant Wistrom and Jason Peter became part of a little drama in the bowels of Husky Stadium. The tunnel to the field, used by both teams, was tight and narrow. As the Huskers headed out, they found the tunnel lined with Husky players not dressed for the game. They started barking: You're in our house now. Get ready to get beat. Then through the middle of it, Wistrom and Peter wordlessly walked through, their heads shaved and in full game-face mode. The two didn't have to say anything. All the yipping stopped at the sight of these two imposing warriors set to go to battle.

Osborne was unusually animated when he spoke to his team just before kickoff. He expressed confidence that Washington would not stand up to the Huskers' physical brand of football. At Nebraska, football is not always fun, he said, because every day we beat up on each other. All these guys do is play catch with the ball. If you go out there and take it to these guys like you do in practice, get after them and hit them right away, you'll own them. The captains' messages poured on the gasoline. Games like this are the reason you come to Nebraska, Peter reminded his teammates. And no one comes up bigger in these games than the Huskers. "These punks don't deserve to be on the same field as us," Peter said. Wistrom reminded the team how

"They ran the option, and they
ran the dive, and it was those two plays
that pretty much killed us."

— WASHINGTON DEFENSIVE TACKLE MAC TUIAEA

everyone in the week after the Central Florida game had been writing the Huskers off. "That's a bunch of crap," he said. "We make a statement today."

The Huskers charged out and did just that, particularly by pounding the bewildered Huskies right between the tackles. Two days earlier during a practice in Lincoln, Osborne called over to Joel Makovicka after the fullback carried on a trap. "You're going to have a big day Saturday," he said. The Washington linebackers and safeties would pursue aggressively on the perimeter to defend the Nebraska option. That would make Washington vulnerable up the middle.

It was music to Makovicka's ears. The junior had followed brother Jeff to Lincoln, both of them walking on out of the eight-man football program in Brainard, Nebraska, pop. 326. He and Jeff had grown up pretending they were Turner Gill and Mike Rozier when they played in the yard. Joel started out at I-back at Nebraska before finding his home at fullback. He loved the blocking demands of the position, which required that he be strong enough to rub out a linebacker and agile enough to take down a defensive back. And he was one of the most determined runners the Huskers ever had. In the season opener against Akron, he had already won over Husker fans with a never-say-die run in which he'd used second, third, fourth and maybe fifth effort to power, twist and barrel into the end zone on a run up the middle. It was another great example of the want-to spirit of the Nebraska walk-on.

True to his coach's word, on the fourth play of the Huskers' first possession in Seattle, Makovicka banged 17 yards on a trap play. You could see both safeties and defensive ends completely taking themselves out of the play pursuing Frost and Green to the outside. Makovicka might have broken the whole thing had a Husky not made a shoe-top tackle, pulling off Makovicka's cleat.

Then after the success of the trap, Osborne unveiled a new weapon the Huskers had been holding on to just for this game. The previous spring, Osborne had first doodled 36 Quarterback Keep, a new running play that perfectly fit Frost's hard-running style. Osborne had almost been tempted to use it when NU was struggling the previous week, but he held off. He sent it in now.

The play was designed to look like the fullback trap, with the same blocking and action up front. But I-back Ahman Green, rather than running down the line to fake an option as he normally would on the trap, would instead serve as Frost's lead blocker. With Green's unusual assignment, Nebraska was simply sending more people right through the heart of the Husky defense than they could account for.

Frost took a step back and faked to Makovicka on the trap, and then followed Green into the tight-end hole. The I-back took to his new assignment, clobbering a linebacker. Zipping around Green's block, Frost bent the run toward the pylon, appearing to shift into a gear Nebraska fans never knew he had. He raced 34 yards untouched into the end zone. It was the end of the field where most Husker fans were sitting, and as they cheered, Frost raised both arms over his head. The score completed a six-play, 80-yard drive — all of it on the ground. Frost would score a half-dozen more times on the Quarterback Keep play over the course of the 1997 season. Years later while Frost was coaching at Oregon, the school's defensive backs coach was still marveling about the design of the play. And it all had been part of a lethal play-calling sequence, each play initially looking to the defense much like the other: the option setting up the trap, and then the trap setting up the Quarterback Keep. Makovicka would later describe it as yet another of example of how while most football coaches were playing checkers, Tom Osborne was playing chess.

Wistrom, Peter and the rest of the Blackshirts made sure the Huskers got the ball back quickly. Playing inspired football against an offensive line averaging over 300 pounds per man, Wistrom and Peter high-lowed Huard, bringing the quarterback down in the shadow of his own end zone. It helped give the Huskers great field position.

That's when Osborne pulled out another new play that would feature his quarterback hitting Washington right in the gut. Showing Osborne wasn't too proud to borrow someone else's work, he'd pretty much taken this one out of Central Florida's playbook. He had been impressed the previous week how Culpepper had burned the Blackshirts with quarterback draws. He thought it would be an equally good play for his rugged, now 220-pound quarterback. In the end, Frost came up with what Osborne considered his best run to date at Nebraska. Taking the snap out of the shotgun, Frost evaded a tackler in the backfield and took it 30 yards through the heart of the defense, diving into the end zone. After just two possessions, Nebraska led 14-0. That jet engine-loud crowd that everyone feared was reduced to only murmurs.

Wistrom further changed the face of the game on the Huskies' next possession when he tackled Huard low just as he threw, rolling up the quarterback's ankle. Huard stayed in for three more plays but then left with a bad sprain. He spent the rest of the game on the sidelines wearing a walking boot and complaining about the alleged cheap shot Wistrom had delivered. Wistrom would try to apologize to him after the game, but Huard didn't really want to hear about it.

"I think he was a little apprehensive
about this game, that if we lost,
people would say it was his fault."

— TOM OSBORNE ON SCOTT FROST AFTER WASHINGTON GAME

Midway through the second quarter, Green scored on a play so well-blocked he could have walked into the end zone, the 4-yard run putting the Huskers up 21-0. Huard's mobile backup was able to make things a little interesting in the second half, but the Huskers held on for a convincing 27-14 win that, thanks to a couple of botched field goals, wasn't nearly as close as the final score.

By the end, the Huskers had run all over Washington, their 384 yards on the ground the second-highest rushing total on record against the Huskies. Makovicka gained a career-high 129 yards on just 12 carries, while Green also ran for 129. Frost would have given the Huskers three 100-yard rushers in the same game for only the second time in school history had he not given up six yards taking knees to burn up the clock at the end. He finished with 97 yards. But numbers didn't come close to capturing the character he showed in leading the team after the week that he'd endured. He had proved to his critics and everyone else that he was a big-game quarterback.

The game also answered a lot of questions about the Blackshirts, who never allowed the high-powered Husky offense to get on track. And the Huskers' revamped offensive line was once again playing like the Pipeline of old. Josh Heskew, Fred Pollack and sixth man Matt Hoskinson had stepped up, joining returning starters Jon Zatechka and Eric Anderson and allowing Aaron Taylor to move back to his natural position at guard. As center Heskew put it afterward, "We shoved it right up their noses."

The comment reflected a Husker team that once again had its mojo back. This game had been the football equivalent of Clark Kent emerging from the phone booth, the bullets suddenly bouncing off Superman's chest. With the Huskers soon after elevated to No. 1 in the polls, that air of invincibility that had evaporated in the desert the previous year returned. As Jason Peter walked into the tunnel after the impressive win, he raised his helmet over his head to salute the Nebraska fans along the rail. "Miami, baby!" he called out — the site of January's national championship game.

Another Husker gave the fans a surprising salute. As he jogged off the field, Frost had a clear path to the tunnel. He could have headed right in. But the Husker fans in the north stands caught his eye. Frost worked his way through a wall of TV cameras and security guards and ran over, pumping his fist in the air.

He took off his wrist bands, the ones with Exodus 14:14 written on the inside, and tossed them into the crowd, drawing more cheers. Some would write about it as a sign Frost was making peace with Husker fans. But Frost saw his gesture as much smaller than that, limited to this group of supporters in the corner of Husky Stadium. The reality of his feelings toward Husker fans remained complicated.

One reporter joked afterward that Frost would need to avoid getting trampled by all the Husker fans who would now be jumping on the Scott Frost bandwagon. Without question, many Husker fans who had doubted Frost were ready to fully embrace him after this one. Sales of No. 7 Husker jerseys picked up considerably at the Husker Authentics store across from Memorial Stadium, becoming a common sight on game days. Many fans who had wanted him benched a week earlier would now want his autograph. "He'll have a lot of new friends," Taylor said. Added Wistrom: "Some people are going to have to eat their words, especially some of our fans who booed him last week."

Inside, Frost did feel vindicated. But that's where he kept it — inside. He declined to gloat about it when questioned by reporters after the game. "My focus is on the football team, the football game," he said. "I care about my teammates, they care about me and we're going to support each other. What other people are saying really doesn't matter. We're proud of the win, and I think we'll end it at that."

Privately, he appreciated the fans who supported him. But he also wasn't about to forget the booing, the threats and everything else he had gone through. Why should he? It was wrong. And after the Washington game, he didn't hear anyone apologizing for it. If most Husker fans were now in his corner, he said years later, he wouldn't have known. He was almost oblivious to them. Frost was going to stick with the small circle of people who had been with him from the start. Days later, he would tell reporters in Lincoln he was taking a vow of silence on any future questions about his treatment by fans. It would be awhile before he could ever forgive.

It's hard to overstate just how much this game had meant to Frost. This was a turning point, with major implications both on and off the field. After he'd done all the postgame interviews, Frost walked back through that narrow tunnel and returned to the field. Huard was nearby wearing his boot and talking to a reporter. Frost stood there in a T-shirt, his shoulder pads off, then looked out over the now silent stadium and the scoreboard that still said 27-14.

Shadowed in smudged eye-black, his eyes turned misty. Stark that day had brought a camera to the game and had been shooting pictures of the quarterback throughout:

Frost talking to Osborne on the sidelines, taking charge in the huddle, celebrating a touchdown, high-fiving teammates. Stark got another shot now. The team psychologist turned the pictures into a collage that he gave to the quarterback. He wanted this game to live on in his memory.

Don't ever forget this day. Don't ever doubt yourself. This is who you are.

The Miracle at Missouri

The play clock running down, Scott Frost and the Nebraska offense ran to the sideline for a quick huddle with Coach Osborne. Several possibilities were discussed, but in seconds they arrived at Shotgun 99 Double Slant — a pass play the Huskers had not run in a game all season. Players scrambled back out to their positions, with freshman receiver Matt Davison barely getting set before the shotgun snap rifled back to Frost. The last seven seconds began to leak off the clock as Frost's eyes darted back and forth across the field. In the stands, his mom could hardly watch, worried that the heavy wrath of the Husker Nation was about to once again crash down on her son's head. Every Nebraska fan, whether in the stands or watching at home on TV, was sitting breathlessly. In this game against Missouri, top-ranked Nebraska's national championship hopes had somehow all come down to one last do-or-die pass.

Almost everyone in Nebraska with a pulse would come to know the play that followed — one that would go down in the annals of college football history and earn Frost, Davison and the deft-footed Shevin Wiggins a free trip to the ESPY Awards. Nebraska and Missouri had been playing football against each other for more than a century. But the 1997 edition of the rivalry would become an instant college football classic.

Nebraska had come into the game in Columbia on November 8 on an absolute roll. Since the win over Washington, the No. 1 Huskers had demolished five more opponents. They battered No. 16 Kansas State 56-26, the only loss on the season for a Wildcats team that would go on to win the Fiesta Bowl. They posted consecutive shutouts of Texas Tech and Kansas, Nebraska's first back-to-back blankings in almost two decades. Kansas gained just 48 yards on 48 snaps, never once penetrating Nebraska territory. It was one of the most dominating defensive efforts in Husker history. The Huskers then demolished Oklahoma 69-7 in Lincoln,

"I dove, and I guess the Lord was watching over me."

— MATT DAVISON

the Sooners' worst loss ever. The game marked the end of the annual NU-OU rivalry — another casualty of the Big 12. But things had gotten so bad for Osborne's old nemesis that by the end he was showing mercy on them. He asked Milt Tenopir to go into the Oklahoma coaching booth to tell them the Huskers would just be handing off to the third-string fullback the rest of the game.

Seemingly on cruise control, the Huskers next would face a 6-3 Missouri team that had not beaten them since 1978 and not won in Columbia since 1973 — Osborne's first year as head coach. In the four most recent meetings, the Nebraska had outscored Missouri by a staggering 199-21. The Huskers were a 29-point favorite. But every week presented new challenges, and there was no margin for error. All it would take was one slip to derail their dreams. "Let's play like we're playing for a national championship," Osborne had said during halftime against OU the previous week. "And, in a sense, you are."

Osborne had been warning since before the season started that this looked like a different Missouri team. With Corby Jones, the Tigers had a quarterback who could hurt the Huskers on the option. Nebraska had recruited Jones hard years earlier, though coaches knew it would be difficult to pull him away from a school where his dad was an assistant coach. Athletically, he was much like Jake Plummer, James Brown and Daunte Culpepper, the kind of mobile quarterback who tended to give McBride and the Blackshirts fits. And Osborne knew this Missouri team would not back down from Nebraska. While the Huskers had won soundly in Lincoln the year before, Osborne thought the Tigers had been one of the hardest-hitting teams the Huskers had faced. Behind Jones, Missouri had pulled off three straight Big 12 upsets this season, including a win the previous week over Colorado in Boulder. They were sitting just outside the top 25. Now in No. 1 Nebraska, they were going after the biggest pelt of them all.

When the game kicked off before a regional ABC television audience, the Tigers and Jones took it to the Blackshirts on their first possession. They gambled and converted a fourth down from their own 41. Then Jones frustrated the Huskers with his elusiveness, spinning out of a near sack to gain 18 and set up a short touchdown dive. Game on. The Huskers came right back, with their all-native-son backfield of Frost, Ahman Green and Joel Makovicka moving the ball down the field. Frost barged his way in from 16 yards on a draw play to tie it. He scored again on a short plunge before the first quarter was out, and then Green ground out another TD on Nebraska's third possession. Frost and Green were showing why the Huskers led the nation in rushing, offense and scoring.

But while the offense was rolling, the Blackshirts were suddenly reeling. A secondary that came into the season young and inexperienced was leaking like an old wooden bucket. Jones and the Tigers put up two more touchdowns and a field goal before the half to go into the locker room leading 24-21. Missouri was hurting the Huskers the most with a play of their own, Jones rolling right on the option and then hitting the tight end dragging across the middle. One Husker defensive back was making so many major errors on simple plays that if you didn't know better, George Darlington said, you'd think he was trying to throw the game. After the player's second major mental bust, other Blackshirts got in his face, causing a dust-up on the sidelines. Darlington years later wouldn't say who the player was. Looking at TV replays, Missouri receivers often were running so wide open it was hard to tell who was supposed to be covering them. But whoever the player was and whatever issue he had that day, he wasn't ready to play. He wasn't the only Blackshirt to stumble. Husker defenders years later would complain of 3-inch-high grass and overwatered sod that was coming up in clumps, believing it was all intended to slow the Huskers down. But regardless, this would be the Blackshirts' worst game of the season, and at a most inopportune time.

Osborne sought to settle things down at halftime. And Frost seemed to restore some order when he took Nebraska on a 99-yard drive to start the third quarter, capping it with his third touchdown run of the day. But even during that drive, the Tigers showed they weren't backing down, pushing and shoving after plays, talking and taking their shots. The game continued to be a dogfight, going back and forth.

Jones shreds the Blackshirts again, scoring the go-ahead touchdown with an acrobatic dive. Mizzou 31-28.

Frost takes Huskers down the field, rarely going down on the first hit, running over linebackers. Nebraska field goal, 31-31. Even if you didn't have a rooting interest, you had to admit: this was one hell of a football game.

It would be kind of lost in the day's zany ending, but Frost had the finest game of his career. He ran for a career-high 141 yards and threw for 175, coming within three yards of the Husker record for total offense in a game. He scored four touchdowns, tying the school record for a quarterback, and passed for another. And he was wildly efficient on third down, converting 13 of 17. But at a critical moment late in the fourth quarter, Frost slipped up. Back to pass, his off-balance throw was behind his receiver, the ball deflecting into the hands of Tiger Harold Piersey.

It was a potential killer. Missouri took over at the Nebraska 30, and Jones sliced through the Blackshirts. On a play-action pass from the 16, he found receiver Eddie Brooks all alone in the end zone. "Again, can you believe it, another wide-open receiver in the Nebraska secondary," ABC play-by-play man Brent Musburger said. The reason this time wasn't so mysterious. The Tigers had run another receiver right into Eric Warfield, the safety who was covering Brooks. If the refs had seen it, it should have been flagged as an illegal pick. But the score stood up. It was 38-31 Missouri with 4:38 left. The Huskers were in serious, serious trouble.

Up in the stands, Scott Frost's mother sunk into her seat, her mind buried in thought. Frost's grandmother, always upbeat, asked her what was wrong. "Oh Grandma," Carol Frost said. "It's going to start all over again." Despite all the plays her son had made, Carol Frost knew that if Nebraska lost this game, the interception that set up Mizzou's go-ahead touchdown would be the only play that would stick with Husker fans. With Nebraska's title hopes wrecked, Scott would never hear the end of it. It would be Arizona State all over again. For Carol Frost, it was almost traumatizing to think about it.

"Ladies and gentlemen, I've been here before," Musburger said after the Tiger TD. "His name wasn't Corby Jones. It was Doug Flutie. And they shot it out one day in Miami in a game that will live forever. Corby Jones is trying to write another chapter that will live forever." Musburger was referring to Boston College's miraculous victory over No. 1 Miami in 1984, when quarterback Flutie completed a 48-yard Hail Mary pass on the final play. It would prove appropriate that Musburger invoked that game, but he did so for the wrong reasons. This one wouldn't end with another upset of No. 1. But it would feature another unforgettable immaculate reception. And it would be Scott Frost, not Jones, who would pen the new chapter in history.

When the Huskers' drive stalled on their ensuing possession, Osborne decided to punt the ball to Mizzou with just 3½ minutes left. He trusted the Blackshirts to make the stop — a leap of faith on this day. The Blackshirts gave up an initial first down, forcing Osborne to burn all three of his timeouts just to keep the clock from draining away. The cameras caught Frost pacing on the sideline, pleading with his teammates to get the ball back. And they came through. The Blackshirts teamed up to stop Jones for no gain on the option on a critical third and 3, and the Tigers were forced to punt. By now the whole nation was watching, ABC having taken the telecast nationwide. In the midst of Missouri's possession, the end-zone sprinklers at the far end of the field inexplicably turned on, briefly delaying the game. It was the first sign there was strangeness in the air at Faurot Field.

Husker Bobby Newcombe then stepped up as a little-recognized hero, fielding a short punt in the face of several onrushing Tigers and taking it up the middle 18 yards to the Nebraska 33. It was a courageous play for a true freshman, especially given all that was on the line. It set Nebraska up in a decent spot with just 1 minute, 2 seconds left.

Osborne gathered Frost and the Husker offense on the sideline. He talked them through what they were going to do. They'd be working out of the shotgun in a no-huddle, hurry-up offense. That meant Ron Brown would be relaying the play calls from the sideline with hand signals. Four receivers, no tight ends or fullback. The Huskers were out of timeouts, so they needed to get out of bounds to stop the clock. And if someone did get tackled in bounds, they'd need to get to the line quickly to ground it. There was no big rah-rah speech, which actually might have rattled Osborne's team. He was his usual unflappable self. And it rubbed off.

At that moment, there weren't many around the country who believed Nebraska was going to pull this off. Even Osborne, Frost and the Huskers would admit later they had their doubts. While Nebraska had a good passing game, it was predicated on its lethal ground attack. This was a sure passing situation, not Nebraska's forte. The odds were definitely against the Huskers. But it wasn't like the offense would be drawing up plays in the dirt. Frost and the Huskers were quite comfortable working the two-minute drill, Osborne having them practice it every Thursday. And they worked it just like they would in games, with Brown signaling from the sidelines and the clock winding down. Frost knew from those practices that the Huskers were pretty good at it. He was particularly compulsive about the clock management part, hating to waste a single precious second. He would get the most out of these 62 ticks of the clock. While Nebraska fans across the country were bundles of nerves at this point, the least anxious people in all the Husker nation were likely the 11 guys on the field. They felt they had some control over the situation. Frost proceeded to take his team on a near flawless drive, one that would have made John Elway proud.

Teammates later recalled Frost's cool as he led the offense into an opening huddle, the only traditional huddle of the drive. Then he jump-started his team on the very first play, rolling right and hitting Kenny Cheatham for 27 yards into Mizzou territory. Cheatham had faked an out route, the defender bit, and he broke it wide open upfield. Frost threw a beautiful ball, feathering a spiral just over Cheatham's outside shoulder. The receiver got one foot just inside the boundary before going out to stop the clock. On the sidelines, Brown couldn't believe the Tiger defender had taken Cheatham's fake. But it was a monster play, giving the Huskers a jolt of momentum.

Frost then rolled left on third down and connected with little-known freshman Davison, picking up 13 yards and a first down. It was unusual enough for a player just five months out of high school to see the field for the Huskers, let alone be out here at a desperate time like this. But Davison had proved that fall that he belonged. He had been recruited by Tom Osborne out of Tecumseh, a small farm town just over an hour from Lincoln. He'd been a good all-around athlete there, but always found catching a football to be about the easiest thing he did in sports. He attributed it not to great hands but great vision, enabling him to pick up the velocity and trajectory of the ball. Were it not for injuries to two veteran receivers, Davison in all likelihood would have redshirted. But after summer drills and the first days of fall camp in Lincoln, he suddenly found himself moving into the varsity locker room, right next to Grant Wistrom and Jason Peter. He learned pretty quickly who the leaders in that locker room were. Then still two months before his 19th birthday, he earned a spot in a three-man receiver rotation with Cheatham and Jeff Lake. Husker receivers, of course, were best known for their blocking, Lake being among the best perimeter blockers Nebraska ever had. But Davison caught three passes for 65 yards in the opener against Akron. This is going to be easy, he thought. Things slowed down from there. The third-down catch on this drive was just his seventh of the year. His eighth career catch would make him an instant Husker legend.

Frost followed the completion to Davison by hitting Cheatham on a pair of short comebacks, netting 15 yards and giving Nebraska a first down at the Missouri 12. The Tiger defense had backed up after the big play to Cheatham earlier, so Frost took smaller bites. But things would be tougher now that the Huskers were in the red zone, with less room for receivers to maneuver. When Nebraska threw the ball down here, it usually was to a tight end. They didn't even have a tight end on the field right now. After Cheatham's catch, Frost hurried to the line and spiked the ball with just 12 seconds left. It set up the final flurry of action.

On second down, Frost tried to hit Davison by the left front corner of the end zone on a deep comeback route, but he had a defender draped all over his back and the ball fell incomplete. Davison got up gesturing for an interference call — "like a whiny little girl," as he later put it. Osborne thought there should have been a call, too. But there wasn't much time to complain. The clock was stopped at 7 seconds, and Osborne wanted to huddle with his team on the sideline before the crucial third-down play from the 12. Davison was on the opposite side of the field from the Nebraska sideline. Fatigue already setting in from the half-dozen routes he'd run downfield in the last couple of minutes, the freshman hustled across the field as the 25-second play clock ran down.

This was great, unscripted human drama — the reason we love sports. As the Huskers huddled up on the sideline to plot their next move, Frost could see the hand in which Osborne clutched his play sheet was actually shaking — something few around the program had ever seen before. There was some talk about surprising Missouri with a sprint option out of the shotgun, but that was risky. If Frost didn't cover all 12 yards to the end zone, the game would likely be over. In the end, it was Osborne who suggested and then called Shotgun 99 Double Slant. On the play, Davison and wingback Lance Brown would run slant-ins from the left side, while Shevin Wiggins and Cheatham would slant from the right. There was no primary receiver. Frost would read the defense and try to get the ball to whoever was open. What Osborne particularly liked was that it called for Frost to unload quickly. He figured it would take just a few seconds, giving the Huskers time for another play if the pass fell incomplete.

By the time Davison reached the huddle, the call was made, and he had to rush back across the field to set up on the left side of the Husker formation. In a matter of about 25 seconds, he'd covered about 100 yards of field, already pretty much gasping for air by the time he reached his spot. He had been set for only an instant when Frost called for the shotgun snap, putting one of the most momentous plays in Nebraska football history in motion.

All four receivers took three steps off the line and than slanted toward the goal posts. The clock ticked down, 6 seconds, 5, 4, 3, and Frost frenetically scanned the field. While the play called for a quick throw, Frost feared the receiver would get tackled short of the end zone if he committed too early. It would be game over. So he held the ball for what seemed an eternity, getting great protection from his line, and let his receivers get deeper into their routes. He first looked left, where his pre-snap read of the defense seemed to give Nebraska its best shot. He saw Brown, the inside receiver on that side, was open. But Frost questioned whether the wingback could reach the goal line if he caught it. He glanced quickly right and then looked hard left again. Then he swiveled to the right and saw Wiggins open in the shadow of the goal line. In an instant, Frost fired the ball in his direction.

The ball hit Wiggins squarely in the chest, and it appeared his momentum might well carry him into the end zone. But when Missouri defender Julian Jones hit Wiggins in the back, the ball popped out and rolled down his body toward the turf.

"I thought the game was over until I saw
Matt running down the field with the ball."

— SHEVIN WIGGINS

In just a matter of a second or two, that ball would take an amazing journey.

Missouri's Piersey thought he was going to intercept it. He had been covering Lance Brown and was right there as the ball fell off Wiggins, so close Piersey could feel the cold leather of the ball on the tips of his fingers. Brown also saw the ball hanging there and dove at it. But both the Tiger and the Husker came up with nothing but air. Because at that point Wiggins desperately kicked at the ball. It was reflexive, but also intentional. His hope was to keep it alive and pop it up to himself. But he overdid it, the ball flying over his head. Then it spun in the air, hanging like a punt. That's when Brown, down on the ground at Wiggins' feet, saw a red streak out of the corner of his eye.

It was Davison. The receiver on the far left side of the play had been well-covered, later believing fatigue from all that running was a factor in his failure to get separation. But he continued his slant across the middle of the end zone. He paused briefly and became a spectator as Frost threw to Wiggins. But then he lurched ahead again when he saw the tumbling football, suspended in the air as if in slow motion. With a dive, he barely got his left hand under it, cradled it to his midsection and rolled. He then popped up from the turf holding the ball aloft, a wild look in his eyes. He initially was afraid no one had seen his amazing grab. But the referee behind him clearly saw the whole thing. He didn't even hesitate to shoot both arms into the air. "Touchdown Nebraska! Davison on the deflection!" Musburger screamed in the ABC booth. Some of the sweetest words Nebraska fans ever heard.

Osborne never saw the catch. When the ball popped up, he thought it was an incompletion. He was as surprised as anyone to see the officials signaling touchdown. OK, he thought. Frost didn't see it, either. When he saw the ball pop out of Wiggins' arms, he immediately looked at the clock to see if there was time for another play. He watched as the last couple of seconds drained off, preparing to complain to the refs about home-cooking by the Missouri clock operator. Then he saw all the officials signaling touchdown and Davison racing up the field in celebration. Frost wouldn't know exactly what had happened until he saw the replay on ESPN hours later. But he lifted his right arm in celebration and jubilantly ran for the sideline.

Lance Brown caught up to Davison and tackled him from behind at the Missouri 30, right in front of the Husker coaches. Ron Brown feared the Huskers were about to get an excessive-celebration penalty. That would have turned the crucial game-tying extra point that was forthcoming into something more like a 32-yard field goal attempt. Brown and Frost tried to shoo the happy Huskers off the field. But there was no way a flag could have been thrown anyway. Because Missouri fans in the sellout crowd of 67,000 already had stormed the field to celebrate their big upset, some even hanging on the goalposts. It was another crazy ending in Columbia, in the same end zone where that fifth-down touchdown had preserved Colorado's national championship season seven years earlier.

Some would question whether Wiggins' kick was legal. The rule book does bar receivers from intentionally striking the ball with a knee, lower leg or foot. And Wiggins admitted afterward he did kick it on purpose. But that admission aside, referees had no way on the field to judge intent. They couldn't tell whether Wiggins did kick it intentionally or if it just incidentally popped off his foot as he was thrown to the ground, one of those fluky things that happen in a game. Big 12 officials said

"When it came down to the end, we sucked
it up and played well when it counted."

— JASON PETER

afterward it would have been virtually impossible for the refs to make that call. The play happened before the age of video reviews by officials. It's hard to say what the result of such a review would have been. There were plenty of replay angles that seemed to show Davison had caught the ball cleanly, but one from behind the play made it look awfully close to hitting the ground. Davison truly believed it was clean.

Kris Brown's point-after kick sailed through a set of uprights that was still swaying, tying the game at 38-all. Nebraska was headed to its first-ever overtime game. Under a new rule instituted by the NCAA the previous year, each team would get alternating possessions from 25 yards out until one came out on top. Missouri won the toss and elected to play defense first. That's the typical strategy, so when it's your turn on offense you know whether you need a touchdown or just a field goal to match or beat the other team. But Frost was happy the Huskers would get the ball first. He and his offensive teammates were feeling so energized by their last amazing drive, the Pittsburgh Steelers weren't going to stop them now. Conversely, the Tigers were completely deflated, drained both emotionally and physically.

Sure enough, it took the Huskers just three plays to get into the end zone. Green picked up 13 yards on two carries. Then on a first down from the 12, Frost ran left on a speed option right into the teeth of the Tiger defense. He ran up Matt Hoskinson's back, broke around and then got a great block from the multi-talented Wiggins. In fact, just about every Husker on the play annihilated his man, Lance Brown picking up a Tiger and planting him on his back. That's how inspired the Huskers were at that point. Frost vaulted the final yards into the end zone. Nebraska led 45-38.

Now it was time for the Blackshirts to take a stand. Stop Missouri, and Nebraska goes home a winner. Charlie McBride figured it was just the time to give the guys some hot words to fire them up. He turned to say something. But Peter and Wistrom just blew right by, their eyes as big as silver dollars. McBride shut his mouth and turned back to the field. "This is going to be good," he thought.

Peter and Wistrom had their own message for the Blackshirts. It's on us now! Four downs! Suck it up! Let's get it done and get out of here! As bad as they'd played, this was their shot at redemption. And the Blackshirts put Jones in peril right away. On first down Nebraska rushed just four but still got pressure on the quarterback, forcing an incompletion. On second down, junior rush end Chad Kelsay, like Davison a southeast Nebraska boy, beat a blocker and cut Jones down on the option after a gain of just 3. Jones missed again on a third-down pass, with linebacker Octavious McFarlin in tight coverage on the receiver.

It once again came down to a single play. Jones dropped back again, McBride blitzed a linebacker, and both Wistrom and Mike Rucker came crashing around the corner from their rush end spots, beating their men. It was fitting that the two Missouri natives combined to take Jones down. Sack. Game over. Nebraska had prevailed, a game that immediately went down as the Miracle at Missouri.

Rucker came away with the ball and went racing down the field with it, tackled by teammates who were now taking Columbia by storm. Frost ran out to the field pumping his fist and then sought out and put his arm around a dejected Corby Jones. The two would become good friends after that. Osborne shook his head as he met Mizzou Coach Larry Smith at midfield. "We were lucky," Osborne told him. In all his years, he could never recall being so close to losing, only to snatch victory from the jaws of defeat. The ESPN Classic sports network, known for its reruns of the greatest games in sports, wasted little time getting this one into the rotation. This was one of the most memorable finishes ever, in any sport.

The Nebraska locker room was equal parts celebration and relief. The Huskers knew they had in many ways gotten away with one here. Darlington, often an emotional guy, was practically in tears, feeling bad about how the secondary had played but thankful Nebraska had won. The Huskers would be punished severely by the poll voters, who clearly focused more on the lucky break than what the late heroics said about this team's character. Nebraska dropped to third in the polls. Michigan took the No. 1 spot after impressively thumping No. 2 Penn State 34-8 that same day. Led by soon-to-be Heisman winner Charles Woodson, the Wolverines were the sexy team in the media's eyes. And because the Big Ten was not part of the Bowl Alliance, the Huskers could not face the Wolverines in a bowl. If the Huskers were going to become the team of destiny they once had appeared to be, they might need some help, and perhaps still more luck. But thanks to a gutsy drive and Davison's desperate dive, the Husker hopes lived on. "Our dream is to win a national championship," Frost told reporters. "Luckily, we found enough deep down inside to keep those dreams alive."

Davison would catch a lot more balls during four years in Lincoln, ending his career second behind Johnny Rodgers on the Husker all-time list. But he never would have a bigger one than this. The stature of Davison's play would only grow as the 1997 season played itself out, becoming the most pivotal single moment in a remarkable year. It was the play that saved Nebraska's season. Davison became an overnight celebrity, interviewed by everyone from ESPN and Sports Illustrated to his hometown Tecumseh Chieftain. "I came here to catch the football," he said in one interview. "Not quite like that." Davison, Frost and Wiggins later went to the ESPY Awards, where "The Catch" was picked as the play of the year. It was an incredible experience, the three Huskers sitting right by supermodel Tyra Banks and singer Darius Rucker of Hootie & the Blowfish. Davison years later went on to become a popular radio color man on Husker football broadcasts, and he always would be asked about The Catch. It was neat to have his own special place in Husker history.

One of the stories Davison would most love to tell about his 15 minutes of fame was what happened when the Huskers boarded the bus outside the stadium that night in Columbia. Osborne already was in his traditional seat at the front when a happy Davison climbed aboard. That's when Osborne flatly spoke the only words he ever spoke to the freshman about his season-saving grab. "Nice catch, Matt."

Over the span of his career, Osborne thought there had been quite a few games where the Huskers had been the victims of some bad luck. The 1982 Penn State game, when NU suffered its only loss of the year after a badly blown call on an out-of-bounds catch. Several games in the 1970s and 1980s when he'd been tormented by Oklahoma's late-game "Sooner Magic," including one where a questionable facemask call had kept OU's winning drive alive. But the Miracle at Missouri would give Osborne a whole new perspective. "Well," he thought to himself, "I guess everything's evened out."

"I know Nebraskans love their football.
And there are very big
expectations for this program."

— FRANK SOLICH

The Promise

Shortly after the Huskers kicked off the 1997 season, Tom Osborne requested a meeting with Nebraska Chancellor James Moeser and Athletic Director Bill Byrne. And one September day, the three met privately around some chairs at a coffee table in Moeser's office in Canfield Hall. Coming in wearing a coat and tie, Osborne swore them both to complete confidentiality. And then he dropped his bombshell.

"I want to retire at the end of this season. This is going to be my last season," the 60-year-old Osborne said. "I don't want to make any announcement yet. I want to wait until the end of the season. But the other thing I'm asking you to do is name Frank Solich my successor."

Tom Osborne was finally ready to begin letting out his most closely held secret. In the midst of one of the most incredible runs of success in college football history, with the gray hair only just beginning to push out the red atop his stately head, he was set to retire.

Moeser and Byrne immediately tried to talk him out of it. He was in the prime of his career, they argued. Even that day, Moeser sensed some reluctance on Osborne's part to step away. But Moeser and Byrne would both recall that Osborne made it clear: He felt duty-bound to step aside now. Because he had made a promise to Frank Solich.

"I don't think Tom wanted to retire," Moeser said in a 2012 interview. "I don't think he was ready to retire. But he felt ethically bound to a promise he had made to Frank. . . . He did make it clear, it was a promise to Frank."

Some 15 years after Osborne's retirement, the mystery was finally solved. Whenever Tom Osborne was questioned in 1997 and thereafter about why he decided to hang up his whistle at the pinnacle of his career, he always related it to a promise he'd made that he felt obliged to honor — a pledge that he would coach five more years and then step down. But he steadfastly refused to say to whom he'd made that rock-solid promise. It was most often speculated that it had been to Nancy. Or perhaps Solich. Or to God. But Osborne wasn't saying.

Even in a series of 2012 interviews for this book, Osborne remained reluctant to say to whom he made the pledge. But after he was read the subsequent accounts of Moeser and Byrne, he finally acknowledged the truth: The promise was to Solich. "It's pretty well documented," he said of his former bosses' recollections. Osborne even seemed a little relieved to be finally freed of the burden.

Osborne in 2012 could not recall exactly when he made the pledge. But he said its intention was simple: to keep the man he planned to succeed him in the Husker fold. Osborne had long been grooming Solich to follow him, naming the former Husker fullback as assistant head coach in 1991. And Solich had turned down other coaching opportunities in hopes of one day coaching the Huskers. Barry Alvarez, Solich's good friend and former Husker teammate, in 1990 had offered Solich the chance to join him at Wisconsin as his offensive coordinator. Under Alvarez, Solich would have been able to draw up the offensive game plan and call the plays, something he'd never been able to do under Osborne. And Solich was known to have been a leading candidate for the head coaching job at Minnesota in 1992. Given the time frame, it seems possible that job was an impetus for Osborne's promise to Solich.

In the 2012 interview, Osborne also confirmed another aspect of his promise never before revealed: While the original pledge was that Osborne would coach for five more years, he would actually go on to coach for six. At Osborne's request, Solich granted him a one-year extension. And the request also had some intriguing roots: the decision by Grant Wistrom and Jason Peter to return in 1997 for their senior seasons.

Under the five-year pledge, 1996 was to be Osborne's last on the Husker sideline. He planned to announce his retirement sometime after the conclusion of that season. It seemed going in like it would be a great way to go out, with the Huskers in pursuit of that three-peat. The season, of course, didn't turn out the way anyone had hoped. Then when Wistrom and Peter told him they were coming back, Osborne got to thinking. He admitted to himself he felt a little like they did. He, too, wanted the chance to end this thing right. And it especially didn't feel right to be jumping ship on two key players who had made their commitment to come back with the expectation Osborne would be there.

Osborne sat down with his coach-in-waiting. "These guys are committed to coming back. I feel I should play out the string with them," he recalled telling Solich. "I want to go one more year." If Solich had said a deal is a deal, Osborne said, he would have stuck with his retirement plan. But Solich agreed to the request, and that was the only reason Osborne was on the sidelines for the 1997 season. (Solich, who still harbors hard feelings about how his tenure at Nebraska ultimately ended, declined to be interviewed for this book.)

At that time, Osborne also made another promise to Solich: that after the extension, he wouldn't be coming around the next year asking for another. Osborne knew from personal experience how frustrating a limbo like that could be. On November 15, 1969, as the Huskers returned from a hard-fought victory over Kansas State in Manhattan, Bob Devaney had called Osborne to the front of the team bus. Devaney told Osborne he was planning to hang it up at the end of the next season. Fatefully, he asked Osborne if he'd be interested in succeeding him. Osborne told him he would. What neither man knew was that the Huskers that next year would go out and unexpectedly win a national championship. That had Devaney asking for an extension, and he asked for another after the 1971 title. To make it clear there would be no more foot-dragging, Devaney finally announced publicly before the 1972 season that it would be his last. Even then, Osborne said, Devaney at times wavered.

It was that memory that brought Osborne to Moeser's office in September 1997. He didn't want to make some big public announcement before the season like Devaney did. He thought that would be very distracting to the team and what it was trying to accomplish. "I wanted it to be business as usual," he recalled. "We had Wistrom and Peter who decided to stay and dedicated themselves to win them all. I wanted to give us every chance to do that." But by secretly telling his bosses, Osborne figured he would be making it firm and official: 1997 would be his final year.

Even with the extra year tacked on, Osborne found keeping the promise extremely tough. He wasn't ready to just go fishing. He was enjoying the Huskers' recent success as much as anyone. And as the years ran down on his self-imposed deadline, the time had not in the least diminished his love for the game, the process or, especially, his players. He knew all along that it would be extremely tough to lose the daily interactions that brought so much meaning to his life. Even as he went to Moeser's office that day, it was hard just thinking about it coming to an end. "But I also think a promise is a promise," he said years later. "You don't go back on your word."

Osborne was going out at a time when he was still relatively young by the standards of other major college coaching icons. Joe Paterno at the time was coaching at age 70. Bobby Bowden was approaching 68. Osborne still had boundless passion and energy, and his health was good. Moeser and Byrne mentioned all those things to him that day, to no avail.

Osborne made it clear in the conversation with his bosses that one of his biggest concerns in wanting Solich to follow him was assuring that the transition was as seamless as possible for his coaches and players. A new coach from the outside would likely bring in the assistants from his former school. Osborne knew that if Solich were named head coach, he would retain all of Osborne's assistants. He had Solich's word on that. That would allow players currently in the program to continue to work with the coaches they knew and were comfortable with. You never even knew how a new coach would treat the players. Would he just see them as pawns on a chess board? Would he abuse them? In making the case to his bosses for such continuity, Osborne said one thing that day that would always stick with Moeser — a statement that spoke volumes about Osborne's commitment and love for his players.

"I don't want someone coming in here and jerking my kids around by their face masks."

Despite the strong case Osborne made, Byrne and Moeser did not immediately accept his recommendation of Solich as his successor. Byrne said later he was not at all rejecting Solich. He considered him a qualified internal candidate, as he did Charlie McBride. He just didn't know Solich very well. And like any athletic director, he already had a list of coaches he had wanted to consider in the event Osborne ever left. There were three names on it: Mack Brown of North Carolina, Phil Fulmer of Tennessee and Jim Tressel of Youngstown State. All three would go on to win national championships over the next decade, Brown at Texas and Tressel at Ohio State. Byrne and Moeser also made it clear that in the hierarchy of the university, the decision on the next coach was not Osborne's to make. Byrne would make the selection, with Moeser's stamp of approval.

But out of respect for Osborne, Byrne told the coach he would spend some time getting to know Solich, a man who could trace his roots to the dawn of the modern Nebraska football dynasty. The undersized but big-hearted Ohio native had been part of Devaney's first recruiting class and once held the Husker single-game rushing record. He'd joined Osborne's staff in 1979, known best for his work coaching some of the game's best running backs. Solich and Byrne subsequently spoke numerous times and also spent some time traveling together. It appears Solich in the end was the only candidate ever seriously considered. Byrne and Moeser said they decided without reservation that naming Solich was the logical choice. Given the successful foundation on which the program was built, it wouldn't have made much sense to dismantle it. A new coach might not understand the culture of the state or how critical the walk-on program had been to the team's success. The NU administrators agreed with Osborne that preserving the program's unique identity was important.

Still, accepting Solich as successor didn't stop Moeser and Byrne from continuing to take every opportunity that season to try to talk Osborne out of retirement. Moeser pulled out all the stops. "The whole state's going to be devastated," he told Osborne at one point. The chancellor also played upon Osborne's disappointment over the Big 12 championship loss to Texas. "You've got Texas at home next year," Moeser said. But each time Osborne was pressed, he brought it back to the promise to Solich and his determination to keep it. "I didn't ever sense that door was open even a crack," Moeser recalled.

The impending retirement made Osborne's 25th season a bittersweet one. As Osborne went through his clockwork-like routine, he did so with the knowledge this was the final go-round. The last spring game. The arrival of his last freshman class. The last kickoff of fall camp. Even his final trip to Stillwater would give him pause, knowing he'd never return to coach in that old Big Eight backwater again. He became more keenly aware of his surroundings. Locker room conversations and rituals he'd long taken for granted became more meaningful. It was even sentimental for him to go into the training room and watch his players get taped. Of course, he cherished all his time around the players that year. Those around him noticed he was more relaxed than ever, laughing a lot. He teased a player about all the jewelry he was wearing, worrying that if he went swimming he might drown. "When I pass him in the hall, he's always making fun of me or joking," Jason Peter said in October. "He's fun to be around."

Osborne also took some time to reminisce. As fate would have it, Devaney died in May of that year, not long after spring ball. It had given Osborne pause during his final year to remember the man who had given him his first chance to coach. Devaney had first brought him on staff at Nebraska in 1962, asking the earnest graduate student to ride herd over players causing trouble in a Selleck Quadrangle dorm. It was Devaney who first recognized Osborne's coaching genius. It was also Devaney who had taught him that it was all about the players. *They're the reason we are out here.* Osborne had had some misgivings back then about following a legend, wondering when he did take over in 1973 whether he'd have been better off making his own way. Then, in a wink, a quarter century passed. Osborne wasn't particularly sentimental. And coaching college football doesn't give you much time to sit back and think about the past. But during this year, Osborne did.

"Coach Devaney had given Tom
quite a lot of responsibility in his
last year or two as head coach."

— FORMER HUSKER QUARTERBACK STEVE RUNTY

In his musing, Osborne tried to look at the bright side of his decision. Keeping the promise did set a date certain for his retirement. So many times you see coaches stay too long, face not-so-subtle suggestions it's time to leave, and hope for one more good year that never comes. Their coaching careers in the end kind of dribble away into oblivion. And he wouldn't be going out the door feet-first, either. He was leaving on his terms. Plus, with the success the Huskers were enjoying, there was no doubt that he now had the leverage to push Solich for the job.

Osborne years earlier had had a different grand plan in mind to make sure things continued as he wished when he left coaching. When Devaney retired as coach, he had slid over into the athletic director's chair. Osborne had always assumed he one day might do the same thing. Nebraska had historically kept things in-house that way. Osborne wasn't sure he wanted the athletic director's job, but he wanted the option. In 1991, when Osborne named Solich assistant head coach, he told reporters he still hoped to coach for several more years before considering becoming the A.D. But Osborne's thoughts on succession were thrown for a loop a year later when Chancellor Graham Spanier named Byrne to succeed the retiring Devaney as athletic director. The chancellor had passed over Al Papik, an internal candidate Osborne, Devaney and many prominent boosters had been hoping would get it, potentially holding it until a time Osborne was ready to step away from football. Osborne didn't feel self-serving in wanting Papik, who was capable, loyal, trustworthy, knowledgeable about the state and very deserving.

It became clear that the hiring of the young and ambitious Byrne made it extremely unlikely the A.D. job would be available when Osborne retired from coaching. To Osborne, it was a deep and personal blow. One Husker booster at the time described the coach as so unhappy with Spanier's decision that he was disoriented. Brown recalled Osborne was so upset he volunteered to speak that night at a Fellowship of Christian Athletes event, basing his talk on Romans 8:28: "And we know that in all things God works for the good of those who love him." Brown believed Osborne spoke the words that night for his own comfort.

Osborne eventually urged everyone to move on and unite. The program was more important than any one person. With Spanier's move, Osborne now would never control the levers that would allow him to name his own successor. Still, he also knew in the end, it would be hard to argue with success.

As Osborne's silver anniversary season wound down, the history-making success continued. Whether Byrne had planned it or not, the November 1 victory over

Oklahoma became a celebration of all things Tom Osborne. It was his 250th career victory, an accomplishment marked with fireworks illuminating the sky over Memorial Stadium. Only six coaches had ever hit that number, and none more quickly.

"I feel honored to play for him — not just for the 250th win, but every time I step on the practice field," Wistrom said. The senior had almost single-handedly made sure the Sooners wouldn't spoil Osborne's moment. His mammoth game included two sacks, four tackles for loss and three forced fumbles, the senior scrambling to his feet to recover one of them himself. After an on-field ceremony in which Peter presented Osborne the game ball, Osborne gave the credit to Nebraska's coaches, players and fans. "A lot of things have gone into what's happened here. I've been a very small part of it — and I really mean that — but it's nice to win the game today." In hindsight, he was talking like a guy near the end of his run.

Win No. 251 was particularly memorable — that was the Miracle at Missouri. Then on a bitterly cold November day, it was time for the home finale against Iowa State. It was always tough to say goodbye to all the seniors as they played their last game at Memorial Stadium. And there were great seniors in this class, players Osborne would always hold dear. But unbeknownst to just about everyone in the chilled crowd of 75,613, this 77-14 blowout would be Osborne's last home game, too. He betrayed no feelings of melancholy that day. It may have in part been because he just didn't feel well.

Osborne first noticed it days earlier during one of his daily post-practice jogs. It felt like he was running with a 50-pound pack on his back. After the Iowa State game, he checked himself into the hospital. The doctors discovered his heart had gone into atrial fibrillation, a non-life-threatening condition in which the upper chambers of the heart aren't beating in sync. It reduces pumping capacity and the amount of oxygen going to the body. Doctors quickly shocked it back into a normal rhythm, and he was back to work the next day (he years later would have a pacemaker installed to keep his heart in rhythm). Initially, his assistant coaches were concerned, but he assured them he was feeling fine. Privately, though, the episode provided Osborne some affirmation. Perhaps retiring now really is the best thing.

Osborne was back on the sidelines as the Huskers played Colorado in their season finale, though his team surely gave his heart cause to skip a few more beats. The Huskers were cruising along late against the disappointing 5-6 Buffs before two touchdown passes in the final four minutes had them barely hanging on for the 27-24 win. The Huskers said they weren't actually that rattled when things got close.

After Missouri, they truly believed they could weather any storm. What Scott Frost would later remember most about the game was a private moment he had with Osborne earlier in the week. Colorado safety Ryan Black had been doing some talking, saying the Buffs were "going to kick the crap out of Nebraska." Osborne suggested to his husky quarterback that he look for an opportunity during the game to run the safety over. Frost later wished the people who always said Osborne wasn't competitive could have heard him then.

Next up was the Big 12 championship game in San Antonio against 14th-ranked Texas A&M. For the Huskers, it was a chance to remove the foul taste in their mouths left over from St. Louis the previous year. Plus, they needed to score some points with pollsters after their close call the previous week in Boulder. Frost and the offense were in a complete groove during the 54-15 bombing, scoring on their first seven possessions. Frost hit 10 of 11 passes for 176 yards in the first half alone and also had the block of the day, peeling back to obliterate one Aggie on a reverse. And the Blackshirts ferociously held the Aggies to just two first downs in the first half. Peter showed his heart, picking up a sack despite painful back spasms that eventually caused him to sag off the field and collapse on the sidelines. Afterward, the Aggies must have known a little of what it was like to be one of the defenders of the Alamo, the hallowed edifice just up the street. "If they're No. 2," one Aggie said, "I'd sure hate to play No. 1."

The win wrapped up Osborne's 13th conference championship and Nebraska's fourth undefeated regular season in the last five years. The chance for a national title was still out there. The No. 2 Huskers would now play No. 3 Tennessee on January 2 in the Orange Bowl, the Bowl Alliance championship game. If the Huskers could win that, and if Michigan stumbled in the Rose Bowl against Washington State, Nebraska would win its third national title in four years. But the Nebraska-Tennessee game was about to take on a whole new level of significance. Because in the wake of the Big 12 title game, Osborne decided it was time to let everyone in on his secret.

At that point, outside of Moeser, Byrne, Solich and Osborne's family, very few knew of Osborne's retirement plans. Due to some unusual circumstances, Charlie McBride had recently gotten in on it. By 1997, McBride was feeling a bit like an old war horse. He'd long had a bad knee and a bad back. And he'd spent so much time on the sidelines standing on his good leg that he'd worn out the hip on that side, too. When he ultimately retired, he actually received Social Security disability payments. During the 1997 season, McBride decided his well-worn body had taken about as much as it could. He went into Osborne's office one morning and told him he had decided to retire at season's end. He figured Osborne would be surprised to hear it. But instead, it was McBride who was caught off guard. "Charlie, you can't retire," Osborne said. "Because I am." Osborne asked the defensive coordinator if he would stay on for another year to limit the disruption for players. McBride agreed, and due to a commitment he'd made to some of his players, actually ended up coaching two more years.

On the plane back from San Antonio, Osborne began individually approaching his other assistants. "I need to talk to you on Tuesday," he said. Several reminded him they would be out on the road recruiting, so they made arrangements to talk by phone. Since George Darlington was about to board a plane for Hawaii and would be out of touch much of Tuesday, he appears to have been the first assistant Osborne spoke with, the two talking Monday night while Darlington was in Oregon. Ron Brown got the word the next day while on a desert highway between San Diego and Phoenix.

All were shocked and disappointed. Milt Tenopir had always hoped to retire with Osborne, but he wasn't ready to go now. He and others were concerned about job security. But Osborne assured his coaches that Solich would be keeping the whole staff together. He said everything from Solich's hiring on down had been agreed to. Darlington even recalled Osborne leaving an out, suggesting he wouldn't leave if anyone reneged on the agreements.

As soon as Osborne started getting the word to staff, the state began buzzing with rumors of his impending retirement. The World-Herald reached Osborne at home Monday night. He dismissed the rumors while not actually denying them. "I'm planning on showing up for work tomorrow," he said. And then at Osborne's regular pre-bowl press conference the next day, he put on the same soft-shoe routine. "I just know when the time comes, you'll be told." He said he would never announce his retirement until he first told his coaches and then his players. So when would that be? "I don't know," he said. "It could happen anytime." The only firm timeline he'd allow was that he didn't expect he'd still be coaching at 70.

But there were other signs if people were looking for them. He sounded like he was speaking with a heavy heart, taking big breaths between sentences. He talked of how he'd stood in the Alamodome before the last game thinking how out of control the attention to his 250th win and 25th season had gotten. He spoke with passion about the contributions of his assistant coaches, their wives, the secretaries, the ticket-takers — everyone. The Huskers' great run had been a team effort. As he said it, his voice cracked, like a guy who was saying goodbye. Some people in the room clearly heard only what they wanted to hear — that Osborne didn't say he was retiring. A TV reporter at one point said, "Well, Coach, now that you've told us you're not leaving, let's go on to football." Except he never said that. The World-Herald's Tom Shatel read between the lines, writing that day, "He certainly sounds and looks like a man who may be coaching his last game."

Osborne didn't tell the reporters he had already performed step one of his pre-retirement ritual — notifying his coaches. Now it was time to tell the players. He well knew that would be the hardest part. A team meeting was scheduled for 2 p.m. the next day, Wednesday, December 10. The players thought they were just getting together to talk about bowl preparations.

After the more than 150 players gathered in the South Stadium auditorium, Osborne held off the inevitable as long as he could. He spent the first 20 minutes cracking a couple of dry jokes and talking about the Tennessee game. Then he turned serious. He told them it was time. The room turned somber in an instant, hearts dropping to the floor. Some of the younger players like freshman Bobby Newcombe cried. Newcombe had chosen to come to Lincoln with hopes of one day playing quarterback for Osborne. Most players just sat in stunned silence, faces of disbelief. Some players would barely recall any of it years later, the whole moment a blur. It was a whirlwind for Osborne, too. Aside from getting through Brook Berringer's death, emotionally this was about the toughest thing he'd faced as a coach.

An hour later, many players followed Osborne to a hastily called press conference in the nearby N Club Lounge. They stood on chairs in the back of the room looking on through eyes tinged in red, joining some 200 others in the room. Also looking on from the wall were painted portraits of all of the Husker All-Americans over the years, more than four dozen of whom had been coached by Osborne. This was a landmark moment — not just in Husker football history, but the state's.

Osborne stepped up to the podium showing about as much emotion as he did when making another crucial third-down call in the Orange Bowl. He was matter-of-fact in telling reporters what he was doing. But his family could tell by looking in his eyes how difficult this was, to walk away from his life's passion. Osborne didn't mention any promises he'd made, mostly saying he just wasn't sure how much longer he could keep up with the 14- to 16-hour days it took to run a top-notch program. Sure, he could step back and let others do the work, become a caretaker

"I don't see him sitting out on the pond with a fishing pole night and day once his time at Nebraska is done."

— NANCY OSBORNE AFTER TOM ANNOUNCED HIS RETIREMENT

coach like some of the game's biggest names. But calling the plays and designing the game plans was something he loved. And if you're going to do that, you've got to put in the time. There are no shortcuts. He also said it was too much to ask of his family to keep up the kind of pace he had for the last 25 years. Significantly, Osborne didn't offer up any concrete plans for the future, portending the many empty days ahead.

Osborne did get worked up a bit a few times during the proceedings. When he asked Nancy, the woman who had known so many lonely times as the first lady of Nebraska football, to come to the front of the room. When Byrne announced Solich as his successor. And when he spoke of his players. "Those are the people that I care a great deal about," he said. "I will miss that very much." But it was better for this to happen than to have a new coach come in who didn't treat them right or who took away all they were familiar with. The program is in good hands, he said. Osborne looked on with pride as Frost, Joel Makovicka and Matt Hoskinson then got up to speak on behalf of the players. Frost talked of what a privilege it had been to play for the greatest college football coach of all time. We don't just learn football around here, Frost said. We learn how to be men. Then he turned and bear-hugged his teary-eyed coach.

As Osborne and his wife abruptly left to catch a plane to Houston — Osborne wanted to be there to see Wistrom pick up the Lombardi Award as college football's best lineman — Frost and other players lingered in the room. Even amid all the tears, the heartbreak and the emotion, a firm resolve was already building. There is absolutely no way we are going to lose Tom Osborne's last football game. It is simply not an option. Hoskinson climbed into an elevator with Jay Foreman to ride to the locker room, the tears and emotion of the last two hours still visible on Hoskinson's face.

"We've got to send him out right," Hoskinson said.

"Damn right, Bro," Foreman replied. "We've got to send him out with a championship."

A Worthy Finish

It was enough to make the Huskers want to throw up. Michigan players danced around with roses clenched in their teeth. They pointed index fingers to the sky. They donned hats proclaiming themselves "1997 National Champions." All after the Wolverines had just hung on to beat No. 7 Washington State 21-16 in the Rose Bowl.

"We would have beaten Washington State by 40," a frustrated Scott Frost said after taking it all in. All the guys were frustrated. And down. They had watched the second half of the Rose Bowl together in the locker room at Miami's Pro Player Stadium after completing their night-before-the-game walk-through — Tom Osborne's last practice as coach at Nebraska. There were cheers when Washington State led late in the third quarter. Then after the Cougars fell behind, it appeared they should have had one more play from the Michigan 16 at the end. But the final two seconds controversially drained off the clock after Cougar quarterback Ryan Leaf quickly spiked the ball to stop it. The game was over. And with it, so appeared the Huskers' chances of sending Osborne out a champion.

Michigan had gone into the bowls solidly No. 1 in both the coaches and media polls, garnering more than 80 percent of the first-place votes. Given it had been 49 years since the traditional football power had won a national title, most observers were saying there was no way voters would take them out of that top spot now. There was nothing the Huskers could do in the Orange Bowl the next night that could change that. "An opportunity to claim their first undisputed national championship in a half-century," ABC's Keith Jackson said of the Wolverines after the final gun. Making it all the harder to take for the Huskers was that Jackson's partner in the booth that night singing the praises of Michigan was former NFL quarterback Bob Griese. His son, Brian, quarterbacked Michigan.

> "They handed us our butts physically in the third quarter. We got mismatched, whipped."
>
> — TENNESSEE COACH PHILLIP FULMER

"On all of our plays, somebody
is going down the field, but Nebraska
took that away from us."

— TENNESSEE QUARTERBACK PEYTON MANNING

Osborne could see his players were in the dumps about their situation. But he still would have to get them ready to play the next day. He tried to console them. If you go out and win the game tomorrow, you will have done all you can do. You will have had a great year, no matter what the polls say. And he tried to offer some hope. There still could be a chance with a convincing effort against Tennessee to finish No. 1. "The door is still open," he said, "at least a crack."

During bowl preparations, Osborne saw one bright side to all the focus on who was No. 1. It was keeping some of the attention off himself. Going into his 307th and last game, Osborne did all he could to keep from becoming the story. He tried to keep the routine as nearly the same as possible for both himself and his team. But when one of football's all-time greats was about to take the sideline for the last time, it was a little hard to ignore. The players and assistant coaches in their public comments mostly downplayed it, too, just what the head coach wanted them to say. But privately it was a huge motivator. Husker players were even getting calls from former teammates. "You'd better not lose this game," they'd say. With all the emotion involved, there was also the risk of getting too pumped up about it and falling flat on their faces. The Huskers were quite familiar with that, often seeing opponents riled up about playing the No. 1 team fall into that trap. It all added a real sense of duty — and some stress — to bowl preparations. Husker players and coaches alike wanted to make sure they had done everything possible to send Osborne out the way he deserved.

When game day broke, Osborne still tried to keep to his ritual. But most of the others around him were making that a little difficult. He started the day at a chapel service. There, former Husker Irving Fryar, an ordained minister, spent much of his sermon speaking of Osborne's influence on his life. Then Osborne himself spent the first 30 minutes of his final staff meeting thanking his coaches. He again credited them with the program's success — "a bunch of baloney," as Craig Bohl later put it. It was an emotional meeting, tough to get through. Then as he traditionally did at bowl games, Osborne had a final meeting with the team's seniors. Osborne told the group that if they ever needed anything, at any point in their lives, they should just give him a call. That message, too, was no different than in the past. But it was particularly meaningful given that Osborne was leaving, too.

For the players, it was a long day waiting for the kickoff. Going over assignments. Watching more film. Worrying. And the Husker locker room before the game would be among the most tense the players would know. They had trouble not thinking the unthinkable — that they could end up sending Osborne off with a loss.

They just could not let that happen. But it would be a challenge. The Tennessee team they faced was stocked with future NFL stars. Volunteers quarterback Peyton Manning had been the runner-up for the Heisman and would become one of the NFL's all-time greats. Running back Jamal Lewis would go on to become the premier back in the league. He was a guy Nebraska had recruited hard. In fact, while Nebraska did have more talent overall, Osborne had recently found himself constantly bumping up against Vols coach Phil Fulmer on the recruiting trail. They were raking in the blue chips, a big reason the Volunteers, even sans Manning, would go on to win the national championship the next year.

A critical matchup would be Manning, one of the most prolific throwers in NCAA history, against that young Nebraska secondary that had now been scorched 27 times for completions of 25 yards or more. "Hopefully we can go out and pick them apart," one Tennessee receiver said before the game. But Osborne overall didn't believe going in that Tennessee could stand up to the pounding Nebraska would deliver on both sides of the ball. One day while watching film of Tennessee with Frost, the coach turned to his quarterback. "You know, these guys might as well play flag football," Osborne said, "because they don't hit anybody."

Minutes before kickoff in the locker room, it was time for Osborne's final pre-game speech. You could feel the history in the air, the team at rapt attention. It started off little different from any other, Osborne going through mundane details like special teams assignments. But then he addressed the discouraging situation the team found itself in with the polls, and he offered his team still more hope. He mentioned his talk the previous night about the door being cracked. "But fellas, as things have developed here and I've thought about it, the door isn't just a little bit open. It's fairly wide open for you." He gestured to his team, his hands far apart.

Osborne said he was convinced that after Michigan's sluggish performance, if the Huskers went out and played a great game against the No. 3 team, he didn't see any way they could be denied. They would come out on top in at least one of the polls. And Osborne said they were ready to play a great game. The team had been tested this season, and some games could have gone either way. But because they had dedicated themselves a year ago to getting here, the opportunity was now there for the taking. "There's no question in my mind we are the best team in the country, but we've got to do it," he said. "Let's make sure we make the thing happen tonight. It will all unfold right there for you."

Ron Brown would later call it one of Osborne's finer motivational moments, helping the team believe in the possible. Of course, Osborne didn't say anything about this being his last game. Any kind of "win one for the Gipper" speech was going to have to come from someone else. And indeed, whenever he wasn't in the room, the talk almost always turned to winning this game for him. Charlie McBride gathered the Blackshirts in the shower for a pre-game talk. "Let's take these next three hours and dedicate it to one of the greatest coaches, if not the greatest coach, there was," he said. In his psych-up tape message to the team just before the Huskers left the hotel, Wistrom played up how Osborne had dedicated his entire life to this team and program. "For us to go out there and not play as hard as we can, sell ourselves out, body and soul, for that man would be just ridiculous," he said. "He deserves nothing less than our best effort for the game he's going to remember for the rest of his life."

Husker coaches could see even before kickoff how jacked up their guys were, actually having to cut back on tackling drills during warmups to keep from getting someone hurt. The powerful feelings then built to a crescendo just before kickoff when offensive captain and tight end Vershan Jackson gave a great locker room speech. He told his teammates the only acceptable way to lose this game would be if every one of them was carried off the field on a stretcher. They needed to give Osborne the game of their lives. The Huskers proceeded from there to run out and deliver an effort worthy of their coach. And it would build into one of the most physical beatings put down by any team in the Osborne era.

It didn't start out that way. The Tennessee defense came out with everyone within four yards of the line of scrimmage, stacking up against the run. Nebraska's first six plays netted five yards. So on the Huskers' next possession, Osborne had Frost come out throwing. He hit three play-action passes in a row for big gainers. First to Sheldon Jackson for 25 yards, then to Davison for 16 more. Then on an option pass, he hit Bobby Newcombe for 22 down to the 13. So much for his shot-put release. Frost was drilling the ball right on the mark. At halftime, his passing numbers would actually be better than Manning's. Then down by the goal line, Osborne had the offense come out in a double-wing, a wingback flanked on either side of the I-back. They had run option out of this formation some against Washington, pitching the ball to the trailing wingback, to no real effect. But the first time they showed it against the Vols, Shevin Wiggins took a pitch and raced 13 yards to the 1. From there, Ahman Green pounded it in. Nebraska led 7-0.

Frost's success throwing the ball got the Volunteers to back off into a more traditional defense. In retrospect, Osborne said, the Volunteers probably should

"I didn't think I'd be able to play,
but I played through it."

— JOEL MAKOVICKA, WHO HAD PULLED A HAMSTRING

have kept jamming the box to stop the run. Forcing Frost to throw all day would have made things tougher on Nebraska. "But they didn't," Osborne recalled 15 years later. "And we started taking them apart."

The Huskers got the ball back quickly when Eric Warfield intercepted a tipped pass, getting knocked dizzy afterward by an excited Jason Peter. It was already the Blackshirts' second takeaway on the night. Ralph Brown had ended Tennessee's second possession by putting a huge lick on Lewis, jarring the ball loose. After Lewis recollected himself and headed for the sideline, Jay Foreman sidled up to the former Husker recruiting target. "Dude, you should have gone to Nebraska." Such turnovers were big, keeping Manning and the potent Vols' offense off the field. The Vols liked to control the ball with their short passing game. Yards after the catch were also big for Tennessee, so tackling would be at a premium for the Blackshirts. They would put on a tackling clinic this night. While Manning for the game would complete 21 of 31 passes, they would amazingly net only 134 yards. Not a single completion went for more than 20. Blitzing and mixing up coverage, McBride's men in black held Manning in check.

Early in the second quarter the Huskers picked up another turnover, a muffed punt giving Nebraska the ball on the 13. Osborne again went to the double-wing down by the goal line, and Wiggins went in from 10 yards for his first touchdown as a Husker. Already ahead 14-3, the Huskers late in the half had a chance to deliver a real back-breaker, driving deep into Vols territory. But on an option, Frost held the ball too long and got hit, losing a fumble. "Gol dang it, Scott," Osborne uttered in frustration. In a game where Nebraska was trying to impress, those were huge points Nebraska had left on the field. But when Frost and the offense got to the sidelines, the coach didn't dwell on it at all, offering only encouragement. "All right, let's go," he calmly said, giving Frost a reassuring pat on the shoulder. Osborne's coaches had never heard him utter profanity in a game. They'd certainly never seen him browbeat or ridicule a player. And that wasn't going to change during his last game. It was a vintage Tom Osborne moment.

The 14-3 lead at the half wasn't the kind of dominating performance Nebraska needed. They would have to step it up in the final 30 minutes. And Matt Hoskinson had some ideas on how. He wanted the Huskers to just start firing straight off the ball. As the offensive lineman walked toward the locker room, he caught up with Milt Tenopir. "Coach, they don't like to get punched in the mouth," Hoskinson said. "We've got to run the ball right at these guys."

"We pounded and pounded and pounded on them ... that's Nebraska, black-and-blue football."

— AHMAN GREEN

"Go talk to the redhead," Tenopir told him. So Hoskinson did, standing by the locker room door to grab Osborne as soon as he came in. "Well, Matt," Osborne replied, "maybe we'll give you that chance in the second half." And sure enough, the Huskers did plot a second-half strategy to run it right at the Volunteers, hitting them right between the tackles. "We've just got to knock them down again," Osborne told his players just before they returned to the field. "Just keep hammering them."

The Huskers came out of the break and proceeded to rip off consecutive touchdown drives of 80, 73 and 80 yards. The Huskers ran 22 plays during the assault, every one of them on the ground. On each snap, there would be a series of collisions up and down the line, the ultimate result usually being a big hole and a Husker running back streaking downfield. And even as the hits and yards mounted, Osborne picked up the pace of his play-calling, pushing Tennessee's defense back on its heels and ever closer to the breaking point. "They're getting the heck knocked out of them," he observed to his coaches at one point early on. This was Tom Osborne's brand of football, about as efficiently savage as it had ever been played.

Makovicka got the first drive started, going 24 right up the middle into Tennessee territory. Frost capped it with a plunge from the 1, the Nebraska front pushing the entire Tennessee line back into the end zone. It had been a 12-play demolition, 11 of them run right between the tackles. "That's a good way to start the second half," Osborne said. "If we can keep it going, guys, we can win it. We can get one poll."

Osborne turned and urged on the Blackshirts as they took the field. This was a big series. And Mike Rucker came up big, the defensive end stunting up the middle to sack Manning and force a punt. Peter leaped over Manning's prone body to give the Blackshirt a whack on the side of the head. The Nebraska offense continued to ram the ball down the field. Green took it 43 yards on an option pitch from Frost. And then from the 11 Osborne went back to Quarterback Keep, the play that had come up so huge against Washington. Same play, same result: a Scott Frost touchdown. The quarterback charged through a tackle and then dove in to make it 28-3. The Big Red machine was now rolling.

Manning was then able to mount a nice drive to pull Tennessee within 28-9, but the unrelenting Husker offense came firing back again. "How many yards do you have?" recent Outland winner Aaron Taylor asked Green. "And how many do you want?" Green responded he didn't care about the yards. He just wanted to stick it in the end zone. And with Taylor and his line mates chopping down everything in their path, Green did. He broke yet another long one, and then he took it the final

22 without anyone laying a hand on him. That put Nebraska up 35-9 as the third quarter ran down. The Huskers could see the Vols were tired, sore and weary from all the punishment. The surest sign of that, they'd later say, was that the Tennessee players had started treating them like old pals. Nebraska teams of this era got used to seeing the unusual dynamic in games like this. Opponents would come in fired up and talking big. But after a half or so of getting minced up by the Huskers, their demeanor would completely change. They'd strike up friendly conversations, often complimenting the Huskers on what a nice team they had. During the first half, defensive tackle Leonard Little had been telling the Husker offensive linemen they were too short and fat to block him. Now Little was telling Taylor, "Man, you guys are great. You're an unbelievable football team." Some Huskers would even recall a Vol suggesting it was time for the Huskers to "call off the dogs." But Osborne wasn't going to be letting up in the final period. Style points mattered here. He knew his team still had more work to do if it was going to reach its goal. The Huskers continued to pour it on.

When the Blackshirts prepared to return to the field the series after giving up the score, Osborne let them hear it. "Hey, now let's go, let's get after these guys," he said. "That was ridiculous last time." Wistrom, Peter and the Blackshirts did get after them. The only points Tennessee would score the rest of the way would be a meaningless touchdown in the final minute against the reserves. Wistrom personally forced a punt on one late fourth-quarter series, blowing up a screen play and then pressuring Manning into a bad throw. He left the field pumping his fist.

That set up one final Nebraska score. Green went over the 200-yard mark on the four-play, 80-yard drive en route to an Orange Bowl record 206 yards. The Omaha native who had entered the season with big questions about his toughness and durability was capping one of the best careers ever by a Husker I-back. There was a brief scare when Makovicka fumbled inside the 10, but Eric Anderson alertly pounced on it. If indeed every point counted, it may have kept NU's hopes alive. On the next play, Frost found the end zone again on the trusty Quarterback Keep, his third score of the game. It was now 42-9 Nebraska. Osborne and his coaches were hopeful they had done enough. In football, hitting 40 was kind of a magic number. It was now all up to the poll voters. "They're going to have to give it to us on that one," Frank Solich told Osborne after Frost's score. "Our players did everything they could, I'll tell you that."

As Frost jogged off the field, he flashed the No. 1 sign to the cheering Big Red faithful. Ron Brown sought him out on the sideline, giving him a squeeze and words of praise. The touchdown was Frost's last play as a Husker, and what a way to go out. He was putting the finishing touches on a dream senior season. He'd become the first Husker ever to both run and pass for 1,000 yards in a single year. But more than that, he had set the tone for the offense with his rugged play and dogged determination to win. Osborne didn't think he'd ever had a quarterback who ran harder. Frost's 24-2 career record as a starter stacked right up there with Frazier's 33-3. Not bad for a player who was booed four months earlier.

In fact, Frost could now finally make his peace with Nebraska's fans. "Love you guys," he'd be heard yelling to the chanting scarlet crowd at game's end. It didn't happen overnight. But since that Washington game, fans had been giving Frost their adoration and love. By now he was reciprocating. He'd grown a lot over these last two years. "It made me a man," he'd say years later of his personal challenges at Nebraska. "We're supposed to rejoice in our suffering and trials. I don't think any success would be as sweet if it came easily." Fighting adversity to finish the way he had on this night, Frost was leaving behind one of the most inspiring personal stories in Nebraska football history.

But the legacy of any Husker would pale in comparison to that of their coach. Tom Osborne was poised to put the final touches on a dominating five-year run in which his teams went 60-3 — one of the highest five-year winning percentages ever and the best for a coach finishing out his career. And as the final minutes and seconds began to tick off on his 255th career victory, the Huskers turned their attention from the field to him. Osborne was still intently watching the action, oblivious that Peter and Wistrom were rounding up a cooler of ice water. They worked 30 yards up field and then back-tracked 10. Then with 58 seconds left, they struck. Osborne gasped from the shock of the frigid bath, and then turned to see the culprits. It was those two seniors who had come back just for this moment, the big reason Osborne was standing there now, too.

"Geez, that's cold!" Osborne exclaimed, flashing a big smile. Peter gave his coach a hug. Correll Buckhalter carried on the game's last play and just dropped the ball on the field. Frost ran and grabbed it, refusing to give it back to the official. Fifteen years later, the ball that was used on the final play of Tom Osborne's career sat proudly on a mantle in Frost's home.

As the final gun sounded on the Huskers' 42-17 win, Osborne was engulfed by security guards and well-wishers. He headed to the podium for the Orange Bowl trophy presentation. CBS had gotten backed up on commercials, so they waited an eternity for the thing to begin. The crowd passed the time by chanting, "T-O! T-O!, T-O!" and then "We're No. 1!" But when the cameras finally came on, Osborne declined to make such championship proclamations. All he'd say is the Huskers played 13 games and won them all. They'd done as much as they could. And despite efforts by the interviewer to wrest some shred of emotion out of the legend who had just coached his final game, Osborne never cracked. She finally just gave up.

Osborne smiled and waved at the crowd as he headed to the locker room for interviews. There he would continue to refuse to campaign. He likewise had been telling his players to let their play on the field speak for them. But this was one case where Frost decided to openly defy his coach. He thought there were some things that needed to be said.

As distressed as Frost was by the thought of going 13-0 and not winning a title, his brother was losing even more sleep. So Frost had asked Steve to do something about it, suggesting he write down some talking points for why Nebraska deserved at least a share with Michigan. Steve gave his thoughts to his brother the day before the game. And on the bus on the way to the stadium, Frost pulled out the paper, tweaking the remarks and committing them to memory. Now here on the Orange Bowl field, in front of the national TV cameras, Scott made the case in what came to be called The Speech.

Frost conceded the writers in the AP poll had pretty much given the title to Michigan. It was now up to the coaches. So while clutching his treasured football in his hand, Frost directed his entreaty right to them. "I basically have two points for the coaches. One, if you could look in the mirror and say if your job depended on playing either Michigan or Nebraska, who would you rather play? The Rose Bowl ended in a controversial play. We took apart the third-ranked team in the country. Two, I can't see how any coach outside the Big Ten or Pac-10 could vote for Michigan. If the other coaches finished undefeated and won the Alliance Bowl game, they would expect to share the national title. It's been split before. It's OK to split it again."

Other Huskers took up the same call with reporters afterward. "Don't give it to Michigan because they haven't seen a national championship in (49) years," Peter said. "Give it to us because we're the best team in the country." He jokingly challenged Michigan to a rumble in his backyard in Jersey. As Peter and his blood brother Wistrom met with reporters, they appropriately sat side by side, whispering to each other and smiling while others spoke. It remained to be seen if the duo had

"To play that well as a team, we really
showed ourselves to be champions."

— SCOTT FROST

"This was a great way to end
25 enjoyable years."

— TOM OSBORNE

successfully ramrodded this team to a third title. But they and the other seniors on this team had finished their careers 49-2, the best four-year record in NCAA history. Without Wistrom and Peter, the Huskers almost surely wouldn't have been sitting where they were right now. Wistrom addressed their friendship, telling reporters he and Peter would be friends for life. Wistrom spoke of how wonderful the last four years had been. And of what an honor it had been to play for Tom Osborne. "Every time we went out on that field tonight, we knew we were playing for him," he said. "We could see it in his eyes that this game was different."

The night's proceedings left Osborne with a great feeling of satisfaction. This 1997 team had been special. It was more talented than the 1994 team, probably not as much as the 1995 Huskers. But in great contrast to that 1995 team, this had been the easiest group he'd ever coached. Self-motivated. Doing the right things, both on and off the field. Working with this team had been one of the most gratifying things he'd ever done in coaching. He showed that appreciation in his much-anticipated final talk to his team. The locker room fell completely silent as he for the last time addressed his players, coaches and staff in the calm monotone they knew so well.

Ring or no ring, they should be proud of what they had accomplished. "In my mind, you guys are clearly the national champions, and in your hearts you know you are, and really that's all that counts," he said. "The ring is nice, the trophy is nice. I hope we get it. I think we deserve it. But if we don't, we did everything we could." And then in his typical understated, sincere fashion, he said his final goodbye. "Thanks for all you've done for me and the university," he said, his voice barely betraying the emotion in his eyes. "And for you guys coming back next year, keep it going. That's all I want to see. Keep it going, maintain this tradition. . . . So we'll go from here, and thanks for all you've done."

There were tears all over the room as his players and staff applauded their steadfast-to-the-end leader. They knew nothing around the program would ever be the same. And they knew in the rest of their lives they'd never know another man quite like him. This night truly marked the end of an era.

Long after midnight, the Huskers bused back to the Sheraton Bal Harbour, and once again Osborne snuck in the back door. He certainly knew the way by now. And now more than ever, he wanted to quietly slip away into the night. While most of the team went to a ballroom for a late-night post-game meal with their families, Osborne retired to his room with his family. The ballroom gathering was winding down around 3 a.m., Frost still hanging out with his parents. That's when there was suddenly an eruption at the far end of the room, where the TVs were. It built and quickly moved in a wave over the crowd. This perfect season was going to have a perfect ending after all. Chris Fowler of ESPN had just come on and made it official: the Nebraska Cornhuskers had finished No. 1 in the coaches' poll. "We got it! We got it!" Frost exclaimed, hugging his brother in the exhilarating moment.

Wistrom and Peter had been in their room when the announcement came over. They at first sat in stunned silence. They couldn't believe their ears. Then they heard the whooping all over the floor. They leaped to their feet, jumped up and down on the beds, hugged each other and screamed. The entire hotel exploded into euphoria. A bunch of players bolted out of their rooms into the hallway, causing so much of a ruckus they had to be shooed away by security guards.

As it turned out, the Huskers had done it by the slimmest of margins. Going into the bowls, Michigan had 53½ first-place votes in the coaches' poll to 8½ for Nebraska. But in the wake of Nebraska's victory, Nebraska finished with 32 first-place votes to 30 for Michigan.

Michigan fans and other critics would immediately begin to gripe that this championship had been a parting gift to Osborne. It was like a gold watch, recognizing a career of achievement. Several coaches disputed that such sentiments played any part in it. The Huskers' complete destruction of the No. 3 team was a little hard to ignore. "As I watched Nebraska play last night and saw their team out there, I felt like I had to vote for Nebraska, and hopefully they could get a tie in this thing," said Colorado State Coach Sonny Lubick, one of the coaches to swap Nebraska and Michigan on his ballot. "Coaches go on fact and observation more than emotion," said Air Force Coach Fisher DeBerry, who decided to split his final ballot. "The coaches vote for who they sincerely believe is the best team."

To be sure, it's doubtful any coach would have voted Nebraska No. 1 had they not thought the Huskers deserving. Still, sentiment toward Osborne can't be dismissed as a factor in the final voting. Osborne was held in high regard among his peers, well-liked and respected as an innovator and class act. Just the year before, as Osborne's team had been pounding Lubick's Rams in Lincoln, Osborne had summoned a ball boy and told him to let his friend Lubick know he'd just be handing it to the fullback the rest of the way. Could such a gesture of goodwill and

Lubick's respect for Osborne have come into Lubick's thinking? And would coaches have been less likely to switch if they considered Osborne a scoundrel or a bad sport? Sure. Maybe nice guys sometimes do finish first.

Regardless, if there was ever a good year for a split national championship, this was it. There would never again be another time when No. 1 and No. 2 would fail to meet on the field at the end of the year. The 1998 season marked the beginning of the Bowl Championship Series, or BCS. No longer would ties to the Rose Bowl keep a Big Ten or Pac-10 team from playing for a national championship. The change was intended to avoid just the kind of scenario that had transpired in 1997.

And both teams were certainly deserving. Both had great defenses, Michigan's ranked No. 2 and Nebraska's No. 4. But while Nebraska had the No. 1 offense, Michigan's only cracked the top 50. Nebraska arguably played a tougher schedule, beating five teams that finished in the top 25 of the final polls to just three for Michigan. And while Nebraska had its close calls on the road against Missouri and Colorado, Michigan won four games that were decided by a touchdown or less. That included barely hanging on twice to beat unranked teams on their home field. Looking at both teams, a Las Vegas oddsmaker the day after NU's convincing bowl win said the Huskers would have been 6½-point favorites in a mythical battle against Michigan.

Years later, that same Sagarin computer that after looking at strength of schedule and performance ranked the 1995 Huskers as the No. 1 team of all time put the 1997 Huskers at No. 20. Conspicuously, Michigan was nowhere to be found on that list. Any objective analysis would suggest the 1997 Huskers merited a title every bit as much as the Wolverines. In the end, the Huskers took great satisfaction that the championship they won came with that crystal Sears Trophy — the award that had come to symbolize college football's finest. As the Associated Press champion, the Wolverines got a very nice wood and brass trophy. But it could never shine as brightly as the trophy the Huskers brought back to Lincoln to proudly set beside the other two.

After celebrating the championship announcement with his family, the faint traces of eye black still on his cheeks, Frost went up to Osborne's room. Frost didn't think he'd find Osborne jumping on the bed. But he thought this was one time the coach would at least show some emotion. Frost was wrong. Osborne was his dispassionate self, quietly content. The coach had actually been in his pajamas packing for home when he heard all the commotion in the halls — the first sign he had just become

"I'm proud of this team and proud
of Coach Osborne, and I don't want to see
him go out without a championship."

— SCOTT FROST

the first coach since Knute Rockne to go out in his last game a national champion. Frost again thanked and congratulated his coach and headed for the beach with his teammates for a moonlight frolic in the Atlantic surf.

Throughout the past day, week and month, the fastidious Osborne had been so focused on his game plan he hadn't allowed himself to become caught up in thinking about his coaching days coming to an end. At some point that morning as he and Nancy were alone together, it kind of hit them: "Oh, that's it."

For 25 years, Tom Osborne had adhered stubbornly to his routine, one of the things that made him one of the most consistent human beings on the planet. Now he wasn't even sure what he'd be doing next month. Osborne had always told his players that this game wasn't about the winning. It was all just part of their personal journey. But for one of the greatest coaches to ever walk a football sideline, this glorious journey was at its end.

Long Road Back

When Tom Osborne stepped in as athletic director at Nebraska in 2007, he went to work in the Tom and Nancy Osborne Athletic Complex, NU's gleaming new home for athletic administration. Near the front door, the living legend walked past a statue of himself giving instruction to Brook Berringer, a poignant reminder of both the greatness and sadness of Nebraska football's glory days. Osborne soon made a baffling discovery. All the portraits of Nebraska's All-America football players — from old greats like Guy Chamberlin and Ed Weir to later heroes like Johnny Rodgers, Mike Rozier, Tommie Frazier and Grant Wistrom — had been stashed away in a storage room. Nothing better symbolized how the Nebraska football program had somehow lost its way, almost inexplicably turning its back on its history and tradition. Both Osborne and the football program had followed tortuous paths to reach this lamentable state.

The Huskers did "keep it going" for a while after Osborne left. They lost four the first year under Frank Solich, including the first loss at home in 48 games, a streak dating back to 1991. But it wasn't surprising, given the Huskers were breaking in a new quarterback, had some huge graduation losses (honor winners Wistrom, Jason Peter and Aaron Taylor among them) and suffered one of the worst seasons for injuries ever seen in Lincoln. Osborne had no doubt his record wouldn't have been a lot better. The 1999 team very well might have been the best in the country and could have played for a national championship had its I-backs not been so fumble-fingered. A late drop at the goal line against Texas sealed the team's only loss. Charlie McBride retired after that season, and the Blackshirts never really were the same again. That was a big reason the Huskers took a little step back in 2000.

> "That legacy question is a tricky one.
> I'd rather you guys wrote it than me."
>
> — TOM OSBORNE TO REPORTERS IN 2012

Then in 2001, Eric Crouch, one of Osborne's last prize recruits, won a Heisman and took Nebraska to the national championship game. They ended up over their heads against a Miami team loaded with some 40 future NFL players. Still, people could see the program was on a gradual decline.

It was likely no coincidence that the 2002 team — the first squad virtually devoid of players who originally had been recruited by Osborne — finished 7-7. That ended a string of 40 consecutive winning seasons and had Husker fans on the warpath. Feeling the heat, Solich made major changes to his program and staff, among them pushing Milt Tenopir into retirement and firing George Darlington to bring in more young blood and re-energize recruiting. The 2003 Huskers went 10-3, but Solich wasn't around to see the end of it. Athletic Director Steve Pederson fired him just before season's end, the final blow having been an embarrassing loss in which K-State joyfully romped all over Tom Osborne Field. Pederson said he would not allow Nebraska to gravitate toward mediocrity. The firing created a huge rift among the Husker faithful. Some believed Solich should have been given more time with his revamped staff to see if he could put Nebraska back among college football's elite. Others thought it had become apparent he was no Tom Osborne. But after seeing what would follow in the next four years, most fans would come to believe Pederson had made a horrible mistake.

After a bizarre monthlong search in which barely a word came out of the athletic director's office, Pederson hired Bill Callahan, recently fired as head coach of the NFL's Oakland Raiders. Callahan came in with plans to transform Nebraska football, NFL-style. The option game that had been Nebraska's bread and butter for a quarter century was scrapped in favor of a West Coast passing offense. No longer would the Huskers rock their opponents. They would dazzle and finesse them. Part of the idea was that the blue-chippers would flock to Lincoln to play in such a system.

Callahan's practices also followed the NFL model, with little of the hard-nosed physical contact for which Nebraska was famous. Gone also was the four-station system that under Osborne had been so critical to player development. The focus in practice would be the starters, with most of the rest of the players standing around. And with the Huskers no longer running four stations, there no longer was a need for all that "personnel." The walk-on program was scaled back considerably. While there's more than one way to win, much of what made Nebraska unique had fallen by the wayside. In a state with big-time aspirations but none of the geographic advantages, Callahan's methods were hardly a recipe for success. During Callahan's disruptive first year, Nebraska went 5-6 and lost its streak of 35 consecutive bowl appearances. Callahan declared it was just one year, one season, which only underscored how little he understood how the very identity of the state was tied to football. The loss of such a treasured streak — and there would painfully be many more to come — had been a huge blow to state pride.

Osborne looked on from afar with much distress. He thought Solich had been a good man and deserved better. And he was distraught that all the systems and traditions he'd created, particularly his treasured walk-on program, were tossed on the scrap heap. By this bitter time, Osborne was largely estranged from the program and serving in Congress — the refuge he had taken to get away from the game he missed so desperately. When he first retired, the university gave Osborne an office and a secretary who couldn't take dictation. The thought was he'd do some fund-raising, but his heart remained with his team and his players. He trod the difficult line of trying to stay close to the program but not hovering over Solich's shoulder. He even had game tape delivered to his home every week so he could watch it on his own. "It's very difficult when something you did for 36 years is no longer part of your life," he said.

While at loose ends, he still refused in interviews to consider it a mistake to have retired when he did. "No," he said. "Because I made a promise." Osborne so badly missed the game he was twice tempted by other college jobs, coming close to saying yes to Michigan State in early 2000. But he knew it wouldn't be the same as it had been at Nebraska. It would have seemed kind of strange wearing green. And after receiving a phone call from a 6-year-old grandson devastated over the thought of his grandparents leaving Nebraska, Osborne knew his coaching days were over. That's when he turned to politics. The best thing about going to Congress: It got him out of Lincoln for much of the football season.

Then there was a serendipitous convergence of events that brought Nebraska football and Tom Osborne back together. After six years in Washington, Osborne made a run for governor, and many had considered him a shoo-in to win. He had some things he wanted to accomplish for the state he loved. But what he found was that on this level, politics, like football, was a contact sport. In the Republican primary, seated Governor Dave Heineman hammered him on a pair of issues. Osborne supported a law that allowed high school graduates who were the children of illegal immigrants to pay in-state tuition rates at the university. And he refused to take sides in a school district boundary dispute in Omaha, saying the issue raised legitimate questions about educational equity for poor inner-city children. What both positions had in common: Osborne was looking out for kids, particularly those most in need. But they weren't exactly winning stances in a GOP primary, Heineman winning big among the conservative wing and suburban voters. The election in the end wasn't even that close.

That defeat left Osborne available in 2007 when it became clear the Nebraska football program had become lost in the wilderness. Callahan had some moderate success in 2005 and 2006, with the expectation that year four of his regime was going to be the year Nebraska regained its footing at the top. Everyone in Nebraska had a September date when national power USC was coming to Lincoln circled on their calendars — the day Nebraska would show it was again a powerhouse. Instead, the Huskers got drilled. And then they proceeded to lay down weeks later in Lincoln against Oklahoma State, a former Osborne whipping boy. By halftime, NU trailed 38-0, angry and devastated fans fleeing the nightmare in droves. Chancellor Harvey Perlman fired Pederson two days later, and his NFL sage coach followed him out the door at the end of the 5-7 season. It was a little shocking how fragile it had all been, that a school so steeped in tradition and just a decade removed from a national title could fall into such an abyss.

Osborne answered Perlman's call to come in as athletic director and clean up the mess, ironically gaining the job he had always hoped for. Many Nebraskans wanted him to turn around and name himself head football coach. That wasn't going to happen. "At this point," Osborne said, "Nancy would get a gun and shoot me." He instead hired Bo Pelini, a torrid young defensive whiz Solich had uncovered during his last year at Nebraska. The new post had Osborne once again trying to strike the balance between not butting in while keeping an eye on things. Five years in, he remained a regular spectator at Husker practices. He also watched tape of every game and scrimmage, saying he'd offer input only if Pelini requested it. But he loved again being close to the Huskers. Pelini quickly got Nebraska back on track, securing a winning record his first season and the next year coming within a second of winning a conference championship. Pelini also pumped some life back into the walk-on program. But in his fifth season in 2012, Pelini still was searching for the win that would propel the faded power back to relevance at the highest levels of college football.

As the 2012 season began, Osborne believed he had done all he could to put things back in order. He announced September 26 he would step down January 1, 2013, a half-century after he first became associated with Big Red football. His legacy was sure to live far longer than that.

To Nebraskans looking back on the rough road their beloved football team had traveled, the end of Osborne's coaching run appeared all the more remarkable. It had once seemed it would go on forever. And even after the program slipped, fans several times were sure the Huskers were right on the brink of getting back. But over time Nebraska fans came to see Osborne's final years were a uniquely magical time — one that may never be seen again in Nebraska or anywhere else. Can you imagine? Over five years, they went 60-3. They won three national championships. They were one play away from claiming a fourth. If things had broken right in a couple of games, they could have played for and won five straight titles. It boggles the mind.

"It's crazy to think we were a few plays away from five championships in five years," Jason Peter said in 2012. Peter and his teammates say even though they witnessed the whole thing, just what they accomplished really never sank in until long after their playing days were over. "When you're living in it, you don't feel the greatness of the era," Tony Veland said. "But after all these years have gone by, and you see where the program is now, you get a sense of how great it was and how it won't ever come around again."

As for why they were so successful, the players always took it back to Osborne. Jason Peter found it a little ironic that the coach who cared about his players as human beings and looked to send them off prepared for life was the one winning all the championships in the end. Then again, it really wasn't a coincidence.

Husker fans still treasure the Osborne years, fondly remembering the glorious fall Saturdays and how they enriched life in a hard-working state. That it was done with a native son head coach and a heavy dose of home-grown kids made them all the prouder. But in the intervening years, fans also couldn't help but wonder: Just how many games and championships could Tom Osborne have won had he followed his heart rather than the dictates of his promise? His players didn't doubt at all that there would have been more hardware. But for his own part, Osborne refused to engage in that exercise. He had moved on.

Like their coach, Osborne's players moved on, too. Some played pro ball for a while, usually learning why they say NFL stands for Not For Long. They started careers. They married and had kids. They grew older. The linemen trimmed down and the backs expanded around the middle, their profiles with each passing year growing more alike. Each Husker would create his own unique life story.

Lawrence Phillips' post-Nebraska life became an open book for all to see. Behind bars in Kern Valley State Prison in Delano, California, in 2012, he did not respond to an inquiry for this book. Paul Koch, a former Husker strength coach and friend of Phillips, said the former Husker star once told him during a visit, "Right now, I'd rather everybody forget about me." But Osborne continued to hope that the intelligent man — in one recent year he read 200 books — would finish school while in prison and one day lead a productive life on the outside. In fact, in 2012 Osborne said he truly believed Phillips would. "It ain't over until it's over," Osborne said. "Lawrence is still a human being. You don't know where it's all going to end." After Osborne's visit to Phillips in 2009, the two regularly corresponded.

Wistrom went on to a distinguished nine-year NFL career. And it would surprise no one that he won a Super Bowl championship with the St. Louis Rams in just his second pro season. Winning and Wistrom always went hand in hand. But he'd also say his pro days could never compare with playing at Nebraska, the most treasured four years of his life. He'd go back and do it again if he could. In 2012, he was devoting his time to his family and his charity that helps pediatric cancer patients — a cause he first became interested in while making hospital visits as a Husker. "It set the stage for my entire life," he said of his days at Nebraska. "I hope my kids get to experience something along those lines that brings them as much joy as it brought me."

Wistrom remained buddies with Jason Peter, who like Wistrom was a first-round NFL draft pick. But Peter's road from there proved much rockier. The root of the problem was the back trouble he suffered late in his senior year. He was prescribed pain pills and liked how they made him feel. Once he had a pro contract, he had the financial means to obtain all the pills he wanted. Injuries and a spiral into drug abuse quickly destroyed his pro career and had him contemplating suicide. After five trips to rehab, he pulled his life back together, returned to Lincoln and wrote a riveting and gritty tell-all book about his life on the edge. Working as a sports talk radio host, he daily lamented that they still had not been able to get things right down in Lincoln.

As dogged as he was by his past when he left Lincoln, brother Christian Peter generally acquitted himself well in his post-Husker days. He spent several years in the pros, still fighting his past. Upon retirement, he returned home to a quiet life in New Jersey. He would seldom speak publicly of his days at Nebraska, often expressing personal regrets when he did. In 2012, he had his own insurance agency, four kids and a wife quick to come to the defense of her husband's character.

Barron Miles went on to have the best pro career you've never heard of. The mighty mite had a Hall of Fame career in the Canadian Football League, continuing to make the big plays. He retired ranking No. 2 all-time in interceptions and No. 1 in blocked kicks. And he continued to justify the opportunity Osborne gave him as a Prop 48, going on to a coaching career north of the border.

Frazier left Nebraska as one of the greatest college quarterbacks of all time, and he hoped to play pro ball in the NFL or Canada. But those hopes were dashed when his blood clot problems returned. His playing days were over, but he again took it in stride. "Things happen," he said. He dabbled in some coaching, for a time joining the Baylor University staff of Kevin Steele — the man who first brought him to Lincoln. The Florida native eventually settled into a business career in Omaha. He continued to take pride in having been part of a group of men as diverse as America that came together in Lincoln to do special things. "When you walk out of that locker room, you're not just teammates," he said. "You're brothers. You're family." Around Husker football, they still call him Touchdown Tommie.

Scott Frost enjoyed some success in the NFL as a safety and then also went into coaching. As of 2012, he was receivers coach at the University of Oregon, a new power perennially ranked higher than Nebraska. In his line of work, Frost was surprised to find just how rare the coaches are who truly care about their players. That's a lesson from Osborne he'd always keep. And when Frost coached his receivers on how to block, he'd show them a 100-play clip Osborne once prepared for him of Husker receivers throwing down. None did it better. Frost's dream job: to come back to Nebraska. "A big part of my heart is in Nebraska," he said, "and I'd love to coach there someday." And it would mean a lot, he said, to follow in the shoes of his mentor. "I am the man I am today because of Coach Osborne," he said. "And most of the guys would say that."

Indeed, to a player, former Huskers said the lessons they learned in Osborne's program served them well. Most valuable, they'd say, was the ability to persevere in the face of whatever life threw at them. That was one that helped them get through some of the most challenging times of their lives. "Even now when I have a tough day or a tough week, one thing I think about is third and 3 in the Orange Bowl," 1994 tight end Matt Shaw, a Lincoln doctor, said in 2012. "It taught me if you can do that, you can do anything."

Bonds between the players indeed remained strong. They'd go years without seeing or talking to each other. Then they'd get together at a golf outing or on the sidelines

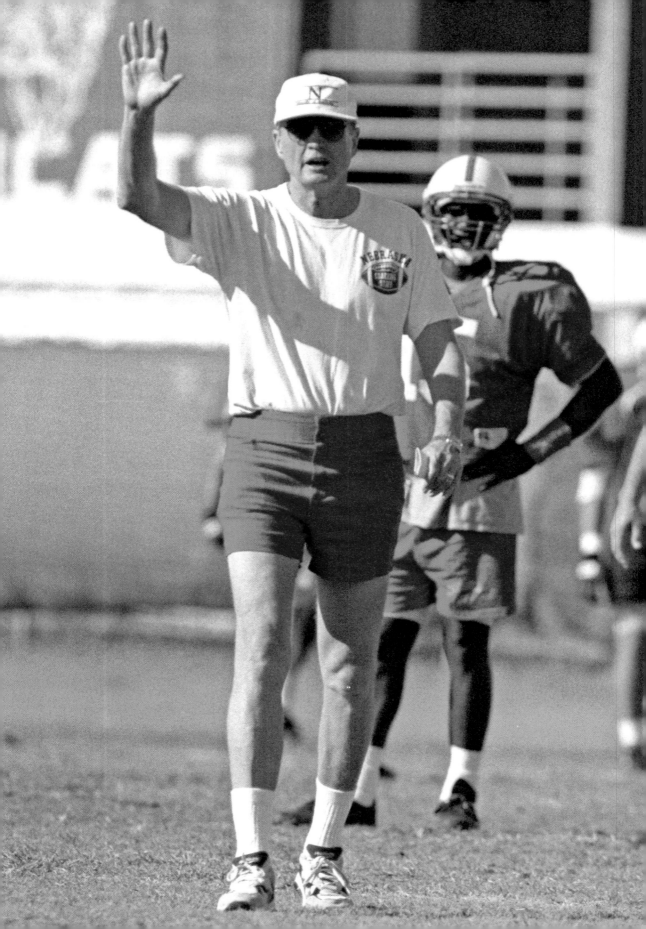

on game day in Lincoln, and it was like being back in the locker room all over again. The players said Osborne was right — it is the journey and the people you meet along the way that are most important. But they said they did disagree with their old coach on one thing: Those trophies still meant a lot. "You'll never duplicate the time spent in the locker room with the guys and the bond with your teammates," Jason Peter said. "But there's no better feeling than at the end, when you're the last man standing."

The three crystalline trophies in 2012 gleamed from a big case right by the front door of the Osborne Complex. But the man most responsible for them would rarely see them. Osborne came to work each day through the back door. He still didn't have a lot of use for trophies. But he was proud of what those symbolized.

"They represent a lot of hard work by a lot of players and coaches," he said. "There was a lot of focus on excellence and achieving great things. Every year, they were after a national championship, and that made a lot of differences and potential conflicts fall away.

"There was generally a good feeling among the people involved. People cared for each other. That was probably the most satisfying thing."

The three championship trophies were on display when the Cornhuskers returned to Lincoln to celebrate their 1998 Orange Bowl victory.

Acknowledgments

This historical narrative relies heavily on the memories of Tom Osborne and some three dozen other former Husker coaches, players and staff members, collected in more than 120 hours of interviews over a six-month period. Tom was very generous with his time, he alone sitting for nearly 15 hours of interviews over 10 sessions (all graciously scheduled by Anne Hackbart, his assistant). He answered every question but one — and even on that one he finally relented. Just as work on this project was wrapping up, Tom announced his plans to retire. As a news reporter in Nebraska for a quarter century, I can't count the number of times I've had the opportunity to interview him — and not always under the best of circumstances. But he never shied away. I'm proud that publication of this book will coincide with the culmination of his incredible career.

Tommie Frazier, Ron Brown, Kevin Steele, Deepak Gangahar, Milt Tenopir, Doak Ostergard, Jason Peter, Clinton Childs, Matt Vrzal, George Darlington and Scott Frost also were particularly generous with their time. In hearing Scott Frost's amazing back story for the first time, I couldn't believe he'd never written a book himself. I'm pleased that he allowed us to tell it here first. Paul Koch generously shared transcripts of several interviews he previously had conducted with notable Huskers from the era. Special thanks also to Jack Stark, who had great stories to tell and introduced me to the world of the Husker psych-up tape.

Understanding that memories can fade and become distorted, their words were backstopped when possible against the archives of The World-Herald. In fact, the detailed accounts and reporting of Lee Barfknecht, Tom Shatel, Eric Olson, Steve Pivovar, Doug Thomas and others represent the framework on which the narrative rests. Information was drawn from more than 500 individual newspaper stories. It's been said that to write daily journalism is to write the first draft of history. That was certainly true here. Other original sources also proved valuable, including Osborne's "On Solid Ground," Frazier's memoir "Touchdown Tommie" with Bob Schaller, Jason Peter's "Hero of the Underground" and past issues of Sports Illustrated. Thanks to HuskerVision's Chris Pankonin for dubbing DVDs for me.

I also have to thank my editors here at The World-Herald, including Executive Editor Mike Reilly, for believing this project worthy and freeing me up to pursue it.

Henry J. Cordes has spent more than 25 years as a reporter for The World-Herald, covering crime, the Statehouse, politics, regional and national public policy and, on occasion, Nebraska football. Four times he has received the University of Nebraska-Lincoln's Sorensen Award for distinguished Nebraska journalism. A graduate of Omaha Central High School and the University of Nebraska at Omaha, he lives in Omaha with his wife and twin daughters.

Special thanks also to my wife, Susan, and daughters, Thelma and Lucy, for likewise indulging me in this pursuit. They probably can appreciate Tom Osborne's reference to how a football coach mentally resides in a foreign country for six months of the year. That was certainly me for much of 2012.

Ironically, I was covering the Nebraska Unicameral for The World-Herald in the early 1990s when I first came to appreciate what an important institution Cornhusker football represents to the state of Nebraska. It's more than just a welcome fall diversion. It's a shared source of pride that binds a wide and diverse landscape, from the campuses of Omaha's Fortune 500 companies to the scrubby ranch lands of Crawford. That pride never surged higher than it did during the run of Tom Osborne's 1990s championship teams. That makes the story of those great football teams part of the fabric of the state's history, worthy of being retold. The fact that there was so much drama associated with the era, both on and off the field, only makes the telling all the richer. Not all the memories were happy ones. But there is no doubt today: In Nebraska, those truly were Unbeatable times.

— Henry J. Cordes

Index

Great Finish

Tom Osborne's final five seasons stacked up with some of the best five-year runs ever by a major college football coach. Nick Saban of Alabama entered 2012 with the chance to equal Osborne's feat of three titles in four years, though his teams still would have lost at least four games in that span. No coach ever finished his career on a more successful run than Osborne.

YOST ROCKNE BIERMAN LEAHY BRYANT

COACHES WITH THREE NATIONAL TITLES IN FIVE YEARS	RECORD	WIN %
Tom Osborne, Nebraska, 1993-97	60-3	.952
Bear Bryant, Alabama, 1961-65	49-5-1	.900
Frank Leahy, Notre Dame, 1946-50	40-4-3	.883
Bernie Bierman, Minnesota, 1934-38	35-5	.875

BEST CAREER FINISHES	NATIONAL TITLES	RECORD	WIN %
Tom Osborne, 1993-97	3	60-3	.952
Fielding Yost, Michigan, 1921-26	0	33-3-2	.868
Knute Rockne, Notre Dame, 1926-30	2	40-6-1	.862